Stolen Future, Broken Present

The Human Significance of Climate Change

Critical Climate Change

Series Editors: Tom Cohen and Claire Colebrook

The era of climate change involves the mutation of systems beyond 20th century anthropomorphic models and has stood, until recently, outside representation or address. Understood in a broad and critical sense, climate change concerns material agencies that impact on biomass and energy, erased borders and microbial invention, geological and nanographic time, and extinction events. The possibility of extinction has always been a latent figure in textual production and archives; but the current sense of depletion, decay, mutation and exhaustion calls for new modes of address, new styles of publishing and authoring, and new formats and speeds of distribution. As the pressures and re-alignments of this re-arrangement occur, so must the critical languages and conceptual templates, political premises and definitions of 'life.' There is a particular need to publish in timely fashion experimental monographs that redefine the boundaries of disciplinary fields, rhetorical invasions, the interface of conceptual and scientific languages, and geomorphic and geopolitical interventions. Critical Climate Change is oriented, in this general manner, toward the epistemo-political mutations that correspond to the temporalities of terrestrial mutation.

Stolen Future, Broken Present

The Human Significance of Climate Change

David A. Collings

( )

OPEN HUMANITIES PRESS

An imprint of Michigan Publishing
University of Michigan Library, Ann Arbor

2014

First edition published by OPEN HUMANITIES PRESS 2014

Freely available online at http://dx.doi.org/10.3998/ohp.12832550.0001.001

ISBN-13 978-1-60785-314-5

OPEN HUMANITIES PRESS is an international, scholar-led open access publishing collective whose mission is to make leading works of contemporary critical thought freely available worldwide. Books published under the OPEN HUMANITIES PRESS imprint at Michigan Publishing are produced through a unique partnership between OHP's editorial board and the University of Michigan Library, which provides a library-based managing and production support infrastructure to facilitate scholars to publish leading research in book form.

MICHIGAN
PUBLISHING
www.publishing.umich.edu

O
OPEN HUMANITIES PRESS
www.openhumanitiespress.org

Contents

Introduction

Lately the news about climate change hasn't been good.

Once upon a time, not long ago, the scientific consensus held that the northern polar ice cap, under the pressure of global warming, would melt eventually—"in the latter part of the 21st century."[1] That estimate, released in 2007, appeared around the same time as Al Gore's documentary, *An Inconvenient Truth,* and reaffirmed a widespread sense that if we did not act soon to curb our emissions of greenhouse gases, the worst effects of climate change could be dire indeed—but would transpire some decades into the future.[2] The threat from that ice melt, and from climate change more generally, was real but not absolutely imminent: we had time to fight for change through the familiar processes of public debate, the gradual formation of public opinion, the eventual forging of a coalition for Congressional action, and the patient negotiation of an international treaty.

That estimate turned out to be much too optimistic. Only two years later, new estimates suggested that the Arctic Ocean would be free of ice in the summer as soon as 2030 or 2040.[3] Thanks in part to the blistering pace with which global economies were emitting greenhouse gases into the atmosphere, the climate was reacting far more quickly than most researchers had previously projected. That shift in the forecast—along with similar shifts all across climate science—had immense implications for anyone who hoped to preserve the biosphere in anything like its present state into the future. The threat no longer loomed far off, near the end of the century, but was only two or three decades away. In the wake of this and other developments, those following the science on climate change felt a greater sense of urgency, knowing the international community better act immediately to ward off severe changes to the global climate. That imperative strained against the limits of national and international political traditions, raising difficult questions. How could scientists bring this news to bear on the thinking of leading politicians, who for the most part still used the estimates and targets set in the early 1990s? Furthermore, how could nations alter their fossil-fuel economies so dramatically in such a short period? What could possibly break through the impasse?

But as it now appears, even *that* estimate has turned out to be too optimistic in its turn. Three years later, the stunning melt of Arctic sea ice in the summer of 2012 prompted scientists to rethink those earlier studies and to propose instead that the Arctic might be ice-free in late summer before 2020. Peter Wadhams, head of the Polar Ocean Physics Group at the University of Cambridge, who researches the thickness of Arctic sea ice, now estimates that the Arctic will become ice-free in the summer well before the end of this decade, and perhaps as early as 2015 or 2016.[4] So in five years, the threat of that dire event moved up from the last half of the *century* to the latter part of this *decade*, almost obliterating the opportunity for serious action. The year 2020, it seems, is the new 2100. So much for having time—even *minimal* time—to address this crisis. The questions instantly multiply: What are we supposed to do now?[5] What political actions are even feasible? And how exactly are we to alter our economic systems to meet this challenge in time?

The news about the Arctic sea ice is bad enough: it tells us that a massive transformation in the climate of the northern hemisphere is well on its way. As the Arctic warms, the difference in temperature between the far northern zone and the temperate regions decreases, causing changes in the jet stream, which now moves more slowly and more often zigzags on its course to the east. As a result, it might swing over Texas, then pull warm air straight north over the Dakotas, causing midwinter warm spells all across the Midwest, or pull Arctic cold down into the Carolinas or even Florida, freezing areas that in the past hardly experienced such frigid weather. Furthermore, because it is moving more slowly, it can stall over certain regions and cause them to be hit with weather over longer periods—leading to longer spells of rain or snow and thus to more flooding or harsher winter storms. The same situation applies all across the northern hemisphere. Such is the "new normal" of our time.[6]

But that is not all. Much worse news awaits. The melting of the Arctic sea ice will lead to substantially higher temperatures in the sea itself, high enough potentially to melt methane clathrates—frozen remains of organic life—deposited on the seabed on the East Siberian Arctic Shelf and cause the resulting methane gas to escape through the sea and into the open air. Scientists have long known about these submerged deposits of clathrates, but since most such deposits around the world rest far beneath the ocean surface in cold waters, they were not overly concerned that climate change would cause them to melt any time soon. But the situation on that Arctic continental shelf is different: it is so shallow—often only around fifty meters below the surface—that the clathrates there are vulnerable to rising temperatures on the ocean's surface. So it is not surprising that the warming in the Arctic has already triggered the initial stages of this process.

In March 2010, a team of Russian scientists led by Igor Semiletov and Natalia Shakhova published a study documenting a major clathrate melt on the East Siberian Arctic Shelf, a melt that is releasing quantities "on par with previous estimates of methane venting from the entire World Ocean."[7] Because methane is around twenty-six times more potent as a greenhouse gas than carbon dioxide, though much less short-lived in the atmosphere, and because there are enormous deposits of frozen methane crystals in that region of the sea, as in many of the world's oceans, the National Science Foundation issued a press release stating, "Release of even a fraction of the methane stored in the shelf could trigger abrupt climate warming."[8] On returning to that region of the Arctic in summer 2011, the research team found much larger "torch-like structures" of escaping methane than before, some a kilometer across, suggesting that they may have to raise their estimates of the volume of the clathrate melt; the most recent rate of methane emissions astonished the very scientists who have long been researching this phenomenon.[9]

But even that is not all the bad news. The Arctic ice melt is driven in part by what scientists call a "positive feedback loop": as the ice melts, open water appears, absorbing sunlight; as a result, it warms up, causing more ice to melt and repeating this process in a kind of death spiral. Now that the Arctic Ocean is melting rapidly, that process will build on itself no matter what we do. Such a vicious circle applies to the melting clathrates as well. The more clathrates melt, the more the global temperature rises, causing further warming in the Arctic and more clathrates to melt.[10] In the Arctic, one positive feedback loop (the melting of the ice) may eventually trigger another, and both, taken together, may trigger similar vicious circles elsewhere on the planet. Once these processes kick in for good, they will bring into play such powerful physical forces on such a wide scale that nothing human beings can do will make much difference.

One can thus entirely understand why a group of scientists formed the Arctic Methane Emergency Group to draw the world's attention to this situation and its potentially catastrophic consequences. In the wake of the huge ice melt in summer 2012, and Peter Wadhams's new estimate that a full summer melt will occur as soon as 2015, that group now states openly that without a huge geoengineering project to *increase* Arctic ice, global climate catastrophe is inevitable.[11] So far this is a minority view, albeit from those most directly involved in Arctic climate research. The scientific community as a whole has not yet endorsed those findings. Nevertheless, the fact that researchers closely attuned to this crucial region of the planet have arrived at such dire conclusions is a good sign that we've reached the final moments in which we might salvage a future for the biosphere we know.

The news about the Arctic is so bad that we must all be forgiven for asking two or three questions almost immediately.

Why didn't anyone tell us this was happening? Major media outlets have at times covered the astonishing ice melt in the Arctic, but they have seldom discussed its wider implications or its potential impact on the future of the planet. But their relative silence in this regard is not surprising. The national media in the United States, at least until the recent past, has pretended that there are "two sides" to a "debate" as to whether climate change is real and whether human activities are causing it—questions that have been settled in the scientific community for over twenty years. Their hesitant, half-hearted, and often inaccurate reporting on climate change is so notorious it has led scientists to issue firm, even resounding statements on the subject, to ponder at length how they might get the message out—and to throw up their hands in frustration that all their efforts in this regard have gone for naught.

Why has the situation changed so fast? Isn't climate change supposed to be a gradual process? The response of the biosphere can take many forms, not all of them gradual. But we could assume that at least *our* contributions to the problem might increase at a steady pace. As it turns out, however, that assumption is wrong. A few years ago, we might reasonably have expected global greenhouse gas emissions to rise at a gradual pace. But as it turns out, those emissions have risen much more rapidly since the early 1990s than anyone expected. Scientists have been warning us for a long time to change our ways, but instead we have dramatically *worsened* the problem. Why should we be surprised when the biosphere responds accordingly?

What are we supposed to do now? Do we have time left to do anything at all? Anyone who tries to answer these questions is in a real dilemma. To say that we *do* have time is to endorse what might be a false optimism, supporting the belief that our usual approach to political problems—the slow, incremental task of building support and crafting a coalition for Congressional and international action—will work in time. Nothing could be less sure. In fact, given our deplorable track record in recent years and the enormity of the challenge, our chances for rising to this challenge in time seem ridiculously small. On the other hand, saying that we are truly out of time is to pretend to have a knowledge we don't actually possess. Things are not looking good for planet Earth, but we cannot yet be *certain* that all hope is lost. Our understanding of the clathrate melt in the Arctic, for example, is still at its beginning stages, as further comments from the primary researchers on that topic suggest.[12] Moreover, the global climate is so complex that certain geophysical patterns might be emerging of which we know even less. We can't claim to have mastered the situation. Without that mastery, it would be foolish to declare with some fanfare that we are truly out of time.

For the last decade or two we have known that we live at the crossroads of history, charged with the task of deciding the fate of the Earth and thus of humanity. So far we have been incapable of resolute action, still caught within the tides of our traditions and habits, as if utterly disabled in the face of the task.

In the meantime, time is passing. The developments in the Arctic—and elsewhere—suggest that we may have already made our choice, that we are now venturing down the path of destruction. We can't be sure this event has taken place, but we certainly can't proceed with the confidence that we still have time. We are now caught in a surpassingly strange, horrific moment—a moment when we cannot help but think, is it too late? Do we still have a future?

Other books have described the physical realities of the climate. Others have reviewed the host of things we could do to reduce our greenhouse gas emissions and discontinue other practices that damage the biosphere. Still others have explained very well our options for using new technologies, converting to renewable energy, and adopting new policies on the national and international scales for making those transformations possible. All of these books and others have urged us to take action in time.

This book will take up those themes as well; it must do so to describe the basics of our present situation. Without question, we must grasp the essentials of the problem, the practical dimensions of the solution, and the implications of both for what we should do.

But the emphasis of this book ultimately lies elsewhere. If we stick only to the scientific, technical, and political questions, if we imagine that we can face this challenge as knowing and planning creatures, we neglect the implications of this moment for *every* level of our human being. Moreover, if we urge action now, as we must, and then stop there, we sidestep the wider implications of the possibility that, despite all the warnings and efforts of the past couple of decades, we will not take action in time. What if it is now too late? What if we now face a disappearing future?

Once we ask these questions, the entire conversation changes. We have long known what is at stake; no one aware of climate change has doubted that it threatens the viability of the world we know. Climate change is not just a crisis for the biosphere; it is a crisis for our very significance and purpose as human beings. It represents a stunning change in the climate of all human emotion. But now we face the possibility that we will not be able to avoid passing the point of no return—of triggering severe, irreversible climate change.

In the past those who have commented on climate change have warned us to act before reaching this point, drawing on this dire threat to motivate us. Nearly every book on climate change has ended on an optimistic note, explaining how this crisis is ultimately an opportunity, a chance to turn things around, to create an environmentally friendly economy and a newly responsible society. This way of thinking about the challenge corresponded well to the nature of the threat over most of the last two decades, when we still had confidence we had time to make a difference. Over that period, it made sense that we could scarcely confront the dire realities of climate change without a certain optimism, without that shift from horror to the possibility of transformation. As a result, we have seldom if ever truly looked into the prospect of a disappearing future.

To some extent this way of thinking must still apply: after all, the demand for urgent action is now greater than ever and has, if anything, become a supreme ultimatum. Without question, we must do everything humanly possible to change our society and to avoid triggering ultimate calamity.

But if we are honest, we must admit that the events of the past few years undermine the prospects of a happy ending more than ever. Nearly all of the time for action has slipped by. It is thus time for us to face this crisis in a new way—not to abandon our efforts for change, not to forget the range of excellent initiatives for shifting our economies onto a new basis, but to contemplate, for the first time, what it means for us if we fail. Doing so will be difficult; it will require new resources of honesty, new capacities to endure dark thoughts, and new reserves of patience for the intolerable. It may ask more of us than we have to give.

If we continue to insist that we have time in the face of increasing evidence that it is running out, we would be less than honest: sticking with that familiar optimistic scenario to the exclusion of all else would commit us to a form of repression, defensiveness, willful blindness—indeed, to a version of denial itself.

This moment thus requires us to do something we seldom imagine: fighting for the planet *even if* it may be too late, sticking with all our efforts—and increasing them—precisely when we begin to admit that the cause may be lost. The developments of these recent years suggests that our whole way of imagining the crisis must change: these days we are stuck with the anguish of the last-ditch effort, the attempt to snatch victory out of the jaws of defeat—with that minimal, desperate slogan: never say die.

We cannot turn away from the new realities of this moment. We now face questions not simply about the scientific, technological, economic, or political dimensions of this crisis, although they remain crucial, but also about its *human* significance. If we cannot face them, we will have lost something precious: our capacity to live with at least a minimal dose of integrity and truth.

These questions are among the toughest we will ever have to face. In some sense they are impossible to answer. But in this book, I will attempt to face them nevertheless—not to answer them, not to give the illusion we can truly know what we are doing under their pressure, but to explore what it is like to dwell with them, to live under their weight and darkness: What is the present for, if the future is on the verge of disappearing? How are we to live if that future is in doubt?

Those questions are supremely tough in part because they come to us *in addition to* the demands that our existing discussion of climate change impose on us. Those demands are already considerable; they have been so stark that we have scarcely been able to engage them well. Before taking up the core questions of this book, then, it may be wise to linger over these latter demands, familiar as they are.

Why have we been so stuck? What has made it so hard for us to face the current crisis as if we were actually sane and responsible people?

The honest answer, I think, is that this is an unprecedented crisis, posing challenges to us that we have never faced before and in response to which we are utterly at a loss.

First of all, if we are to tackle the fundamental aspects of climate change, nearly all of us are forced to examine realities well outside our expertise, to read, learn, and judge scientific findings for which we often have little preparation. Previous crises did not demand this task of us. For most of the modern era, people could read the newspaper or speak with friends to assess for themselves the state of public affairs; no special expertise was necessary. Even in the nuclear era, citizens did not have to learn the physics of the nuclear reaction to realize what had taken place at Hiroshima and Nagasaki: those events were real and the devastating effects of those weapons palpable.

In our era, however, we are asked to grapple with a phenomenon that is not a singular event, not a known threat, but the *context* for possible events—a context that we must learn about through the careful work of hundreds of scientists. Moreover, it is never obvious whom we can trust to mediate that work to us, to explain what the science has actually found: since so many participants in the debate deny that there is a problem, or suggest that there is genuine disagreement between scientists about whether climate change is real, we are not sure whom to believe. For no previous crisis has a similar situation been the case.

Our hesitation in accepting the reality of the challenge arises as well from the tendency to trust our own experience. If our lives and environments feel mostly familiar to us, it is hard for us to accept that something is dramatically amiss. Intuitively, we hesitate to act on any claim that is not evident to us in our own experience, not visible to the naked eye, not confirmed by authorities we have already chosen. In this regard, climate change is truly unprecedented: it touches us right where we live, calls us to consider our moral responsibility to ourselves, to others, and to the future—without offering us any obvious confirmation. It asks us for a serious moral commitment without providing us with the foundations we usually ask for when taking that kind of step.

But that is not all. If we *do* accept the reality of climate change, and our responsibility for causing most of it, that realization is so wounding that we may not wish to grapple with it any further. The prospect that the planet's future is in danger is most likely to fill us with anger, horror, and desperate hope. Underneath all these responses lies a sense of great dread. And we have almost nothing to help us live with that dread.

There is little or no precedent for that emotion. Even at the height of the nuclear arms race, when people were forced to contemplate the possibility of global annihilation, at least they were aware that the conflagration could erupt from something *other* than the ordinary course of their lives. A nuclear war would be a devastating interruption of the way things were. Climate change is different: it threatens to transform our entire world if we stick to our *current* habits, founded as they are on the extravagant use of fossil fuels. Our way of living threatens *itself*. No previous generation of human beings has ever confronted that possibility—at least not on the planetary scale.

This shift from a singular horror to everyday disaster is hard for us to accept: somehow, a cataclysmic event is easier to understand than climate change. After all, such an event isn't that different from the thought of our own deaths. Most of us are quite aware that our lives might go horribly wrong at any moment. We know that a random accident could kill us, disfigure us, or change our personalities before we have any warning at all. Even worse, a freak event could destroy all the people we love. That's just the way things are.

But climate change is different. Nowadays, *our everyday lives are the source of the problem*: everything we depend upon to live as we do—the energy we use to get around, to heat or cool our homes, to power the industry that produces the goods we use—is also pumping enough greenhouse gases into the atmosphere that eventually our climate will be transformed. The societies in which we live are causing events to take place that could directly threaten how we live. It's not that there is a *chance* something horrible might happen; this time, we *know* it will happen if we stay calm and carry on.

Even worse, once we decide to confront this pain and take action, we realize that the task may be beyond our capacity. The most dire challenges of the past look easy in comparison to what we face. Consider the long drive to abolish slavery in the United States. Abolitionists fought for generations to eradicate that institution without success. Slaveholders, however moved by moral appeal, often felt incapable of liberating their slaves because in doing so they would lose too much "property"; to treat their slaves as free human beings would simply cost them too much. Most chose prudence over humanity, allowing financial considerations to trump ethical principles. The same thing is happening today: we in the developed nations are the equivalent of slaveholders, resting easy on the fierce subordination of the world's ecosystems (and more).

In the United States, it took a war to bring about abolition. That event came at a great cost and nearly tore the republic apart. Yet that fight could succeed in part because abolition sought to undo an institution that was closely linked to one region of the nation. Today, climate change arises from the actions of people throughout America and around the world. No force will wage war against us to force us to change. As a result, we in the United States and elsewhere will have to renounce our privilege *voluntarily*. We will have to call on all our ethical reserves to make a wholesale renunciation of privilege. There really is no historical precedent for our doing anything of the sort.

The problem is not that we are uniquely corrupt, hopelessly selfish; it is rather that history now confronts us with a challenge to which *no prior generation* has ever arisen. We're being asked to do the impossible.

No wonder we'd rather do virtually anything to evade the task. None of us really wants to believe it is happening. We almost automatically put up great resistance to accepting it. Even those of us who react with despair or anguish typically move on quite soon to the realities of ordinary life. On some level, *all* of us are in denial. Who would welcome the thought of such a profound transformation? Facing the facts is the *last* thing any of us might wish to do.

If that is the case, then the strangeness of our response to it begins to make sense. The prospect of climate change is so unwelcome that the widespread outcry against its reality seems virtually inevitable. Climate change is nothing less than an assault on who we think we are: it exposes the fact that the economies of the developed world are founded on a lie, that our way of life takes for granted the eventual destruction of the Earth, and that persisting with it makes us complicit in a great crime. Nobody wants to accept those realities. It is thus remarkably satisfying for many people to turn our instinctive denial into a full-fledged, explicit, and articulate claim that nothing is amiss.

It is quite obvious that in doing so, we would cease to function as sane and responsible adults. At this stage of the evidence, to embrace denial is ultimately to *choose* the destruction of the Earth. But it does not follow that doing the opposite—choosing a sane response—is welcome to us, for it asks us to transform the foundations of our lives. To overcome denial requires us to accept that we have been living a lie for many generations, that our entire civilization is on the course toward committing ecocide—a crime much greater than genocide, though intimately bound up with it—and that our most intimate assumptions are monstrous if not worse.

If we do manage to rise to this challenge, we will have accomplished a feat virtually unique in human history. If we do not, our failure will be understandable, even if it will make us uniquely horrific. Either way, our generation will be the only of its kind in the history of the species. No wonder this moment feels so strange.

But the difficulty of our situation is still greater. Even if we are entirely persuaded we must do something and we attempt to do so on our own, it's not as if any one of us, or even a large social movement, has the power to do enough. In our own lives, we might take many steps to do much less to harm the biosphere, but those individual actions can never be enough as long as industrial and agricultural enterprises, and indeed entire nations, continue on with business as usual. As a result, we are caught in the contradiction between our willingness to act and the radical limits of our agency, between ethical principle and pragmatic reality. We might fight hard to push beyond that contradiction, to force the nations to change, but so far very little transformation has taken place; accordingly, we have little choice but to live within a social context still shaped by a denial we may not share, still caught up in habits we wish to break. Because we cannot produce the infrastructure of our society on our own, or manufacture the goods we use, we may end up inhabiting an economic system we deplore.

Faced with these seemingly impossible odds, we may resort to any number of plausible responses. We might, for example, simply throw up our hands in despair. In all bitterness, we may conclude that the task is too huge, the cost too great, the resistance so formidable, that it is impossible to worry about climate change any further. After all, we might argue, its worst effects won't happen until after we are dead: let later generations face them.

But here again, climate change won't let us pass it by. True enough, the idea that those effects will take place well into the future is surprisingly familiar across the political spectrum. Many people evidently assume that climate change will really come down hard on someone *else*, probably their grandchildren. Even James Hansen, one of those who first brought the concept of global warming to the attention of Congress and an advocate for greatly decreasing our greenhouse gas emissions, titled his recent book *Storms of My Grandchildren*. And James Garvey, in his excellent book, *The Ethics of Climate Change*, bases his analysis on our ethical obligation to others, especially to those in future generations.[13]

But do we really think that what happens to later generations is only a matter of our ethical obligation to them? The attitude we display as we carry out most of our activities tells us otherwise. If we build a city, don't we want it to endure? If we enjoy our local traditions, don't we want them to retain their charm? If we educate the young, don't we want them to flourish? If we bring about a medical breakthrough, don't we want it to help people live long and healthy lives? If we create a work of art, don't we want it to be enjoyed by posterity? If we write a book, don't we want it to be read? If we cherish the great cultural and historical achievements of the past, don't we want to pass them down to others after us? In short, what actions do we take that do *not* imply a relation to the future? What would be the point of our lives if the future were to disappear?

The future is never just for the people of the future; without that future, what we do now loses its force. Without a future, there is no present and not much of a past. Climate change isn't just about our obligation to others. It's about our *own* lives, too.

If we give up on climate change, we cancel the present. We choose to make all of our ordinary activities meaningless, as if we want to become shadows of ourselves, or as if we want to float forever in a world without foundations. None of us would choose such a fate. Yet choosing the opposite—a radical change in who we are—is immensely difficult as well. One option is horrific, the other impossible. But no other options are available.

At every turn, climate change puts us in new situations. It is truly unprecedented, not just as a material reality, but in its impact on our ordinary lives, our ability to understand it, our willingness to face its implications, and our capacity to discuss those implications for our societies. If it throws us off, if it inspires odd reactions in us or others, we shouldn't be surprised. Climate change is intrusive, insidious, anonymous, implacable. Yet it won't let us turn away. Endlessly, ruthlessly, climate change *interrupts* us, throws us off, and asks of us what we barely know how to give.

To take the full measure of that challenge, this book must of course bring into view the practical realities of our time. But the purpose in doing so is always to ponder their further dimensions, to *think* about their implications for all that we are.

In the chapters that follow, the first key step is to assess our current situation as honestly as possible, confronting it without denial and without reserve. Only on this basis can we begin to ponder the full implications of our dilemma. The task is not simply to review the facts but to allow them to sink in, to speak to us where we live, and to overcome our resistance to their full implications. Accordingly, I will first go back to the basics and grapple with climate change itself—to understand its impact on any one of us where we live. The next step, equally essential, is to consider what we can do to remove the causes of climate change and to ask whether we can take action in time to make a difference. The third step, key to any understanding of our present dilemma, is to consider why we are so hesitant to take action on the scale required—and whether, given our enormous population as human beings on a small planet, doing so will finally solve our environmental crisis. These initial steps will be the concerns of chapters one through five.

After exploring the physical and political realities as directly as possible, the book will then take up its core challenge of thinking about the human implications of the dilemma before us and to delve into their ultimate consequences. It will ask, what is it like to be alive at this strange moment? What is the present for, if the future is disappearing? How can we respond, if the point of our lives is dissolving, yet we live on? In exploring these questions from chapters six through eight, the book will bring forward the impact of the environmental crisis on our own lives, sketching the outline of an intimate disarray we are now beginning to experience in full force.

Having considered these tough, harrowing questions, the book will then seek a way through that disarray to a basis for living with integrity even in the midst of the ruins. What can anchor our actions on behalf of others and for the sake of all living things if the damage to the Earth is nearly irreversible, if the prospects for warding off disaster are dimming? How might we respond to natural forces with respect if they now threaten us with greater violence than before? Here the book will propose that our best option is to own disaster, to accept responsibility for what humanity has done to the biosphere, and thus commit ourselves to making reparation—and on that basis, to take concrete ethical actions in our own lives no matter what others may do. It will suggest as well that we may greet the ferocity of the whirlwind with awe, accepting at last our limited place within the biosphere and finding a renewed foundation for enduring whatever may come.

Notes

1. See the Fourth Report of the Intergovernmental Panel on Climate Change (the IPCC), Working Group I: The Physical Science Basis, Chapter Ten: Global Climate Projections, Executive Summary, on Snow and Ice, http://www.ipcc.ch/publications_and_data/ar4/wg1/en/ch10s10-es-4-precipitation-extremes.html - 10-es-5-snow-and.

2. I will use "climate change" more often than "global warming" throughout this book, not because "climate change" is a less offensive term but because it is more accurate. While "global warming" inevitably suggests that what we face is largely a matter of rising temperatures, "climate change" indicates that such warming has a wide array of varying consequences over time—including unusually cold snaps, large rain or snowstorms, and general transformations of regional climate systems. In short, "climate change" captures the big picture much better.

3. See Richard Kerr, "Arctic Summer Sea Ice Could Vanish Soon But Not Suddenly," *Science*, volume 323, number 5922 (March 27, 2009), 1655, doi:10.1126/science.323.5922.1655 and Bill McKibben, *Eaarth: Making a Life on a Tough New Planet* (New York: Times Books, 2010), 4.

4. See Fen Montaigne, "Arctic Tipping Point: A North Pole Without Ice," Yale360, August 30, 2012, http://e360.yale.edu/feature/tipping_point_arctic_heads_to_ice_free_summers/2567/ and David Spratt, "Big call: Cambridge prof. predicts Arctic summer sea ice 'all gone by 2015,'" Climate Code Red, August 30, 2012, http://www.climatecodered.org/2012/08/big-call-cambridge-prof-predicts-arctic.html.

5. I will use "we" throughout the book in describing most activities and choices to reflect the fact that all those alive today face the core dilemmas and will live with the consequences as well. In the context of climate change, many differences between people melt away. Typically, when describing how "we" must act, my emphasis will fall on those who live in developed nations, especially the United States, whose possibility for action will provide the context for many discussions to follow. Although people in nations around the world by no means have equal impact on the climate or an equal voice in advocating for change—for on the contrary, they suffer from a continuing structural inequality—they nevertheless have the responsibility to act as they can in their own circumstances to ward off the harm that will befall them and thus must also be included in the term.

6. See Andrew Freedman, "Arctic Warming is Altering Weather Patterns, Study Shows," Climate Central, April 3, 2012, http://www.climatecentral. org/news/arctic-warming-is-altering-weather-patterns-study-shows and the underlying study, Jennifer A. Francis and Stephen J. Vavrus, "Evidence linking Arctic amplification to extreme weather in mid-latitudes," *Geophysical Research Letters*, Volume 39, issue 6 (March 2012), L06801, doi:10.1029/2012GL051000.

7. Natalia Shakhova and others, "Extensive Methane Venting to the Atmosphere from Sediments of the East Siberian Arctic Shelf," *Science*, volume 327, number 5970 (March 5, 2010), 1246–1250, doi:10.1126/ science.1182221.

8. "Methane Releases From Arctic Shelf May Be Much Larger and Faster Than Anticipated," National Science Foundation, March 4, 2010, http://www.nsf. gov/news/news_summ.jsp?cntn_id=116532.

9. Steve Connor, "Vast methane 'plumes' seen in Arctic ocean as sea ice retreats," *The Independent*, December 13, 2011, http://www.independent. co.uk/news/science/vast-methane-plumes-seen-in-arctic-ocean-as-sea-ice-retreats-6276278.html. For more information about the Arctic clathrate melting process and its implications, see Sam Carana, "The potential for methane releases in the Arctic to cause runaway global warming," *Arctic News*, December 20, 2011, updated January 29, 2012, http://arctic-news.blogspot. com/p/potential-for-methane-release.html.

10. On the interplay between these feedback loops, see Peter Wadhams, "Imminent collapse of Arctic sea ice drives danger of accelerated methane thaw," *Arctic News*, March 7, 2012, http://arctic-news.blogspot.com/2012/03/ rebuttal-imminent-collapse-of-arctic.html.

11. See the Arctic Methane Emergency Group website, http://www.ameg.me and Peter Wadhams, "Geoengineering May Be Our Best Chance to Save Sea Ice," *Scientific American*, November 14, 2012, http://www.scientificamerican. com/article.cfm?id=geoengineering-last-chance-save-sea-ice.

12. See John Mason, "Arctic methane outgassing on the East Siberian Arctic Shelf. Part 2. An interview with Dr Natalia Shakhova," *Skeptical Science*, January 19, 2012, http://www.skepticalscience.com/arctic-methane-outgassing-e-siberian-shelf-part2.html and IdiotTracker, "Semiletov and Shakhova report," December 27, 2011, http://theidiottracker.blogspot. com/2011/12/semiletov-and-shakhova-report.html.

13. James Hansen, *Storms of My Grandchildren: The Truth About the Coming Climate Catastrophe and Our Last Chance to Save Humanity* (New York: Bloomsbury, 2009) and James Garvey, *The Ethics of Climate Change: Right and Wrong in a Warming World* (New York: Continuum, 2008). For an instructive and amusing discussion of how often speakers associate climate change with their grandchildren, see Bill McKibben, *Eaarth*, 11–13.

Chapter 1

Climate Change Will Happen to You

By now, many of us have some sense of the basics of climate change. We've seen images of melting ice, stranded polar bears, and calving glaciers. We've examined the charts depicting the rise in atmospheric carbon dioxide or heard about them. We've surmised whether Hurricane Katrina and various floods or droughts were caused by global warming. Maybe we've seen *An Inconvenient Truth* or read books about climatology. In fact, if polls are to be believed, most Americans accept the basic reality of climate change and would like the nation and the international community to do something about it.

But many of us might also hesitate to accept aspects of the science about climate change—whether it's actually happening or whether human activities are causing it. Since nothing I will say in the rest of this book will make much sense unless readers grapple first with these questions, if you are still cautious in these respects I recommend that you turn now to the Appendix, where I discuss them, and then return to this chapter.

Working through those concerns carefully is essential: if our decisions are to have a firm basis, if we are to live with real deliberation, we should not skip over any stage of the process. It's not likely we can become fully conscious of our situation as human beings without having paused to learn the fundamental physical facts of climate change. If you have already done so, keep reading: this is the chapter for you.

As it turns out, recognizing the reality of climate change—and its being caused by human beings—is only the start of a deep engagement with what confronts us. The further we go and the more we recognize the potential impact of climate change on our own lives, the more we may try to protect ourselves from what we learn so that we can continue with our lives in good conscience. Often it is quite easy to do so. For good reason, the typical discussion of global warming sticks close to the science; the difficulty of the subject for lay readers and the need for an explanation that can cut through the fog of rancorous debate require that the subject be handled with as little fuss as possible. But as a result, even the best presenters of the science write as if the facts will speak for themselves, as if there are no obstacles in our lives that would interfere with a full acceptance of what they say. In fact, few of us are free of such obstacles; most of us filter what we hear in some fashion or indulge a tendency to simplify or deny, misconstrue or exaggerate, the full import of the facts—at least in part, and perhaps unconsciously.

Delving further into climate change, in short, requires an increasingly direct confrontation with realities that we would rather ignore. Accordingly, for nearly all of us, the chief task is to break through the tendency to keep the entire problem at a distance from our actual lives. The challenge is to identify and confront the most representative ways we evade what the scientific research teaches us and thus to encounter the truth as fully as we can.

So let's begin with perhaps the first key objection one might make to the notion that climate change is a serious and immediate threat to humanity.

Yes, a voice protests, *climate change is real and will have serious consequences, but not right away; we have plenty of time to figure out what we'll do to keep its worst effects from taking place.*

To some extent, my discussion of our current situation in the opening pages of this book may provide an adequate, if hasty, reply. But to respond more fully to this objection, it may be valuable to slow down here and outline the overall context of contemporary scientific thinking on this question.

This objection relies on the scientific uncertainty with regard to exactly how much harm greenhouse gas emissions will eventually have. The estimates in the assessments of the Intergovernmental Panel on Climate Change (henceforth IPCC), the international body that assembles and summarizes the current state of scientific knowledge for the benefit of the world's governments (and was awarded the Nobel Peace Prize, along with Al Gore, in 2007), have indeed varied widely. More importantly, however, the sense that we have time to put together a response is also implicit in the slow pace of negotiations over international agreements about emissions—not to mention the even slower pace of compliance with the cuts already specified in the Kyoto Protocol. (Very few nations that signed those accords have begun to make substantial cuts in their emissions, despite the publicity over their promise to do so.)[14] The same patience is evident in the fact that these negotiators either set modest cuts in emissions (as at Kyoto) or distant dates for compliance.

The greatest virtue of this patient approach is its realism about the difficulty of finding agreement, changing our carbon-based culture, and cutting emissions deeply enough to make a difference. Anyone who reflects on how difficult it will be to transform our societies to the necessary degree must empathize with the bone-deep pragmatism of negotiators, their acceptance of the political conditions we face and the necessity of working within them to achieve anything that will matter.

But very little in the scientific research can justify such patience. For one thing, a portion of the carbon dioxide we emit remains in the atmosphere for a century or more. As a result, even if we soon curtail the amount of carbon dioxide we produce, levels of that gas will remain high throughout the rest of this century at least, forcing changes to the climate throughout that long period. In effect, our actions long ago are being felt today, and our actions today will be felt for many decades to come. The longer we continue our current habits, the greater the difficulties future generations will have to face. Unless we are fairly certain that today's emissions will do no harm later on, we should do what we can today.

Moreover, although views differ about the effects that will follow from our emissions, it would be foolish to assume that only the more optimistic projections are true. If the science is uncertain in this regard, we should listen to the full spectrum of considered judgment before opting for a slow-motion strategy. If we listen in this way, we will soon discover that things may be substantially *worse* than we might think.

The major debate among climate change scientists today is not whether climate change is real but whether it will have a more severe effect on Earth's ecosystems in the future than we previously thought. One element contributing to this debate is research into the problem of positive feedback loops of the sort I mentioned at the beginning of this book. These vicious circles emerge when the warming temperature causes the release of more greenhouse gases into the atmosphere, which cause a further increase in temperature, and on around again. Once these vicious circles become strong enough, they constitute "tipping points" that lead to an irreversible sequence of events and an unstoppable rise in temperature. The more gases we emit and the longer we wait to change our habits, the more likely we will cross these tipping points, making it even more difficult to postpone the arrival of serious climate change with all its consequences.

In his book on the subject, *With Speed and Violence: Why Scientists Fear Tipping Points in Climate Change*, Fred Pearce reviews a wide array of potential "positive feedback loops" that could arise in a number of regions of the world. Some of these tipping points may indeed be decades away. But we threaten to cross others in the fairly near future, if we have not done so already.[15]

Several key examples of tipping points are those I explored at the beginning of this book. As I mentioned there, the stunning melt of the Arctic sea ice in the summer of 2012 suggests to many observers that this process has now crossed the tipping point and become irreversible.

A second example, also related to the discussion in the introduction, is the possibility that the methane clathrates on the seabeds around the globe will begin to melt and release gas into the atmosphere.[16] If this feedback loop gets going on any large scale, we are in for big trouble, for there are untold quantities of methane capable of being released in this fashion. One estimate suggests that the methane in the clathrates in all the world's oceans is around four thousand times the amount in today's atmosphere.[17]

Researchers typically guess that such a clathrate melt will take place only at much later stages of climate change. In 2008, Mark Lynas suggested that this potential clathrate melt might take place on an Earth that had warmed 5° Centigrade over preindustrial temperatures.[18] But already, as I mentioned above, the clathrate melt is beginning on a shallow continental shelf of the Arctic Ocean. That relatively local event does not suggest that the clathrates around the world are about to melt as well. But because clathrates exist in such huge numbers, even a melt in only a small fraction of their total bulk would be enough to shift the Earth's climate severely. We are already seeing what might be the beginnings of that event, in which case it is making itself felt at temperatures far lower than we expected, and several decades earlier as well.

There is yet another worrisome instance looming not far from the arctic region. One of the most pressing instances of a possible tipping point is the melting permafrost throughout the far North—in Siberia, Alaska, and northern Canada. When it melts, it releases immense volumes of carbon dioxide and methane. Once the release of these gases hits a certain point, it will cause so much further warming—and further melting of the permafrost—that the results will be irreversible.

The tipping point for the permafrost is not far away. One study that appeared in January 2011 strikingly predicts that the feedback loop in the far North will cause the arctic permafrost to become a net source (not sink) of carbon and methane after the mid-2020s and will be strong enough to cancel between 42 and 88 percent of the planet's land-based capacity to absorb those emissions.[19]

These examples may imply that only the feedback loops of the far North—the Arctic ice, the clathrates, the permafrost—are of concern. But consider what is transpiring in the Amazon region. Rising temperatures and an associated decline in rainfall have led to the drying of the Amazon rainforest, causing trees there to grow less and making them more vulnerable to decay and to wildfires, as well as to the very serious droughts of 2005 and 2010.[20] This process has gone so far by now that by some estimates this ecosystem now *releases more carbon dioxide into the atmosphere than it absorbs.*[21] Think about it: the Amazon, once famous for being one of the Earth's best ecosystems for soaking up immense quantities of carbon dioxide—and for pumping huge quantities of oxygen into the atmosphere—may already be helping to *drive* global warming rather than alleviate it, and if not, is likely to do so very soon. Once we cross that tipping point for good, an entire array of planetary systems that dominate not far from the Equator will be transformed as well. That example suggests that the Earth's systems *in every region* are vulnerable to severe disarray; no area of the biosphere is safe.

As realities like this suggest, if we ignore the causes that set these vicious circles into motion, we will face an impossible challenge, for in the following years, the results could wipe out any gains we might make in reducing our greenhouse gas emissions. The Arctic sea melt is already irreversible. If any one of these other processes crosses the tipping point, we are in for major trouble. Yet all of these tipping points are drawing nearer every day. Our contribution to climate change right now is significant enough, but once very large ecosystems get into the game, they will dwarf what we can do.

There you go again, another voice objects; *you are sounding much too loud an alarm. Climate change is real and is caused by human beings, but don't make any reckless statements about its potential effects. Don't get carried away; cut back on statements that go too far, that warn against all kinds of horrible and devastating consequences.* Some "skeptics" apply this advice to nearly all discussions of climate change, advocating what they regard as a "moderate" estimate of global warming's dangers; others, such as Claire Parkinson, a clear-sighted scientist well within the mainstream who otherwise has a great deal to teach us, targets more narrow claims.[22]

No doubt it is best for all participants in the debate to stick as closely as possible to demonstrable findings. But because this argument places far more emphasis on curbing wild talk than the danger of the crisis itself, it ultimately treats caution and politeness as more important than the future of the planet. Such a preference reveals an excessive distaste for the language of crisis. This kind of talk, some think, is *always* irresponsible, just a form of panic-mongering. Evidently, a responsible, sane person should avoid speaking of an emergency or doing anything reckless, like proposing that we consider modifying our way of life. But to focus on excessive statements rather than the underlying threat of climate change diverts attention from the most pressing concerns to relatively marginal ones. It's as if these authors live in a house that is starting to burn down, but would do anything rather than actually sound the alarm: that would be noisy and rude!

This preference for understating the severity of the threat, as it turns out, is shared not only by a handful of scientists but may characterize the general tone of climate science overall. One recent study suggests that "scientists are biased not toward alarmism but the reverse," toward "erring on the side of less rather than more alarming predictions," possibly because researchers generally adhere to the "scientific norms of restraint, objectivity, skepticism, rationality, dispassion, and moderation." The authors of this study argue that climate scientists have more often under-stated the potential impact of climate change than the opposite, fearful of coming across as alarmist or incautious in their findings.[23]

While in many contexts this bias toward caution may serve scientific research well, in the arena of controversy over climate change it may rein-force our belief that the situation is not that dire after all. In short, it can feed into our sense that things are all right and will work themselves out in some fashion. Such a viewpoint is clearly a mode of denial, even if one who espouses it is otherwise remarkably insightful. As Parkinson herself admits late in her book, she is less concerned about the future than oth-ers because she believes that "surely" inventors will create new energy alternatives that will make fossil fuels a thing of the past, and by implica-tion will do so in time for us to avoid the ill effects of climate change.[24] But it is naive to suggest that a solution will simply appear or that it even if it does it will take effect immediately. Inventions take time to manu-facture and even longer to produce on a massive scale that this occasion requires. Only a supreme confidence, however unjustified—only a belief in the secular equivalent of a miracle—can explain such a distaste for talk of crisis.

All right, one might say, *it's happening, we're causing it, and it may be worse than we thought. But from what I see, it may not happen* **here**. After all, most of the images we associate with climate change depict what is happening elsewhere—in the Arctic, for example, or around the distant islands that will soon be swallowed by rising waters. Seldom do we see images of the effects of climate change on us where we live. Of course, we are aware that our summers are warmer than before, our growing seasons longer, our climate more erratic and surprising. But so far very few of us have been lost on melting sea ice or swamped by the rising tides.

Most of us are so used to thinking about climate change in this man-ner that it is very difficult for us to get beyond it. Perhaps only a brutal restatement of our situation will get us out of the habit and help us focus on what will happen to us in our own immediate surroundings. So here it is: climate change is devastating, absolutely powerful, undismissible, *even if* in our darker, most selfish moments we might want to say "damn the ice caps" or "the hell with Tuvalu," *even if* we might wish to mutter so as no one can hear, "pfft to plankton" or "good riddance to the coral reefs." Climate change won't just harm others, forcing the Peruvians to suffer from thirst or sweeping more Bangladeshis away in flooding seas; on the contrary, we better pay serious attention, for our *own* way of life is on the line.

For one thing, as I mentioned in the introduction, the changes in the Arctic are already altering weather patterns over the northern hemisphere. Just consider the strange events in the United States in 2012: the huge thunderstorm and tornado complex—the derecho—that swept over central and eastern portions of the country starting on June 29; the vast wildfires in the West beginning as early as April; the massive drought in the Midwest, threatening food crops and on occasion closing Mississippi River traffic; and Superstorm Sandy that wreaked havoc over major parts of the Northeast in November. In that single year, the altered climate caused significant harm to nearly every region of the country. And that's just 2012: the same pattern is borne out by the bizarre episodes—too many to list—in the seasons since then. Researchers now state outright that there is a strong link between climate change and these extreme weather patterns. According to the Environment America Research & Policy Center, the frequency of extreme precipitation events has increased by 30 percent from 1948 to 2011.[25] Are you confident that you will escape such events in the forthcoming years and decades?[26]

Climate change will be just as real where you live as anywhere else on Earth. In the United States, it will raise average temperatures; increase the amount of moisture in the air, making heavy precipitation events (of rain or snow) more likely, thus causing an increase in flooding and landslides; increase the number of blisteringly hot days in the summer; change the water cycle and increase evaporation, in most regions resulting in a drier landscape and more frequent droughts; and create the conditions for more insect and waterborne diseases. It will force the migration of local species into new habitats further north, as well as the absorption of species moving from the south, thus altering the balance between mutually dependent forms of life within each local ecosystem. The changes to the water cycle will alter the rivers, streams, and open landscapes throughout the country and the fundamental character of each region. These changes, and many more, are likely to have an adverse effect on food production, outdoor activities, seasonal rituals, the physical structures we have built, public health, and local and regional economies. We may end up living in natural systems that are not only rapidly changing, but also much weaker and in some cases dying out altogether. We'll be far less comfortable right where we live than we once were.[27]

At first changes of this kind may seem overstated. For example, the fact that the zones with a particular average annual temperature will be shifting northwards might not initially sound so bad. After all, one might argue, ecosystems further south hang together quite well; wouldn't they fare equally well if they moved to the north? But many species are less able to compete with or displace species that already live in regions to the north, to reproduce quickly and thus adjust to new living conditions, and to move across miles of territory in a few years, suggesting that some portions of an ecosystem will migrate successfully while others will not. Some species might be mobile enough to move on, but if they did so, would lose access to their sources of food or to the habitats (river valleys, mountains) where they previously flourished. Forms of life that flourish in mountainous terrain may have only so far up the mountainside to migrate before running out of room. Unlike animals or birds, plants rooted in the soil might find it difficult to move quickly into new terrain. Many species will adapt to new conditions, but many others will not. Studies show that in the second half of the twentieth century, species on average migrated toward the poles at the rate of four miles per decade, while the zones in which they live—those defined by specific average temperatures—have migrated far more quickly, about thirty-five miles per decade.[28] Over time, as warming continues, the species that can't move very fast will find themselves within much warmer temperature belts, will be unable to flourish within a climate too hot for them, and will succumb to natural forces.

Such pressures can take many forms. Consider the changes taking place in the pine forests of western North America, especially in British Columbia. The pine beetle, a native insect in those regions, is now reproducing at a much greater rate than before; thanks to the warming winters, the warmer summers, and the reduction in summer precipitation, it is becoming a much more dominant species in those habitats than before. As a result, it is killing millions of acres of trees, converting the boreal forest of British Columbia from a carbon sink to a net emitter of carbon.[29]

Such vast damage in those forests, needless to say, will have profound impacts in the entire ecosystem, changing the water cycle, the growth patterns across the formerly wooded landscape, and much more. This transformation is largely due to the activities of a *single species* and perfectly illustrates how the complex interactions between species in ecosystems make them terribly vulnerable to climate change.

But changes due to the expansion of single species throughout a region are relatively subtle compared to the even broader transformations that every ecosystem will have to undergo. The effect of pine beetles in western forests pales in comparison to the even more dramatic effects of rising temperatures on the water cycle. The warming of the ecosystem increases evaporation and causes the gradual drying of the land, killing trees even where they are not vulnerable to insects. Recent research into the state of forests throughout the western United States shows that they are already experiencing a demographic shift—an increase in the number of trees dying and a decrease in the number of new trees growing per year—and that as a result they are approaching "thresholds for abrupt dieback." The drier conditions as well as the increasing activity of various species of insects is leading to rising mortality in those forests.[30] Evidently, climate change often works through several effects at once, each compounding the impact of others, creating conditions that are worse than any single process could bring about.

Similar changes are taking place in every region of the United States. In the Northeast, for example, climate change will drive the maple forests further north, eventually depriving the region of the autumn colors distinctive to the region, and the rising seas and increasing intensity of storms will lead to greater storm surges, damages to wetlands, coastal flooding, and erosion (as the stunning effects of Superstorm Sandy have made abundantly clear). The Southeast will become so hot and dry that its pine forests may disappear; oxygen depletion in the region's lakes will kill off fish in lakes and streams; and more powerful tornadoes and hurricanes will damage inland regions and coastal areas alike. The Southwest faces a dramatically altered future, one in which droughts will be longer and more intense than they were in the past, causing rivers and lakes to diminish and fires to spread more easily. The reduction in the snowpack over the Sierra Nevada in eastern California will lead to severe water shortages in much of that state; in mid to late summer, people there may turn on the tap and find no water coming out. Needless to say, these and other changes will harm each region's food supply, sources of energy, distinctive landscape, and quality of life—if such a drab list of consequences can possibly capture the scale and intensity of what will take place.[31]

It's not difficult to extrapolate this pattern to the rest of the planet. Clearly, climate change will have severe consequences for ecosystems around the world. Forests all across the world are in serious danger.[32] Moreover, the stress on ecosystems is putting a fair portion of the planet's species under terrific pressure. Although it boggles the mind to sum up the possible effects on the Earth as a whole, some scientists have attempted to do so: one often-cited study by scientists on several continents who examined 1000 species concluded that under a mid-range estimate of the severity of climate change—that is, with an increase of only around 2° Celsius above preindustrial levels, and only 1.2° over current temperatures—15 to 37 percent of Earth's land species could be "committed to extinction" by 2050, although a more recent study qualifies those findings and provides a somewhat less pessimistic assessment.[33]

What about the sea? We often forget that climate change acidifies the oceans, harming organisms that rely on calcium carbonate to form shells or skeletons, including the coccolithophores, one of the most abundant types of plankton. The prospect that the further absorption of carbon dioxide into the oceans could damage the plankton, the first links of the marine food chain, is especially chilling. Scientists do not understand the potential effects of further acidification well, but given what we do know already, we have little reason for optimism.[34] One study states that the oceans are acidifying at a rate ten times faster than they did 55 million years ago during a period of mass extinction for marine life, and another finds roughly a 1 percent decline per year in plankton since 1950 due to warming temperatures at the ocean's surface.[35] A recent study conducted by the International Programme on the State of the Ocean found far greater declines in oceanic life than expected; Alex Rogers, its scientific director, stated, "[A]lmost right across the board we're seeing changes that are happening faster than we'd thought, or in ways that we didn't expect to see for hundreds of years."[36]

So far I have emphasized how climate change will put nearly all ecosystems into severe disarray and force a good portion of the Earth's species into extinction. But for human beings, these biological realities are only part of the picture. For us, such vast damage will also deplete the pleasure we take in natural beauty—in the blossoming of a tree, the cry of a bird, the subtle coloring of a fish, the scent of bark, the interweaving of forms on a tangled bank. The devastation of Earth's living forms is also a traumatic blow to the beauty of the common day, the poetry of everyday life.

So what, someone might respond; *we've always had extinction, and we always will; there is nothing here to be upset about.* But this time we're not talking about one species giving up its habitat to another over many decades or being pushed out under ordinary processes of natural selection. We're talking about a volatile combination of factors: wiping out the ecological niche of many species; making complex biological interrelations vulnerable to unforeseen interactions; and putting entire ecosystems under duress. In fact, extinction at *this* pace and at *these* numbers deserves a stronger term; it is not just extinction, but the death or at least decay of entire natural systems, if not of the Earth itself. Some previous events in the planet's history caused a similar devastation—the impact of meteors, for example—but do we really want to compete with meteors to see which force can mess up the Earth the most?

All this is bad enough. But at the moment we are causing much more than climate change. If you factor in everything *else* that advanced industrial civilization is doing to our local and regional ecosystems, the situation becomes even more difficult. All kinds of familiar practices on which we in the United States rely today—monoculture agriculture; the depletion of water aquifers; the release of vast quantities of nitrogen into ecosystems from fertilizer; large-scale farming of chickens, pigs, and cows, creating unprecedented quantities of manure effluent; the destruction of wetlands; the expansion of cities, suburbs, and exurbs; strip mining, mountaintop coal mining, and oil drilling in formerly protected areas; the release of untold quantities of plastics into the world's waterways and oceans; overfishing; and the inadvertent importation of exotic species, to name a few—already place our ecosystems under duress. To add climate change, with all its consequences, to this pressure simply multiplies the danger.

All these factors make it clear that the transformations to ecosystems will take place right in our own neighborhoods. If you need an image to capture the relevance of climate change for you and yours, take a look at the natural life that surrounds you wherever you live and imagine it damaged or disappearing. Then remember for a moment that if climate change decimates an ecosystem, it won't come back—at least not in the form we know, and not for millennia. It will be gone for good.

Very well, someone might reply, *that may be true for most regions, but some areas will no doubt benefit from climate change: their growing seasons will expand, more life will flourish there, and the winters will be more temperate. Isn't climate change good news for* **some** *people?*

It's true that climate change models have suggested that some areas may experience warming that will improve the growing season, for example, or reduce the discomforts of winter. But it's naive to imagine that these changes are truly beneficial. As we've already seen, the warming climate has *devastated* the boreal forest of British Columbia; the loss of those cold winter nights, and of the shorter growing season, has *not* been a benefit there. Any so-called benefit to other regions is likely to have similar effects.

Nevertheless, it's worth taking this objection seriously and thinking it through with another thought experiment. If we imagine that some region would actually benefit, then what might follow? For one thing, can we suppose that the people who live in the lucky region rely exclusively for their well-being on what happens there? Or do they live in houses built of imported materials, drive cars manufactured in other regions, eat food grown elsewhere? Conversely, do they sell their own wares to people who live elsewhere? What supports the economy of their region? If ecosystems in other regions are suffering, so also will the economic base in those regions, and the trading relationships will suffer as well. No region can imagine that it would survive easily on its own.

But for a moment, let's take this experiment to a second level and imagine that it could thrive all by itself. Perhaps people in a particular region would be very good at creating a self-sustaining economy. Very well. But if residents of other regions are suffering, doesn't it seem likely they would migrate to the areas that lucked out? As a result, wouldn't those better-off areas be overwhelmed with people seeking a better life? What's more, does it seem likely these migrants would have been able to sell their homes at a good price? Would they always have secured jobs that paid them as well? The people in the lucky zone might find themselves trying to accommodate an inflow of stressed-out, disadvantaged people hoping to find a good place to live. If nonhuman species will have to migrate, people will too. What's more, they will often have to migrate across national borders, leading to a whole range of crucial political questions. Once you factor in human mobility, you change the entire dynamic: a region whose *climate* might not be bad will have to face a massive *social* transformation, one that may stress out the region's ecosystem in turn.

So it simply isn't credible to suggest that climate change would benefit anyone in the long term. Because of the intricate web of our economies and the inevitability of migration, there are no guarantees. Perhaps if those who lived in this hypothetical lucky region put together a self-sustaining economy—*and* declared political independence, surrounded the entire zone with a thirty-foot fence to keep everyone else out, and taxed themselves silly to create a state-of-the-art military that could defeat any invaders—*then* they could live in relative abundance (if also in a state of perpetual selfishness and paranoia). Does *that* sound like a good future?

All right, says one last voice, *even if everything you say is true—even if climate change will alter the ecosystems where I live or cause a massive social transformation in my region, what difference does it really make to* **me**? *I don't care about nature; if a lot of species go extinct, it's not going to affect* **me**. *Ecosystems may come and go, but in the modern world, what does it matter? I don't really object to social change in my neighborhood, either; by now we're all used to new developments of that kind. As long as I have a job and can live in my urban environment, with a car, a cell phone, a nice Internet connection, good heating, a working air conditioner, and plenty of food at my local supermarket, everything's going to be fine.*

The voice that speaks here is at last the distinctive, perhaps mostly unconscious, voice of our own innate, indestructible narcissism. That profound cluelessness arises in all of us at the prospect of our own mortality: though we acknowledge the reality of our eventual deaths on some level, we don't often live in accordance with that insight. The same applies even more to the thought of what may happen to the Earth. Perhaps the greatest help to our narcissism in the face of global warming is the air conditioner: evidently, as long as we are assured we'll be able to live in a relatively comfortable indoor temperature in perpetuity, we sense that there is nothing much to worry about.

This version of the near future may seem surprisingly plausible. Perhaps even if the seas rise, the planet warms, and vast portions of the Earth are devastated by climate change, wealthy people living in some places will live in circumstances not entirely different from what they are used to. If they wish, they might well ignore the bad news arriving from around the country and the world—at least for a while. They might even dismiss the changes to the climate of their region, the dying forests on nearby mountains, the shrinking local rivers, and the new vulnerability of many plants, birds, and animals that live in their vicinity. But eventually they will find it difficult to ignore the dust storms that may result from the drying of vast regions; the dwindling water supply; the much harsher snowstorms, rainstorms, tornadoes, hurricanes, or windstorms; the occasional severe floods (surprising, no doubt, given the general drying of the landscape); or the landslides and avalanches in nearby terrain.

But natural disasters will only be part of the story. The slow devastation of ecosystems around the world will eventually take its toll. We are not likely to welcome the consequences of stress to agricultural regions, leading to rising food prices; nor of stress to the local water cycle, resulting in a lower water supply and perhaps water rationing; nor of global warming itself, causing occasional summer days with brutally high temperatures. We will not be happy that climate change will cause long-term difficulty for many industries, including fishing, forestry, tourism, and outdoor recreation, and will impose immense costs on regions recovering from natural disasters. Nor will we be pleased when climate change begins to eat away at the nation's economic growth rate—or more likely, cause a perpetual *negative* growth rate, forcing us into a permanent and devastating Climate Change Depression. It will be especially challenging to deal with these and other difficulties while also helping an increasing number of retirees meet their monthly expenses and pay for their medical care. Moreover, the consequences of international chaos on ordinary lives might be painful as well. When nations begin to enter severe domestic crises, endure new rounds of terrorist activity, or wage war against each other over basic natural resources, food supplies, population pressures, or rights of migration, one may find one's own nation at war as well—or suffering the economic or political consequences of that unrest in other ways, even potentially within its own borders.

To imagine that we can shield ourselves from all these trends by retreating to living spaces, turning on the air conditioner, and entertaining ourselves in some fashion simply ignores reality. In one way or another, the transformation of the planet will seep through those walls. We may find ourselves incensed at the result and might even mutter: *why didn't they* **tell** *me it would be like this?*

There really is no evading it: climate change is well under way, caused by human beings, *and it will happen to you.*

Notes

14.   Robert P. Semple, Jr., "Remember Kyoto? Most Nations Don't," *New York Times*, December 3, 2011, http://www.nytimes.com/2011/12/04/opinion/sunday/remember-kyoto-most-nations-dont.html?_r=0.

15.   Fred Pearce, *With Speed and Violence: Why Scientists Fear Tipping Points in Climate Change* (Boston: Beacon Press, 2007).

16.   See Pearce, *With Speed and Violence,* 91–98.

17.   Thomas Blunier, "'Frozen' Methane Escapes from the Sea Floor," *Science,* volume 288, number 5463 (April 7, 2000), 68–69. doi:10.1126/science.288.5463.68.

18.   Mark Lynas, *Six Degrees: Our Future on a Hotter Planet* (Washington, D.C.: National Geographic 2008), 220–228.

19.   Kevin Schaefer and others, "Amount and timing of permafrost carbon release in response to climate warming," *Tellus B*, volume 63, Issue 2 (April 2011), 165–180, doi:10.1111/j.1600-0889.2011.00527.x.

20.   On these droughts see Simon L. Lewis and others, "The 2010 Amazon Drought," *Science,* volume 331, number 6017 (February 4, 2011), 554, doi:10.1126/science.1200807; on the only partial recovery of the rainforest from the 2005 drought by the 2010 drought see Yadvinder Malhi and others, "Persistent effects of a severe drought on Amazonian forest canopy," *Proceedings of the National Academy of Sciences of the United States of America,*

volume 110, number 2 (published online before print December 24, 2012), 565–570, doi:10.1073/pnas.1204651110.

21. Fred Pearce, *With Speed and Violence*, 65. For more on the effects of climate change on the Amazon, see Nikolas Kozloff, *No Rain in the Amazon: How South America's Climate Change Affects the Entire Planet* (New York: Palgrave Macmillan, 2010).

22. Despite the inaccuracy of the term, a problem I will discuss in the Appendix, I will use the word "skeptics" because calling this group "deniers" suggests that the rest of us are somehow free of denial – a dubious proposition at best.

23. Keynyn Brysse and others, "Climate change prediction: Erring on the side of least drama?" *Global Environmental Change*, volume 23, issue 1 (February 2013), 327–337.

24. Parkinson, *Coming Climate Crisis?* 321.

25. See Nathan Willcox, "Extreme downpours up 30%. Scientists link trend to global warming," Environment America, July 31, 2012, http://www.environmentamerica.org/news/ame/new-report-extreme-downpours-30-percent and the underlying report, Environment America Research and Policy Center, "When it Rains, it Pours: Global Warming and the Increase in Extreme Precipitation from 1948 to 2011," July 31, 2012, http://www.environmentamerica.org/reports/ame/when-it-rains-it-pours.

26. For a summary of the leading climate change stories of 2012, which includes events that occurred in the United States, see Greg Laden, "Top Climate Stories of 2012," ScienceBlogs, December 28, 2012, http://scienceblogs.com/gregladen/2012/12/28/top-climate-stories-of-2012/.

27. For a brief, readable overview assessing the impact of climate change on each region of the United States, see the United States Global Change Research Program, *Global Climate Change Impacts in the U.S., 2009 Report*, http://nca2009.globalchange.gov/.

28. Hansen, *Storms of My Grandchildren*, 146.

29. W. A. Kurz and others, "Mountain pine beetle and forest carbon feedback to climate change," *Nature* 452 (April 24, 2008), 987–990, doi:10.1038/nature06777.

30. Phillip J. van Mantgem and others, "Widespread Increase of Tree Mortality Rates in the Western United States," *Science*, volume 323, number 5913 (January 23, 2009), 521–24, doi:10.1126/science.1165000.

31. See the assessment at the United States Global Change Research Program, *Global Climate Change Impacts in the U.S., 2009 Report*, http://nca2009.globalchange.gov/.

32. Justin Gillis, "With Deaths of Forests, a Loss of Key Climate Protectors," *New York Times*, October 1, 2011, http://www.nytimes.com/2011/10/01/science/earth/01forest.html?pagewanted=all.

33. Chris D. Thomas and others, "Extinction Risk from Climate Change," *Nature* 427 (January 8, 2004), 145–148, doi:10.1038/nature02121. For a lucid meditation on the implications of these findings, see Mark Lynas, *Six Degrees*, 115–119. The recent, smaller study surprisingly finds that taxonomic groups (rather than species) migrate at an average rate matching the shifts in temperature, significantly complicating the picture; see I-Ching Chen and others (including Chris Thomas), "Rapid Range Shifts of Species Associated with High Levels of Climate Warming," *Science* 333 (August 19, 2011), 1024–26, doi:10.1126/science.1206432. For a general guide to climate change's effect on ecosystems, see Robert Henson, *The Rough Guide to Climate Change* (London: Rough Guides, 2006).

34. For a report on recent research on the consequences of ocean acidification, see Richard Kerr, "Ocean Acidification Unprecedented, Unsettling," *Science*, volume 328, number 5985 (June 18, 2010), 1500–1501, doi:10.1126/science.328.5985.1500, which emphasizes the toll that acidification will take on a wide range of marine organisms. On ocean acidification and the coccolithophores, see Jacqueline Ruttiman, "Sick Seas," *Nature* 442 (August 31, 2006), 978–980, doi:10.1038/442978a; and Dalin Shi and others, "Effect of Ocean Acidification on Iron Availability to Marine Phytoplankton," *Science*, volume 327, number 5966 (February 5, 2010), 676–679, doi:10.1126/science.1183517.

35. Andy Ridgwell and Daniela N. Schmidt, "Past constraints on the vulnerability of marine calcifiers to massive carbon dioxide release," *Nature Geoscience* volume 3, number 3 (March 2010), 196–200, doi:10.1038/ngeo745; and Daniel G. Boyce, Marlon R. Lewis, and Boris Worm, "Global phytoplankton decline over the past century," *Nature* 466 (July 29, 2010), 591–596, doi:10.1038/nature09268.

36. Richard Black, "World's oceans in 'shocking' decline," *BBC News,* June 20, 2011, http://www.bbc.co.uk/news/science-environment-13796479; see the International Programme on the State of the Ocean website for reports and updates at http://www.stateoftheocean.org/.

Chapter 2

What We Could Do

So if climate change is taking place, will intensify further in the coming years, and will hit us where we live, what can we do? If we accept the findings of scientists about climate change, the path before us is clear: since we human beings are contributing to the problem, we should do as much as we can, as soon as we can, to reduce our contributions to climate change. We should do so on every level: as individuals, families, businesses, industries, states, nations, and the international community. We should use every technology already known to us to reduce our emissions; be inventive in finding, testing, and implementing new technologies; create smart and workable public policies and real-world arrangements to help smooth the transition to new practices; and handle the many historical, cultural, social, economic, and political obstacles to this transition with grace and sensitivity—while moving ahead as quickly as is feasible.

The trouble is that we have not taken these steps with the clarity and dispatch we need. In fact, we have done the opposite. Most nations have continued with business as usual, delayed real action, perhaps taken partial steps at most, and waited for others to sign on before starting up a serious effort. But the climate continues to change, and time is waning. Even as scientists warn us that waiting further could be disastrous, we persist in a resolute inertia.

At this late hour, then, we need to take a double approach to the challenge before us. On one level, we must examine carefully the entire range of measures we could take for reducing the harm we do. To this end, we could rely on those expert guides who explain how to use existing sources of energy more efficiently; how to create, distribute, and use new, sustainable sources of energy; and how to reduce or end other practices (outside of energy use) that contribute to climate change.[37]

But doing so is not enough. If we are to be honest about what we must do, we need to take into account the obstacles that prevent us from taking action. Even if we have a set of potential strategies in hand, they will not do much good if they are too expensive, take too long to implement, or harm the environment. Furthermore, what will it take to overcome political opposition, to change actual attitudes and behavior, and to inspire action on the vast scale that is required? This aspect of the question is the most crucial, because so far it has proved the toughest to solve.

Accordingly, we have little choice but to examine our potential course of action taking *all* of the relevant factors into account. A thorough, comprehensive look at energy efficiency and technology, however necessary, cannot take us far without an honest appraisal of our collective willingness to act and to change.

Let's start with a basic principle: we simply must shift from our current heavy reliance on oil, coal, and gas to less destructive fuels. Some might argue that the recent shift from oil or coal to the relatively less harmful natural gas is at least a step in the right direction, but it turns out that enough natural gas (or methane) escapes into the atmosphere during the drilling process to cancel out any such benefit.[38] We can't fix anything by shifting from one fossil fuel to another; our only real option is to rely on renewable energy, if we must use energy at all. But at this point we cannot rely very much on alternative sources of energy; a key task is to figure out what technologies might work best and how soon we can implement them.

Several sources of energy are very promising but may simply create more problems than they might solve. Many experts suggest that nuclear power is an excellent long-term option for providing energy at a comparatively small cost in injury to people, footprint on the landscape, and the storage of waste, especially when compared to fossil fuels. But it's clear that creating a new generation of nuclear power plants would be extremely expensive and time-consuming; since few plants are currently in the process of being built and each plant takes roughly a decade to come on line, nuclear power cannot help us right when we must take huge strides toward cutting our emissions. Furthermore, because of the events at Three Mile Island, Chernobyl, and Fukushima, we all have serious questions about the safety and reliability of nuclear power. Even if the engineering details make nuclear power intriguing, as a real-world matter, implementing it raises too many questions and—even if it should win public approval—would take far too long. It's not a viable option.

Geothermal energy has the great advantages of being inexhaustible, creating no byproducts, remaining constant through time (unlike solar or wind energy), interfering in no natural motion of the winds or tides, and requiring no extraction from the Earth (a claim that not even nuclear power can make, reliant as it is on the mining of uranium). But it, too, requires us to intervene into the Earth's systems, for when we drill some distance beneath the surface, we may risk triggering seismic disruptions, even small earthquakes. A greater problem is that over much of the Earth, bedrock of a sufficiently high temperature (300°) is found very far below the surface; in most of the western half of the United States, for example, geothermal engineers would have to drill down four miles or more, and in most of the eastern half, over six miles.[39] Drilling that deep on a large scale is technically and financially difficult and will be feasible only after a lot more research and testing.

This sort of problem applies not only to alternative forms of energy, but to the possible transformation of our use of fossil fuel as well. Many observers suggest that we cannot rely on renewable sources alone; we will also have to burn coal and natural gas—not as we have done in the past, releasing ruinous quantities of carbon dioxide into the atmosphere, but by capturing and storing it deep in the ground. Although the process of capture and storage will take up part of the energy the plants generate and will thus raise energy costs, at least it will not harm the atmosphere. The real problem in this case—and it's a big one—is that this technology is largely untested; so far not a single coal plant has actually tested carbon capture technology in any serious way. Moreover, just as the Environmental Protection Agency is pondering whether to ban the release of carbon dioxide into the atmosphere from future coal-burning plants in an effort to force them to capture carbon, the low price of increasingly available natural gas is removing incentives for utilities to build such expensive plants at all.[40] Nevertheless, Carbon Engineering has created prototype carbon cleanup systems in Calgary, Alberta, and now hopes to market its techniques to oil companies and others. Experimentation with this technique is still in its early stages; according to one report, David Keith, the president of this company, "says he thinks it may be possible to lower the cost of capture toward $100 a ton as the company grows."[41] Because the study of this technology is at such an early stage and its potential use so expensive, we cannot presume to rely on it in a large scale in the near future. Yet in his mission to find out how to create an energy system that will reduce greenhouse gas emissions 90 percent in the United Kingdom by 2030, George Monbiot suggests that that nation get half of its power for electricity from plants that burn natural gas (not coal) while using capture and storage technology. Think about it: he's suggesting that *half of the electricity* come from a technology that he admits is *largely untested*. Does that sound like a solid plan to you? But what other choice does he have? Renewable energy of other kinds won't supply enough power to keep Britain going. His dilemma is typical of this entire discussion. We need technologies we do not have, and we need them yesterday.[42]

Luckily, bad news of this sort is not the whole story. Other technologies at first do not seem promising but on a second look turn out to be potentially helpful. Biofuels—fuels created from trees or plants—are technologically viable, but creating an incentive for people to tear out native ecosystems and grow crops to be sold for this purpose—especially in Brazil, where their planting has helped destroy vital ecosystems—undermines the whole purpose of this transition, which is to sustain and enhance the ecosystems we still have.[43] Removing crops for food and replacing them with plants for biofuel can also lower the food supply and raise food prices around the world.[44] A more responsible and sustainable practice of using only waste products or byproducts of farming or forest management might work, if conducted very carefully, but would produce only a fraction of the energy we need.

But a related alternative to biofuels has great promise. Burning the methane emissions from public landfills, sewage plants, and farms addresses two problems at once: it reduces those emissions and transforms them into a locally sustaining form of energy. The technology is readily available; cattle and pig farmers use this technology to burn manure to generate electricity for their own use or for sale back into the grid.[45] Moreover, it is being used very effectively in Kristianstad, Sweden, which burns biogas from a landfill, sewage ponds, wood waste, and tree prunings, heating homes and businesses without relying on other renewable energies.[46] This technology burns a bit of biofuel along with the gas arising from garbage and waste and may thus provide a good alternative to the more familiar version of biofuel. A municipal biogas plant has the advantage of potentially being under local control: presumably you wouldn't have to move heaven and earth to get a local biogas plant up and running; you'd just have to create the necessary will in your own community. With enough initiative in cities and towns throughout the world, this technology could be implemented widely.

An alternative to geothermal energy also has real merit. Without drilling deep into the Earth, we can still use its warmth as a source of energy. Below five feet or so, the ground has a constant temperature; if you lay a network of pipes in the ground below that depth and run water through those pipes, you can draw the heat from the Earth, concentrate it, put it through a heat exchanger, and use it to warm or cool your house.[47] While the initial cost is high, this source of energy pays for itself in a few years. The largest obstacles to its widespread adoption are public ignorance, the large initial cost, and the lack of trained technicians in many locations throughout the nation.[48] Governments and utilities, however, provide incentives for homeowners to install these systems, and with greater demand, more publicity, and a concerted public effort, people might be able to use this technology throughout the country effectively.

What about solar and wind energy? These have the merit of being familiar to us, but it will take a major effort to supply them in the abundance we require. Our use of these energies is rapidly increasing, their cost continues to fall, and their advantages are becoming clearer to the public as time goes by. But at current rates of implementation, they will contribute only a fraction of energy needs even in a decade or two. Furthermore, since the sun does not shine forever, nor does the wind blow at all times, we can fully use their energies only when we've learned how to store and release the power they provide on demand. A large shift from gasoline-powered to electrical cars would help out in this regard, since the car batteries would serve as an effective form of electrical storage. But for an effective system, we need to create stations to store the energy these sources provide and relay that energy to consumers on demand. One solution is to pump water into a reservoir when the electricity supply is available, then release the water to flow downhill and generate power when it is needed.[49] These pumped storage facilities—or better alternatives, when they become available—will be necessary components of the overall system. Moreover, to bring these energy sources into a system of sustaining power, we need a smart grid, an updated, high-tech electricity distribution network that can withstand the sudden variations in power provided by the sun or wind, connect all the points in the system, and use the energy contributed by households (from small solar units). In short, we need a lot more than solar panels or wind turbines: we need a new, sophisticated, national grid.

But that is not all. Installing large solar plants will take up huge amounts of open land in the nation's sunny places—land now used by plants, animals, and human beings. Putting in industrial-sized wind turbines on mountaintops, for example, or in promising offshore locations will directly intrude on relatively unharmed ecosystems or pristine vistas. Furthermore, as it turns out, large wind turbines are noisy: they cause a low-level vibration to be heard for a mile or more in the surrounding vicinity. Despite their ability to harness sun and wind for human purposes, these technologies come at a real cost: if we really want to reduce our carbon footprint, we will end up greatly expanding our physical footprint on the land and sea. The reality is that many people will resist these intrusions: the opposition to wind farms around the nation, even from local environmentalists, is substantial. The same will be true once we begin to install industrial-sized solar power plants.

We could, however, decrease the footprint of immense solar power plants by making the generation and use of solar energy an ordinary feature in millions of ordinary households. David Crane and Robert F. Kennedy, Jr., point out that the cost of solar panels has fallen by 80 percent over the past five years and now competes with the cost of the normal electricity supply in twenty states. But few people are choosing it over electricity from the grid because of permitting requirements imposed by state and local governments; complying with those requirements now costs more than the solar equipment itself. If our governments changed the rules, as the federal government in Germany has done, it would be much easier for people to shift their homes to solar energy.[50]

So how feasible is a large reliance on solar and wind energy? Clearly, we have a lot of work to do. Just building a national smart grid is already a massive infrastructure project; to get it done, we'll need a lot of money, greater technical expertise, and several years of concerted effort. Building a sufficient number of wind and solar farms will also require a lot of advance research, time to put them in place, and a lengthy effort to win public approval. We need key technological breakthroughs to make energy storage cheap and viable. We also need to think carefully about exactly how much of a physical footprint we want to impose on the land and sea for these purposes. But the declining cost of solar energy and the possibility of producing it on the household level may make aspects of this transition easier. Ultimately, these forms of energy could be part of the solution, but they may not be available on a sufficiently large scale and with a truly workable infrastructure for many years.

Let's turn for a moment to another key aspect of the question, the reduction in energy use. As it turns out, industrial electric motors use more energy than highway vehicles. As one energy efficiency expert argues, a wholesale turnover to new, much more efficient motors would cut the energy these machines use in half and pay for the new machines fairly quickly (between a few weeks and sixteen months).[51] New methods of casting metal, new technology for industrial pumps, recycling, and combined heat and power systems (CHP) can each have a major impact: according to the Department of Energy, the widespread use of CHP systems, for example, which recovers otherwise wasted heat, would save the "equivalent to the output of 40 percent of the coal-fired generating plants now producing electricity in the United States."[52] Increasing energy efficiency in homes and buildings, in lighting and appliances, would also save a large share of the energy we now consume.[53] All these transitions use existing technology, would pay for themselves soon, would decrease costs, and are already being implemented by smart businessmen and citizens. In short, this is a no-brainer: reducing energy use in these ways alone would make a serious difference.

But reducing our greenhouse gas emissions involves much more than changing our extraction and use of energy. According to the IPCC, forestry practices—primarily deforestation—causes just over 17 percent of all our greenhouse gas emissions.[54] Deforestation damages the Earth twice over: it directly releases carbon dioxide *and* damages a forest's long-term role as a carbon sink. Since forests around the world are *already* under severe stress from climate change, as I discussed in chapter one, slashing and burning forests, clear-cutting them, or replacing them with farms or ranches only contributes to an already acute problem. Deforestation will have to end if we are to have the slightest chance of avoiding the worst consequences of climate change. But it is much easier to envision this change than to carry it out. Even if we added the ending of deforestation to the proposed international climate treaties, there is no guarantee that the signatories would actually carry out their obligations. This is a tough one: somehow, we need to create new strategies that will truly stop deforestation.

Most of us intuitively know how we could meet this challenge. We in the developed nations should protect our own forests, of course, but should also pay less wealthy nations for protecting theirs, help them create effective environmental agencies to monitor those ecosystems, and start buying out local farmers and ranchers on the periphery of forests to return recently cleared land to its prior use. In short, we need serious international initiative, political and financial, to make this happen in a way that will matter. The problem, of course, is that funding these measures will require the adoption of an international treaty on climate change, a goal that continues to be elusive, as well as the consent of a majority of voters in developed countries. In some nations, especially the United States, there may not yet be a majority in favor of sending real money overseas to address climate change. It will take many years of hard work to put the necessary agreements in place and to pass the key legislation.

Our use of soils, while the focus of much less public attention, is also crucial. Since the soil contains three or four times as much carbon as plants and trees, tilling the soil—all by itself—can contribute substantially to global warming, for it releases that carbon through erosion and dust. Over most of human history, plowing the land has contributed more carbon to the atmosphere than the burning of fossil fuels; by one estimate, the latter surpassed plowing as a source only in the 1970s.[55] The mechanization of agriculture, of course, alters the picture; by now, the manufacture of fertilizer and herbicides, the use of fossil fuels to power farm machines, and the release of methane and nitrous oxide into the atmosphere, especially from the application of nitrogen-based fertilizers, makes the situation even worse. The 2007 IPCC assessment estimates that today agriculture contributes around 13.5 percent of greenhouse gas emissions worldwide. Luckily, we already know the basics of how to reverse these practices; according to one study, with smart soil management, the greater use of cover crops, no-till agriculture, manuring, and agro-forestry, we could sequester between 5 and 15 percent of the world's annual fossil-fuel emissions in the soil, transforming a contributor of carbon into a major carbon sink.[56]

But making this shift will require a wholesale transformation in agriculture. In the United States, that's not an industry that yields easily to public pressure, nor is it a political constituency that accepts the urgency of action to save the climate. How exactly are we to bring about the necessary change of attitudes and practices to make a difference? Certainly the federal government could impose new regulations on farm practices or new taxes on certain goods. But farmers could block new rules by litigation or delay new legislation through political pressure. Finding a solution on this one is difficult.

Several patterns emerge from this brief discussion of these questions. For one thing, there are only a few technologies that are ready to go, that can be implemented without difficulty, and that we can build on a sufficient scale to make a real difference. For the most part, new techniques require skills we don't yet have, infrastructure that isn't built, or public approval that will be difficult to gain. As Fred Krupp, President of the Environmental Defense Fund, and Miriam Horn argue, entrepreneurs and inventors are busy creating next-generation technologies that may soon provide solutions to many of our energy needs, but only political intervention to increase the cost of generating greenhouse gases (through the mechanism, for example, of a cap-and-trade system, possibly of the sort that California is now launching) would make it possible for these innovators to generate energy on the scale we require.[57] In a similar vein, Thomas L. Friedman urges the United States to forge into the lead on creating new energy technologies, demanding that our government produce an "ecosystem for energy innovation" by developing "an intelligently designed *system* of policies, tax incentives and disincentives, and regulations ..."[58] But so far, no such system is in place, and as a result the new energy economy has not yet taken off. Some new technologies are available, and in those cases, we should move without delay—to build biogas plants, for example, to shift to a new generation of industrial engines, and to improve efficiencies in our households. But to surmount the difficulty on a vast scale will require enormous political will. Even that is an understatement, since that political will can come from only one place, a huge upwelling of popular support for these changes.

Everything in this discussion thus comes down to the political situation in nations around the world, but especially in America, still the world's dominant economy and one of the leading contributors to climate change, where taking action has proved especially difficult. Yes, the American public believes that human beings are causing climate change by huge margins. But it clearly *hates* any increase in taxes, *even if* a tax is meant to forestall climate change. According to Jon Krosnick, in a poll conducted in early 2009 which found that around 74 percent of the American public thought that global warming was taking place and that it was caused by human activity, majorities of 78 percent and 72 percent, respectively, opposed federal taxes on electricity and gasoline to reduce consumption. But majorities of 80 to 84 percent favored tax breaks of various kinds to encourage renewable energy and energy efficiency.[59] The poll unsurprisingly reflects the public distaste for taxes and love of tax breaks that has been familiar in American politics since the late 1970s. But by sticking with that preference in this case, most citizens choose incremental, piecemeal changes over anything more systematic. They seem to believe that if we improve technology, encourage industries to increase efficiency, and invite people to insulate their homes, we'll be doing fine. Unfortunately, that belief is simply untrue.

We have failed to make progress in shifting to a new energy economy over the last decade because most of us make our decisions according to the laws of the marketplace. We want cheap energy: oil, coal, and gas. The only effective way to change our practice *across the board* is to tax all the sources of greenhouse gas, impose a cap-and-trade system on those sources (as Congress debated in 2009–2010), or create a rationing system that would supply each citizen with a tradeable set of credits to be used in purchasing fuel in a given year (as proposed by Monbiot).[60]

These ideas are a tough sell to a public that hates taxes. We need an alternative. And luckily, there is one. Several observers have proposed what Steven Stoft calls the carbon "untax"—a tax whose proceeds would be refunded *in full and equally* to every citizen of the United States. This idea has the support of people across the political spectrum, from James Hansen, the leading climate scientist, to N. Gregory Mankiw, who served as George W. Bush's chief economist. It resembles the system in Alaska, whose government returns the state's portion of the proceeds from the sale of oil to every citizen.[61] Other advocates tweak this proposal a bit by suggesting that a portion (perhaps a fourth) of the money raised through the tax be spent funding research and development of renewable technologies. Bill McKibben, a leading environmental writer, likes this proposal; it also served as the basis for the bill sponsored by Senators Maria Cantwell (D-Washington) and Susan Collins (R-Maine) in the 2009–2010 session.

Each of these proposals has strengths and weaknesses. But it is not necessary to consider them at length here. Even with the large majority of Democrats in the first two years of Obama's presidency, the Senate could not act on climate change. Republicans were virtually unanimous in opposition to the cap-and-trade bill, and enough Democrats resisted it in the name of protecting the interests of constituents (such as those in West Virginia, a true coal state) that the bill may never even have had majority support, much less the sixty votes required for passage. That bill was already so riddled with exceptions and special favors, so obviously a series of compromises with the demands of resistant industries, that it may not have been worth passing. But all that is ancient history by now. The "tea party" revolt, the shift in power toward "skeptical" or hesitant Republicans in the 2010 elections, and the enduring resistance of many Democrats make it clear that the necessary political action will not emerge from the U.S. Congress any time soon. In fact, the political realities are and will remain dire. Because the substantial bloc of the public that still repudiates the science of climate change constitutes the base of the Republican party, that party will for many years be held captive by a dogmatic "skepticism," as the 2012 Republican presidential primaries demonstrated at length. Barring a stunning change in Senate rules, that body will continue to require a supermajority of sixty votes to pass legislation, giving Republicans and resistant Democrats an effective veto on any serious action. There is little cause to hope that the American Congress will ever approve of workable solutions in the absence of a fundamental political realignment of the sort that is highly unlikely to take place anytime soon.[62] The Obama administration, assessing the situation in Congress well, has scaled back its attempts to address climate change in any forceful way and has made clear its preference for fairly modest measures, even after Superstorm Sandy brought renewed attention to climate concerns in the waning days of the 2012 election campaign. Its plans to take action within existing law, through the President's executive authority or the powers of the Environmental Protection Agency, while welcome, can only chip away at the problem rather than bring about the necessary widespread transformation.[63]

That's just the domestic political situation. Things aren't much better internationally. As everyone knows, developing nations refuse to sign on to a climate change treaty without a much more sophisticated understanding of their dilemma, especially of their desire to continue on the path of economic growth and industrial development and their longing to join in the abundance on full display among the wealthy nations.[64] Their hope, in short, is somehow to combine development and greenhouse-gas austerity. Doing so will happen *only* if wealthy nations help them leapfrog over outdated technologies and adopt the most recent, least damaging alternatives—and to preserve their ecosystems as well.

This demand for subsidies, of course, does not go down easy in the developed West. But that is only part of the problem. Most commentators point out that we cannot blame China for its intransigence on climate change, because historically the developed nations have put far more carbon dioxide into the atmosphere than China and because the per capita carbon footprint in China remains far below that in the West. All these points are true. But it does not follow that China's resistance deserves sympathy. For one thing, emitting greenhouse gases into the atmosphere in total ignorance of the consequences, as developed nations have done for a century or two, is quite different from emitting them *now*, when we *know* what those consequences are. We would not countenance any nation accepting the enslavement of its citizens and justifying the practice by arguing that America once accepted slavery. It is simply unacceptable to use past ignorance to justify present stupidity. Moreover, we should not use the fact that China's per capita carbon footprint remains small to explain why it might be resistant to action: if we do so, we endorse the idea that in all fairness, this footprint *should become larger*— as if developing nations somehow *have the right* to spew huge quantities of greenhouse gases into the atmosphere, simply because *we* have been stupid enough to do so for generations. We can sympathize with their longing for economic growth, but we should *not* submit to liberal guilt. If the rest of the world demands the opportunity to live through the history we have enjoyed, the planet will be toast in short order.

We have to translate China's demands into terms that are just both across nations and to the planet. And justice demands something we may not be able to tolerate: a radical and instant renunciation of what we can now see as extravagant, monstrous stupidity, our willingness to eat the Earth for our own benefit. The point is not to invite the Earth's nations into our greenhouse gas insanity, but to stop *our* insanity and to discover a way of living that is truly sustainable. We should not only make this shift ourselves but also enable developing nations to enter an alternative, more viable modernity as well.

This discussion of the international political scene, of course, takes us right back to the domestic context. Needless to say, the American public has little inkling that such a renunciation is necessary or should even be discussed. The politics of climate change in the United States typically revolves around what we must do domestically to change our practices and whether or how to secure international agreement. But since a workable solution will have to provide substantial subsidies to developing nations, it will also require at least a minimal generosity from American taxpayers *on top* of whatever costs we must pay to transform our *own* energy practices.

It might be plausible to imagine that in a period of robust abundance, Americans could accept both domestic transformation and international generosity at once. But it's hard to imagine that sort of acceptance today. The lingering effects of the Great Recession make aggressive action politically impossible. With high federal debt, state governments recovering from crisis, and elevated unemployment, the public appetite for renouncing our dependence on fossil fuels is virtually nonexistent. The focus on recession or debt will drown out other priorities for many years—at least until the recovery has brought the country well out of the housing crisis and greatly reduced the unemployment rate. Never mind that the actual costs of the transition for an average citizen would not be very large; with the carbon untax, for example, such a citizen would probably come out *ahead*. Never mind that a substantial subsidy to the developing world wouldn't impose a large burden on the ordinary taxpayer. The problem here is not practical, but psychological; it arises from the difficulty of thinking about distant nations, and a presumably distant future, while in the midst of hard times. In a highly polarized political context, actions that are rather inexpensive can take on huge symbolic significance, for taking those actions requires that we accept a new and perhaps unpalatable view of the world and of our place in it.

For some observers, it may be quite easy to denounce the widespread denial of climate change as well as the overwhelming reluctance to act. But it just won't do to blame others. Those who are often the most passionate about climate change—relatively well-off, educated, and literate citizens—are part of the problem, too. Take the question of airplane travel. Let's say an exemplary citizen recycles scrupulously, drives a fuel-efficient car, eats organic food, and votes for enlightened politicians—but takes three plane trips a year (to see parents in California, to vacation in the Caribbean, or to see friends in New York). It's quite possible that just *one* of those plane trips will have as great a carbon footprint as driving that fuel-efficient car for an entire year. Everybody knows, or should know, that plane travel is a serious indulgence, that it cancels out any environmental responsibility that citizens might otherwise display.[65] But everybody in the middle class or above indulges in it anyway. David MacKay brilliantly juxtaposes two quotations from Tony Blair. In the first, Blair says, "Unless we act now, not some time distant but now, these consequences, disastrous as they are, will be irreversible. So there is nothing more serious, more urgent or more demanding of leadership." Two months later, "responding to the suggestion that he should *show* leadership by not flying to Barbados for holidays," Blair says that this idea is "a bit impractical actually ..."[66]

I think most people in the relevant classes can sympathize: nearly everyone who understands what is at stake and can afford to travel really can't *imagine* renouncing the convenience of flying. Let's not point fingers at those other idiots; with few exceptions, we're idiots, too. Blair's reluctance to give up his vacation in Barbados demonstrates quite clearly that political inaction only expresses a reluctance that *all* of us feel to transform our lives fundamentally. However much our minds may be persuaded of the need to act, on a gut level we just can't do it—or can't do it nearly as quickly and thoroughly as the occasion demands. Our experts have long since outlined what we could do to face the present challenge. Slowly and with infinite reluctance, we may be starting to take up the task. But do we have time to spare?

Notes

37. Some of the best examples include Al Gore, *Our Choice: A Plan to Solve the Climate Crisis* (Emmaus, Pennsylvania: Rodale, 2009); George Monbiot, *Heat: How to Stop the Planet from Burning* (initially published 2007; Cambridge, Massachusetts: South End Press, 2009); and David J. C. MacKay, *Sustainable Energy—Without the Hot Air* (Cambridge, England: UIT Cambridge, 2009).

38. Joe Romm, "Bridge to Nowhere? NOAA Confirms High Methane Leakage Rate Up To 9% From Gas Fields, Gutting Climate Benefit," Climate Progress, January 2, 2013, http://thinkprogress.org/climate/2013/01/02/1388021/bridge-to-nowhere-noaa-confirms-high-methane-leakage-rate-up-to-9-from-gas-fields-gutting-climate-benefit/.

39. See the map in Gore, *Our Choice*, 103.

40. Matthew L. Wald, "With Natural Gas Plentiful and Cheap, Carbon Capture Projects Stumble," *New York Times*, May 18, 2012, http://www.nytimes.com/2012/05/19/business/energy-environment/low-natural-gas-prices-threaten-carbon-capture-projects.html.

41. Anne Eisenberg, "Pulling Carbon Dioxide Out of Thin Air," *New York Times*, January 5, 2013, http://www.nytimes.com/2013/01/06/business/pilot-plant-in-the-works-for-carbon-dioxide-cleansing.html.

42. David MacKay, *Sustainable Energy*, differs; in his thought experiment, Britain would not need to rely on power plants of this kind at all. But his suggestions would require a huge increase in the energy-driven footprint on the land and sea.

43. Kosloff, *No Rain in the Amazon*, 145–73.

44. For one example, see Elizabeth Rosenthal, "As Biofuel Demand Grows, So Do Guatemala's Hunger Pangs," *New York Times*, January 5, 2013, http://www.nytimes.com/2013/01/06/science/earth/in-fields-and-markets-guatemalans-feel-squeeze-of-biofuel-demand.html?pagewanted=all.

45. On generating biogas from manure, see Fred Krupp and Miriam Horn, *Earth: The Sequel: The Race to Reinvent Energy and Stop Global Warming* (New York: Norton, 2009), 206–208.

46. Elisabeth Rosenthal, "Using Waste, Swedish City Cuts Its Fossil Fuel Use," *New York Times*, December 10, 2010, http://www.nytimes.com/2010/12/11/science/earth/11fossil.html?pagewanted=all.

47. For a good overview of residential geothermal systems, see U.S. Department of Energy, "Geothermal Heat Pumps," available at the Whole Building Design Guide, http://www.wbdg.org/resources/geothermalheatpumps.php.

48. Patrick J. Hughes, "Geothermal (Ground-Source) Heat Pumps: Market Status, Barriers to Adoption, and Actions to Overcome Barriers," Oak Ridge National Laboratory, U.S. Department of Energy Publications, December, 2008, available as a pdf document online.

49. MacKay, *Sustainable Energy*, 190-94.

50. David Crane and Robert F. Kennedy, Jr., "Solar Panels for Every Home," *New York Times*, December 12, 2012, http://www.nytimes.com/2012/12/13/opinion/solar-panels-for-every-home.html.

51. Amory Lovins and L. Hunter Lovins, *Climate: Making Sense and Making Money*, Old Snowmass, Colorado: Rocky Mountain Institute, online publication, 1997, 6, http://www.rmi.org/Knowledge-Center/Library/C97-13_ClimateSenseMoney. See also the U.S. Department of Energy, Energy Efficiency & Renewable Energy, at http://www.eere.energy.gov/.

52. Gore, *Our Choice*, 253–54.

53. For excellent, detailed estimates of the benefits of energy savings in vehicles, buildings, and households, see MacKay.

54. See the IPCC Fourth Assessment Report (2007), Synthesis Report, 2.1: Causes of Change, http://www.ipcc.ch/publications_and_data/ar4/syr/en/mains2-1.html.

55. Al Gore, *Our Choice*, 203.

56. Rattan Lal, "Soil Carbon Sequestration Impacts on Global Climate Change and Food Security," *Science*, volume 304, number 5677 (June 11, 2004), 1623–1627, doi:10.1126/science.1097396.

57. Krupp and Horn, *Earth: The Sequel*, make this point throughout their book; for example, see 40–44. On the California cap-and-trade launch, see Felicity Barringer, "A Grand Experiment to Rein In Climate Change," *New York Times*, October 13, 2012, http://www.nytimes.com/2012/10/14/science/earth/in-california-a-grand-experiment-to-rein-in-climate-change.html?pagewanted=all.

58. Thomas L. Friedman, *Hot, Flat, and Crowded: Why We Need a Green Revolution—and How It Can Renew America*, Release 2.0 (New York: Farrar, Straus and Giroux, 2009), 293.

59. Jon Krosnick, "The Climate Majority," *New York Times*, June 8, 2010, http://www.nytimes.com/2010/06/09/opinion/09krosnick.html?pagewanted=all&_r=0.

60. For a relevant report on the results of a carbon tax imposed for slightly different reasons, see Elizabeth Rosenthal, "Carbon Taxes Make Ireland Even Greener," *New York Times*, December 27, 2012, http://www.nytimes.com/2012/12/28/science/earth/in-ireland-carbon-taxes-pay-off.html?pagewanted=all.

61. Steven Stoft, *Carbonomics: How to Fix the Climate and Charge It to OPEC* (Nantucket, Massachusetts: Diamond Press, 2008).

62. Of course, if a party with a majority in that body invokes the so-called "nuclear option," eliminates the filibuster or the cloture vote, and thus makes it possible for legislation to pass with a simple majority vote, then a bill addressing climate change might have a chance. But leaders of majority parties have been historically reluctant to take this step, and it's not clear that they would prevail without having a supermajority in hand to do so.

63. See Richard W. Stevenson and John M. Broder, "Speech Gives Climate Goals Center Stage," *New York Times*, January 21, 2013, http://www.nytimes.com/2013/01/22/us/politics/climate-change-prominent-in-obamas-inaugural-address.html.

64. Here and elsewhere I use the language of "development" for several reasons: to avoid using the language of the First and Third World (with its inherently hierarchical notion of geopolitics), to avoid overemphasizing the notion that some nations are wealthy and others poor (since under the pressure of climate change we may have to redefine wealth), and to foreground the concept of development and all it implies (the notion that all nations should imitate modern Western societies and thus should adopt a highly energy-intensive economy).

65. For a discussion of the environmental costs of air travel, see chapter ten.

66. MacKay, *Sustainable Energy*, 222.

Chapter 3

Time's Up

Many observers, long used to the slow pace of political transformation, might agree with everything I've said so far but insist that we need not worry too much: given time, our economy will recover, the superma-jority of Americans will prevail, our political system will work, and we will see real action on climate change. With enough persistence, over the next decade or so we will help forge a genuinely effective international agreement. The research into new technologies will begin to see fruitful results, we'll create the new energy economy, and we'll be on a secure footing at last.

But in the case of this particular transformation, unlike most others, we just don't have the time to let things play out. While we proceed at our usual deliberative pace, climate change speeds ahead. The mismatch is stark and growing. If we're going to get anything done, we should do it now, and preferably yesterday. As Rajendra Pachauri, the scientist who headed the IPCC in 2007, remarked in that year, "If there's no action before 2012, that's too late… . What we do in the next two or three years will determine our future. This is the defining moment."[67]

We're not used to thinking about acting so quickly in part because we tend to accept the pace of political change. The international negotiations for a climate change treaty, building on that premise, takes for granted that we have some time: the proposed agreement sets the target of an 80 percent reduction in the emission of carbon dioxide by 2050. That year is indeed some distance away. But if we take a good look at the most recent information, it's clear that we will have to make the cuts much deeper and sooner than we thought.

But wait a minute, many voices say; *why do you keep insisting that everything has to happen* **now**? *Why not let the country recover economically* *before asking for change? Why not bring everybody on board before rushing into action?*

There are **eight** good reasons why time is up.

First of all, the target—cutting emissions 80 percent by 2050—was chosen for political reasons, not on the basis of the science. 2050 is far enough away to make deep cuts politically palatable. Whenever people suggest that we have to make these cuts earlier, others resist—not because of the science, but because they fear the political consequences. Unfortunately, the change in Earth's climate doesn't particularly care about what is palatable to us. The goals we once set are too far away; if we are honest, we must acknowledge that we must act much sooner.

Second, the science itself has changed since the international negotiations began. Over the past twenty years or so, scientists have been asking what would happen if we doubled the preindustrial level of atmospheric carbon dioxide—around 275 parts per million—to around 550 ppm. This number, chosen in part as a convenient signpost, has determined the shape of countless investigations of climate change as well as much of the discussion of potential future scenarios in the IPCC assessments. As a result, for many years we did not have a sure sense of how much change might take place at lower levels. In a rather different vein, those seeking international agreements initially chose 450 ppm as a target in part because it once seemed that with concerted effort the international community might be able to meet it.

But in the last four or five years, further research suggests that these numbers are too high. One paper (authored by James Hansen and many others) published in September 2009 argues that previous models failed to take into account the effect of positive feedback loops. Models once predicted that a doubling in carbon dioxide concentrations in the atmosphere would lead to a temperature increase of around 3° Centigrade (with a range of from 2 to 4.5°). But current models that include the effects of positive feedback loops estimate that the same carbon dioxide concentration will lead to an increase of around 6° Centigrade (with a range of from 4 to 8°). The implication of this argument is that the widely known and cited estimates of the IPCC are too optimistic—and that in fact we have *already* gone beyond what the planet can tolerate. If Rajendra Pachauri thought we have until 2012, these researchers imply that we should have acted long before even *that* year. They estimate that the boundary for carbon dioxide concentration is 350 ppm; at the time of that article's publication, the concentration was 387 ppm and rising— and was forcing an exit from the Holocene, the stable environment we have enjoyed over the past 10,000 years.[68] Persuaded by this argument, Bill McKibben and many others have formed the group 350.org, which advocates for concerted action to meet that lower target.

Third, although the international community set 450 ppm as its target many years ago, the continuing rise in emissions from most developed nations in the intervening years, together with the huge increase from developing countries like China, has made that target totally unrealistic. In the Kyoto Protocol, most of the world's nations promised to reduce greenhouse emissions by about 5 percent below 1990 levels by 2012. But instead, global carbon dioxide emissions *increased* by 38 percent from 1990 to 2009.[69] Very few observers now believe that we will be able to stabilize carbon dioxide levels at that threshold. In August 2004, Stephen Pacala and Robert Socolow introduced the idea of "stabilization wedges." In their definition, a wedge is the shape on a graph whose top (ascending) line depicts a gradual increase in carbon dioxide emissions and whose bottom (straight or descending) line depicts a potential decrease in those emissions if we adopt new practices. In short, a wedge is a chunk of unemitted carbon dioxide. Pacala and Socolow proposed fifteen possible wedges drawing on existing or nearly existing technologies and suggested that achieving seven of these wedges over the next fifty years would be enough to stabilize those concentrations at 500 ppm, a target they thought plausible.[70] But in September 2010, Martin Hoffert pointed out that because our emissions have been rising much more quickly than Pacala and Socolow envisioned, we would now need to achieve eighteen of these wedges just to reach stabilization and twenty-five to phase out fossil fuels altogether.[71]

Think about it: in six years, the world went from needing to achieve seven wedges to eighteen. We're going in the wrong direction, and going fast: we're *adding* to our challenge by nearly two wedges per year, making the task of reversing the effects of these emissions even more difficult.

It's true that during the recession, the usage of electricity and gas fell, slowing down the increase in our greenhouse gas emissions. But usage fell because of hardship, not from any shift in our fundamental habits. In the midst of the downturn, it was easy to predict that once the recovery began, people would rush back to the behavior they know best. In fact, that is exactly what happened. Researchers found that global emissions of carbon dioxide increased by 5.9 percent in 2010, more than making up for a slight decrease in 2009, the year in which the recession had the most impact.[72] Clearly, the recession did not slow down the steady increase in greenhouse gas emissions.

Fourth, even *this* discussion does not face the full measure of the challenge, for the simple reason that carbon dioxide is not the only greenhouse gas. George Monbiot points out that according to the Potsdam Institute for Climate Impact Research, we should aim to stabilize "greenhouse gases in the atmosphere at or below the *equivalent* of 440 parts of carbon dioxide per million." When the carbon dioxide concentration was around 380 ppm, "the other greenhouse gases raise[d] this to an equivalent of 440 or 450."[73] But in late 2013, the global monthly mean of carbon dioxide approached 400 ppm, so that the overall concentration of greenhouse gases is now well above the equivalent of 450 ppm.[74] *We have already exceeded the upper limit* for our contribution to the greenhouse effect we set some years ago.

Fifth, we must take another factor into account as well. As time goes by and we emit more carbon dioxide, the less the biosphere can absorb; by one estimate, it will absorb fully one-third less as much by 2030.[75] As a result, emitting a certain quantity of carbon dioxide a decade from now will impose a greater burden on the biosphere than emitting it today—and what is more, reducing our output will only keep up with the Earth's capacity to absorb less. In effect, we will have to cut back our footprint *an extra portion* just to take that fact into account.

Sixth, much as these estimates for how *deep* we must cut have to be revised, the guess as to how *soon* we should achieve our target must change as well. Monbiot's already severe estimate—that the United Kingdom would have to cut its emissions 80 percent by 2030—was based on a guess as to when our emissions would be so great that they would trigger positive feedback loops and thus irreversible climate change. But Monbiot relies on an estimate in a paper published back in 2003.[76] It's already clear that in the intervening years we've emitted far more than scientists in 2003 would have guessed. If they thought that business as usual might trigger irreversible global warming around 2030, twenty-seven years later, the reckless emission of greenhouse gases over the last ten years has undoubtedly moved up the date much closer to the present.

These physical facts alone are dire. We have over twice the reductions to achieve as we did only a few years ago and far less time in which to achieve them. Very soon, the present in which we live and the future in which we would cross the tipping point will coincide—and we'll discover we've already passed the point at which those positive feedback loops kick in.

Doing some arithmetic based on these facts may help clarify our situation. In 2003 it once seemed we'd meet our goals by 2030, but we've managed to waste ten years or so. If we once needed to achieve seven wedges, we now need to achieve eighteen—*plus* a further increment to hit a target not of 500 ppm, but of 350. Since we are already above the equivalent of 450 ppm, if we wish not to go too far beyond that level we will have to try to eliminate fossil-fuel use entirely, and thus to achieve twenty-five wedges, as Hoffert suggests. But to do so now, after several years since his study have gone by, we'd most likely need to hit around thirty wedges. Yet we'd need to add a *further* increment to take into account the fact that the biosphere will absorb less of what we emit in the coming years. A back-of-the envelope calculation suggests that *if we acted today* we would need to reduce our emissions by at least thirty-two wedges. Moreover, thanks to our profligacy in recent years, as well as our sense that we must hit a lower target, it's also likely we would need to achieve these cuts many years earlier.

Other ways of estimating the challenge confirm these figures. At the Copenhagen summit on climate change in 2010, a majority of nations endorsed a target of raising the Earth's temperatures no more than 1.5° Centigrade above preindustrial levels. But since we've already raised the average temperature by 0.8°, and the temperature will rise another 0.6° due to the inertia of the world's climate, 1.4 of those 1.5° are already inevitable, leaving us virtually without hope of reaching the target.[77] Even if we acted *today* to eliminate our greenhouse gas emissions *entirely*, we'd still barely meet our goal. And there is simply *no* chance we can eliminate all those emissions so quickly.

Let's take more than the purely physical facts into account here as well. It will take us a few years to pass the necessary legislation and sign the key international agreements, as I suggested above, and a few years after *that* to research and implement an array of new technologies, build the solar and wind plants, create a new energy infrastructure, convert our transportation system, and fund the protection of forests. If we're lucky, perhaps we will begin to see steep reductions in greenhouse gas emissions in about a decade. By then, however, we will have emitted so much more carbon dioxide that we'll have much further to go to meet our targets. How far is impossible to say—but clearly we'd need to achieve many more than the thirty-two wedges I mentioned a moment ago.

From these estimates it seems that if we acted *now*, our change in policy would finally *begin* to take effect roughly ten years from now, somewhere in the early 2020s. But the severity of our situation is clear if we take into account the seventh reason—the fact that, as I've said above, 2020 is the new 2100. As recent research indicates, we've already crossed one tipping point with the melting of the Arctic sea ice and may cross one or two more by the mid 2020s. Nearly all the above estimates take as their fundamental principle the overriding task of *not* crossing through those tipping points; once we reach them, we need not work our way through all those calculations but can sense our situation immediately from the state of those tipping points. We're now witnessing the very events we were trying to avoid, and all this talk of targets, all this arithmetic, however useful it may have once seemed, ultimately distracts us from what is right in front of us. And from the evidence of the melting sea ice, the exploding methane clathrates, the morphing permafrost, and the crackling Amazon rainforest, the essential story is becoming increasingly clear.

So it seems that even under the *best case scenario, even if we acted today* our efforts might take effect in the mid 2020s—just as we may be triggering severe and irreversible climate change. Fortune may smile upon us and allow us a few years of grace to hit our target, but if so, we really must achieve everything in a ridiculously tiny span of time. It is far more likely that we will be in the position of taking action after the feedback loops have already begun—making ourselves poster children for defiant foolishness. We are more than flirting with disaster; we're *inviting* it. It's almost impossible not to think that all is lost, that even if we act, it will be too late.[78]

These realities undermine the premise of a major activist enterprise of our moment—Bill McKibben's drive to encourage many public institutions to disinvest in fossil-fuel companies and thus help prevent the United States from pushing the biosphere beyond the limits of its tolerance. In the *Rolling Stone* article in which he lays out his case, McKibben first explains that the 2° threshold on which international negotiators rely is too high, but then invokes on a specific "carbon budget" derived from that threshold to argue we have time to make a difference through the strategy of divestment.[79] His effort, praiseworthy as it is, relies on a contradiction between his knowledge that we've already virtually met the limit of what the Earth can tolerate and his description of what a certain kind of activism can still accomplish.

Given all these factors, we can no longer assume that our efforts will bear fruit, that the civilizations of the Holocene will survive in anything like their present form. An honest look at the task ahead and the time remaining should disabuse us of our unspoken confidence that the world we know will endure in something of its current form for the rest of our lives.

But hold on, someone might say, *what if we lower our emissions* **after** *that target date? Wouldn't the Earth's temperatures eventually decline as well, getting back down to a level that would not cause extensive climate change? Even if we've been very slow and don't meet the target of 450 ppm, isn't there hope that we can* **eventually** *hit that or a lower target, and all will be well?*

In this question, I hear the voice of the last optimists speaking—the voice of those who hope that, however stupid and cowardly we all are, however slow to act, however likely to botch the entire task for a few more years, we might *still* have a chance. The activists at 350.org, acting on something of this premise, are organizing efforts to reduce our carbon dioxide emissions to that lower number in the long term, hinting that if we can do so, we will avert the onset of serious climate change.

But it simply isn't so. The eighth reason we have so little time is that *once we warm the planet up to a certain point, it will not cool down again* for a very long time. A recent paper showed that "the climate change that takes place due to increases in carbon dioxide concentration is largely irreversible for 1,000 years after emissions stop." If we did manage to stop emitting carbon dioxide, "radiative forcing"—or what we usually call the greenhouse effect—would indeed decline, but that decline would be "largely compensated by slower loss of heat to the ocean."[80]

This finding means that even if we manage to cut our output of carbon dioxide, Earth's temperatures will go up *and stay up*. But wait a minute: as I mentioned above, the rise in temperature lags behind the rise in carbon dioxide concentrations by many years, so that even after we stop emitting carbon dioxide, the temperature would rise another 0.6° Centigrade or so—a time lag that all the above estimates take into account. So the reality is that even after we cut our greenhouse gas output, the temperature level would *continue to rise*—and *then* eventually level off and *stay* at that higher level.

Unfortunately, then, the physics of the climate will not let us reverse the effects of our misbehavior now. If we push temperatures up, they are going to stay there. We have no second chance. And the first one is already slipping away.

It would be nice to pause here and suggest that it is not yet absolutely certain that those vicious circles are under way in full force and for good. That hesitation might have been plausible a year or two ago. But by now, the dire state of the Arctic feedback loop and our sense of its consequences for the entire global climate leave us little room for doubt.

Is there no basis for hope left to us? One last consideration remains, one final bedrock for hope: our general humility in the face of the vast complexity of Earth's dynamic systems. Only the sense that our knowledge is limited, that something may be taking place and might still appear of which we have little inkling, stands between us and a frank acknowledgment that all is lost.

Many others seem to have come to a similar conclusion. Some of them show their awareness of our situation by introducing an entirely new angle on the problem, suggesting forms of geoengineering to address our plight; the Arctic Methane Emergency Group I mentioned in the introduction is a good case in point. But almost invariably such suggestions threaten to harm the planet in their own way. One idea is to inject aerosols into the atmosphere to dim the sun and lower the temperature. But doing so would ultimately cause serious ground-level pollution and could help deplete the ozone layer. What about a shield placed in outer space to lower the amount of sunlight hitting the earth? It would need to be around 4.5 million square kilometers in size—and thus cost a huge amount of money to build and maintain (perhaps as much as 6 percent of the world's GNP, every year). Maybe putting white plastic sheeting over various deserts and reflecting the sunlight back into space would help. But doing so would prevent the circulation of dust, which has a vital role in providing iron and phosphorous to other regions and in supplying nutrients to plankton. What about placing that white reflective plastic over a vast area of the ocean? The objections to *that* idea are fairly obvious: vast quantities of plastic would cut off sunlight to organisms in the sea, would easily be transported by wind and storm, and could affect coastal ecosystems if the plastic were blown ashore.[81] These and other suggestions speak more about our current desperation than about any genuine attempt to address our dilemma.

Other suggestions seem quite sane. The leading climate scientist Wallace Broecker has concluded that there is no realistic chance we'll be able to replace fossil fuels with renewable sources in time. Accordingly, he proposes that we fix the climate by withdrawing carbon dioxide directly from the open air and injecting it deep into the earth. As I mentioned in chapter two, Carbon Engineering is putting similar ideas to work and is hoping to market its technology soon. But here again, there won't be enough of a commercial incentive to do so on a sufficient scale until there is a carbon tax (or untax)—until there is political action to make fossil fuels more expensive.[82] Sound familiar? We need political action before we get the new technology—and in this case, the technology is in a very preliminary stage.

Other observers, seeing our dilemma, do not imagine we can find a technological fix. They turn in a different direction, encouraging us to adapt to the massive transformations that are coming our way. Bill McKibben, for example, took a big step when he entitled his book *Eaarth*: in his view, we're no longer living on the planet Earth, for thanks to climate change, we find ourselves on another planet, one we're not used to at all. Earlier writers, like Al Gore or Monbiot, who discussed our dilemma in 2006 and 2007, still had reason to be optimistic. McKibben, writing in 2010, abandons the attempt to tell us how to avoid a dire fate.

Instead, he prepares us for that new planet and gives us advice about how we might live there. This shift in itself is a signal of how far we've come. Unfortunately, even his advice about adaptation cannot do justice to what we face. In the last half of his book, he suggests that we should create strong small communities, produce food locally, and rely on the resourcefulness and creativity of towns rather than the nation as a whole. These suggestions are remarkably sane. But doing so would hardly enable us to survive the events he describes so well in the first half of the book. How well will local communities raise their own food in many regions, when rain falls less regularly, the landscape retains water less well, and the plants may not have the chance to mature? How will towns flourish in the midst of dying forests and drying streams? Where exactly will these small communities succeed?

Not long ago, people who studied climate change could emphasize the possibility of transforming our fossil-fuel economy. A few years later, the tone has shifted: now they emphasize the prospect of engineering the Earth or offering up a localist ethic as a counterbalance. As I have suggested, I do not think these suggestions provide actual solutions. But they do have the merit of pointing out the problem. The challenge, then, is to face that problem without looking away, without escaping to increasingly less credible responses. A crucial shift has taken place in the last few years, and yet for the most part we avoid it; we hasten to move on, to find *some* pretext for optimism. There must *still* be comfort available to us, wherever it may be. But these responses fail to take into account the real implications of what is before us.

I do not discount the need for us to begin assessing the task of adapting to a changed Earth. Here again, the IPCC reports perform a valuable service. The 2007 assessment takes great care to describe the potential effects of various levels of warming on ecologies and societies around the world—and on how they might adapt. Because of our increasingly dire situation, many observers now treat these sections of the report more seriously than they did in the past. But as the focus shifts toward adaptation, we should pause and think about the implications of that change in emphasis.

For one thing, "adaptation" is a misleadingly gentle term for the task before us. "Adaptation" suggests that we can adjust some of our practices, rethink how our ecosystems and economies will survive, and find a "new normal" in which to live. But this implication is simply too optimistic. Unless we make severe, thorough, and uncompromising changes soon, temperatures will climb to a high level. The longer they remain at that level, as they will, the more likely they are to trigger positive feedback loops—and thus create a *further* round of warming, with a further series of harsh consequences for the climate. These possibilities were not incorporated into the projections of climate change provided in the IPCC report in 2007, nor were they a factor in the scenarios of adaptation sketched there. The reality we face, then, is somewhat tougher than we thought a few years ago. The most likely scenario we face is that changes to Earth's climate systems will accelerate and get steadily *worse*, step by lurching step, for decades—as various feedback loops kick in and impose devastating effects. The release of methane gas from the permafrost in the far North, for example, if it takes effect on a large scale, will lead to a rapid round of global warming, which in turn could trigger a wholesale collapse of the Amazonian ecosystem, with all its consequences for weather in the Americas, and a general increase in carbon concentrations in the atmosphere, which could in turn trigger feedback loops elsewhere. Once we pass the first tipping point, we cannot have confidence we will escape others and still others. What we face, in short, is *perpetual* adaptation— the task of making a wholesale adjustment to our reality, then doing it *again* ... then doing it *yet again*. It would be better if we admitted that if we make the necessary changes too late, we will have to *adjust radically, and at uneven and unpredictable intervals, for as long as we can imagine.*

That prospect is quite dire. But we should not therefore leap to the popular image of a planetary catastrophe. The future we face is *not* as simple as a full-out, planetary disaster that will simply defeat us. If that were the case, it would indeed make all our efforts vain, all our best strategies hopeless. But climate change is not a single, devastating event, like a nuclear holocaust. If irreversible, devastating climate change takes place, in the long term it will displace many societies, change the ethos of our cultures profoundly, cause untold suffering to millions of people, and reduce the Earth's population by a major fraction. It will do so over generations, altering the world decade by decade, allowing us to accommodate certain changes and be defeated by others. As a result, it will not allow us to relax into any particular mode of response. It may proceed at an incremental pace for many years but at other times strike quickly.[83] It will be an ongoing horror unlike any we have faced before. Planetary in scale, unfolding over a long span of time, it will at times give us room to change and at others interrupt our projects without mercy. It will allow us to have the illusion we are adapting successfully, then undercut our efforts with further ecological transformations. We cannot assume these events will necessarily finish us off soon, but neither should we pretend we can master them or survive them unscathed. Climate change, in short, will never quite allow us total hope or utter despair: we will be caught endlessly between conflicting possibilities.

In realizing that *this* is our most likely future, in turning from the hope we might ward it off to accepting the task of adapting to it, we are taking no small step. In doing so, we concede that our future will consist of living in a worsening world—a world that may get incrementally, steadily *less* habitable as time goes by.

This change will be much tougher on all of us than the most likely consequences of severe climate change, such as storms and floods, rising food prices and disappearing water supplies, economic distress and wars. Modern life has always been premised on the notion of progress—on democratization, economic growth, increasing cultural interchange, and improvements in the lives of ordinary people. America as a nation, borrowing on the promise of the Enlightenment it shares with many other traditions, has always looked ahead, building its identity on the promise of eventual liberation for its citizens and for the people of the world. For many generations, parents in modern societies have assumed that they were making better lives for their children, confident that their hard work and sacrifice would benefit their offspring. Even in dark times, at the depths of the Depression or in the midst of war, Americans have kept this hope alive. Participants in movements for social and economic justice have always cast their eyes far ahead, knowing that activism might pay off only decades into the future. All these hopes, in turn, have tacitly relied on the promise of economic growth, a promise that all advanced capitalist nations now rely on for their legitimacy—the hope that over time, all incomes would rise, and everyone would eventually flourish.

To give up the dream of progress and accept the prospect of a perpetually worsening world would be an immense loss for all of us. Without the promise of better lives for everyone, few of the attitudes of modern life survive intact. Facing the reality of our present moment, then, requires much more than an assessment of how we are doing in reducing our greenhouse gas emissions. It requires nothing less than a wholesale reexamination of the progressive attitude we inherit from the Enlightenment, a rethinking of the most basic attitudes we take for granted about our relation to the future.

Looking at our present moment in this way does not force us to give up our fight to ward it off in the first place. Nevertheless, as people begin to admit more and more that we have come to the final years in our effort to avoid irreversible climate change, as the emphasis falls ever more on adaptation, the question of how to be honest about our situation without giving up on the battle becomes more pressing. Al Gore once commented that "an astonishing number of people go straight from denial to despair, without pausing on the intermediate step of saying, 'We can do something about this!'"[84] He's absolutely right. I would only add that despair can be a form of denial: it, too, allows us to dismiss the problem, to assume we're not responsible. Since nobody can do a thing, we're off the hook.

But what if we have been dedicated to doing something about it—and nothing happens? What if we do what we can, join an activist community such as Repower America, the group Gore founded to agitate for political action, encourage the nation to shift to renewable sources by the end of the decade, and help individuals to take voluntary actions to reduce their carbon footprint—but ultimately realize the necessarily big shift will not take place in time? What then?

That question is what this book is about. Here we are now, fully aware of climate change and what it can bring, well aware of what we can do, but thwarted from real action. We're stuck in a holding pattern, as if we must simply accept our fate. It would be the height of foolishness at this key moment simply to give up and abandon the effort. It's devastatingly clear that our first task is to *intensify* the effort. After all, we are talking about the world's greatest crime, ecocide, an assault on our entire planet's ecology. It far outweighs genocide, the destruction of a people, for it threatens to ruin the support system for all living things, and along the way displace, impoverish, or destroy a major portion of the human race. It undercuts our hopes for the future. It alters our understanding of the religious, cultural, and political traditions we inherit, for the future on which their validity relies threatens to disappear. We simply *must* fight on.

But as we do so, we should begin to confront the possibility that whatever the results of our efforts, the future we have always taken for granted is in danger of disappearing. We could once rely on the notion that the basic ecosystems of the Earth would still be present and flourishing for decades and centuries into the future. We can do so no longer.

As I mentioned in the introduction, the best thinking about our current situation almost always hesitates to acknowledge this fact. Inevitably, with only one or two exceptions, those who tell the truth about the dimensions of the challenge and the lateness of the hour lay great emphasis on the steps we can still take to alleviate the crisis or the best strategies we might use to survive the changes in the biosphere when they come. Providing a note of optimism is key; thanks to that gesture, we can handle an honest assessment of our situation much more productively. I too would emphasize that not all is lost, that we can still take action—if we do so immediately and on a vast scale. But anyone who stops there is not telling the whole story. In actual fact, given the slow pace of political change and the immense inertia of our economies, the probability we will do what is necessary in time is extremely low.

To face our situation without evasion, then, we must do the apparently impossible, break a very strong taboo, and begin to ponder what it would be like to live in a world undergoing severe climate change. None of us would ever seek out thoughts of this kind. Nevertheless, to block them out is ultimately another form of denial, another way to protect ourselves from the realities of climate change. Any such defense ultimately contributes to our complacency, our willingness on some level to accept things as they are. In contrast, the sanest, most humane, most transformative course of action is to face our situation as fully as we can.

Doing so will not undercut a commitment to changing our societies; on the contrary, it will help us understand the real stakes of the current fight. The goal is not only to safeguard the future of the biosphere; it is also to preserve our *idea* of the future, on which so much of our lives and traditions are based. We are battling to preserve not only the ecosystems in which we live, but the *hope* for an expansive and joyous life for ourselves and others—the very hope on which we ultimately stake nearly everything we do. Let us face the abyss together, then, in the coming chapters, knowing that in doing so, we may be catching a glimpse of our actual future—or perhaps learning so much from that glimpse that we will fight even harder to keep it at bay.

Notes

67. Elisabeth Rosenthal, "U. N. Chief Seeks More Climate Change Leadership," *New York Times*, November 18, 2007, http://www.nytimes.com/2007/11/18/ science/earth/18climatenew.html?pagewanted=all&_r=0.

68. Johan Rockström and others, "A Safe Operating Space for Humanity," *Nature* 461 (September 23, 2009), 472–475, doi:10.1038/461472a.

69. Robert B. Semple, Jr., "Remember Kyoto? Most Nations Don't," *New York Times*, December 3, 2011, http://www.nytimes.com/2011/12/04/opinion/ sunday/remember-kyoto-most-nations-dont.html.

70. S. Pacala and R. Socolow, "Stabilization Wedges: Solving the Climate Problem for the Next 50 Years with Current Technologies," *Science*, volume 305, number 5686 (August 13, 2004), 968–972, doi:10.1126/ science.1100103.

71. Martin I. Hoffert, "Farewell to Fossil Fuels?" *Science*, volume 329, number 5997 (September 10, 2010), 1292–1294, doi:10.1126/science.1195449.

72. Justin Gillis, "Carbon Emissions Show Biggest Jump Ever Recorded," *New York Times*, December 4, 2011, http://www.nytimes.com/2011/12/05/ science/earth/record-jump-in-emissions-in-2010-study-finds.html. This report was based on the report at the Global Carbon Project released on December 5, 2011; for its current report see http://www.globalcarbonproject. org/carbonbudget/.

73. Monbiot, *Heat*, 16.

74. See the data at CO2now, http://co2now.org/.

75. Monbiot, *Heat*, 16.

76. Monbiot, *Heat*, 15; see note 122 (page 227), which refers to a paper cited in note 86 (page 226).

77. See Mark Hertsgaard, *Hot: Living Through the Next Fifty Years on Earth* (Boston: Houghton Mifflin Harcourt, 2011), 70.

78. For a well-known discussion that comes to a similar conclusion, see James Lovelock, *The Revenge of Gaia: Earth's Climate Crisis & the Fate of Humanity* (New York: Basic Books, 2006). For a more recent, exemplary treatment that reaches conclusions similar to those outlined in the present chapter, see Clive Hamilton, *Requiem for a Species: Why We Resist the Truth about Climate Change* (Washington, DC: Earthscan, 2010), 1–31.

79. Bill McKibben, "Global Warming's Terrifying New Math," *Rolling Stone*, July 19, 2012, http://www.rollingstone.com/politics/news/global-warmings-terrifying-new-math-20120719. On the second page of this article, he writes, "Scientists estimate that humans can pour roughly 565 more gigatons of carbon dioxide into the atmosphere by midcentury and still have some reasonable hope of staying below two degrees." But if the two-degree target is already too high, as McKibben suggests, this carbon budget is too generous as well.

80. Susan Solomon and others, "Irreversible Climate Change Due to Carbon Dioxide Emissions," *Proceedings of the National Academy of Sciences of the United States of America*, volume 106, number 6 (February 10, 2009), 1704–1709, doi:10.1073/pnas.0812721106.

81. For a helpful discussion of these and other geoengineering schemes, see Parkinson, *Coming Climate Crisis?*, 165–191.

82. Wallace S. Broecker and Robert Kunzig, *Fixing Climate: What Past Climate Changes Reveal About the Current Threat—And How to Counter It* (New York: Hill and Wang, 2008), 186–233.

83. For a representative discussion of the possibility of abrupt climate change, see Richard Alley, *The Two-Mile Time Machine: Ice Cores, Abrupt Climate Change, and Our Future* (Princeton: Princeton University Press, 2000).

84. Gore, *An Inconvenient Truth: The Planetary Emergency of Global Warming and What We Can Do About It* (Emmaus, Pennsylvania: Rodale, 2006), 276.

Chapter 4

The Impossible Revolution

So far I have been arguing that climate change is real and that its irreversible form is virtually upon us. The moral imperative to act is overwhelming. Yet we do not. Why are we in the United States incapable of acting even under this immense imperative? If we are to understand this crossroads in time, we must grapple with whatever in our collective habits makes it so difficult for us to face this moment with genuine foresight and sanity. At first glance, it is not all that clear why we are so stuck, why we seem incapable of addressing a threat that has such enormous consequences for us all. What features of this crisis have led us to such an impasse? What attributes of our political culture might explain our hesitation? And what does our inability suggest about our overall dilemma and its consequences?

The practical steps we could take to address our crisis seem rather simple. We just need to raise the price of fossil fuels—as well as the cost of generating greenhouse gases through the poor management of farmland and forest—so that the market reflects the physical realities in which we live. If we do so, we will all have a practical incentive to shift to new and less destructive practices. If we increase these prices in further steps over the ensuing years, we would change our practices even further, eventually reaching the point where we would not be contributing to the planet's warming at all. We should also fund research into developing and implementing new technologies so that solar, wind, tide, wave, and geothermal energy can become readily available; the mechanisms for capturing and storing carbon dioxide can be installed on a large scale; and our agricultural and forestry practices can become ecologically sustainable. These ideas of raising the cost of unsustainable practices and funding new research are fairly straightforward and by now thoroughly familiar to climate change scientists, technicians, policy experts, and legislators; we just need to carry them out and do so soon.

To make these changes, however, is not so simple. Imagining a course of action is much easier than actually pursuing it. For those of us living in the United States, taking these key steps will require a fundamental reorientation of our attitudes and practices all across the nation. That change will have to operate on many levels if it is to work at all. It will require a shift in our understanding of our place in the world, a willingness to endorse unprecedented public policies, a revision of our industrial and agricultural practices, and a change in our individual daily habits. It will have to be ideological and legislative, technical and financial, large-scale and individual, all at once. To ward off the prospect of severe climate change requires us not only to change our thinking but also to participate in an everyday, detailed endeavor that will often seem utterly tedious and banal; at every turn, we will have to overcome our comfort with things as they are, our resistance to inconvenient interruptions, our preference for cheap living, and our ignorance of alternatives.

How best might this transformation come about? Only something very powerful, systemic, and persuasive could possibly succeed—something like climate change itself, except within the political domain. The challenge is to translate the reality of climate change into terms our culture can understand and accept. But doing so is no simple matter. Most policy experts take for granted that introducing any radical new principle is bound to fail, at least at first. Doing so, they argue, forces one to advocate for positions that are not politically viable. In their view, we must be more strategic, more circumspect; we must find means of subtle encouragement that nudge people toward more responsible behavior. An outright intervention would simply provoke a repudiation of the entire effort. After all, as Aristotle said, politics is the art of the possible; if you demand too much, you won't get a thing. One version of this attitude is voiced by Mike Hulme, who reviews the various reasons why people disagree about climate change and suggests that we will make headway only when we can reconcile our divergent beliefs.[85]

But climate change does not compromise. For us to ward off severe disturbances to our ecosystems, we cannot compromise either. But without compromise it is virtually impossible to change democratic societies.

It takes several generations for social movements in the United States to achieve their primary goals; activists in this nation have always been forced to accept small gains over many years until the prize is won. So far the debate over climate change is following this pattern. Activists point out what must be done, "skeptics" refuse to act, and the nation edges forward, slowly and cautiously, toward the goal.

This time around, however, the slow and steady approach will not do. We do not have the luxury of awaiting the reconciliation of beliefs that Hulme envisions. Because climate change proceeds apace, we must act as soon as we possibly can. Hesitating to act in *this* case seems foolish. Although all of us by now have a healthy respect for the ponderous rate at which political change comes in modern democracies, we also know that in this particular case, the problem gets worse with each passing year.

Is it possible that something is wrong with the best solutions proposed to this point? Are they simply too much to take? If so, what about them seems to go too far? As I have suggested, the basic approach is straightforward enough: raising the price of emitting greenhouse gases would do the trick, especially through the mechanism of a greenhouse tax or untax. (As I mentioned in chapter two, following the usage of Steven Stoft, an untax is a tax whose entire proceeds are distributed equally to all taxpaying citizens.) But to be fair, even this relatively simple approach would require an important transformation in our political culture.

In the United States, we tend to place great faith in the rationality and efficiency of the market. We interfere, if at all, by making certain transactions illegal, imposing regulations on business practices, and encouraging various endeavors with tax breaks. But for the most part, we allow the market to set its own priorities. We regard any widespread attempt to shape market forces with suspicion, having decided many decades ago, at least by the time of the Cold War, that any collective control over the market constituted socialism and therefore (in a major leap) totalitarianism. For us, it seems, the liberty of the market is as sacred as any other freedom, no matter what the consequences. But as a result, we tend to let many abuses fester for generations; even though we can see that the market creates a wide array of social problems, we refuse to consider many ways to fix them out of the fear that intervening would look like socialism. Ironically, of course, through our government we have subsidized the extraction of fossil fuels, interfering into the market to *lower* their cost, creating as we so often do a kind of warped socialism, stretching out a helping hand to the staggeringly wealthy. The first thing we need to do, then, is to eliminate these subsidies entirely. But that step in itself would simply restore the market to its own equilibrium and would fail to address the problem at its core.

A greenhouse gas untax cuts through this impasse. Ordinarily, the low cost of fossil fuels makes them the default source of energy; as long as these sources remain cheap, the market will forever reinforce our current fossil-fuel habits. By raising the price of sources of energy that contribute to climate change, an untax modifies this dynamic entirely. Because it incorporates the collective good into the pricing mechanism, it enables us to bring about a massive shift in our practices simply by following the laws of the market. Once fossil fuels become more expensive than renewable alternatives, we'll all have the incentive to power our industries, heat our homes, and fuel our cars with sustainable sources of energy.

The result will be an explosion of technological innovations to create a new energy economy. When this untax raises the cost of agricultural and forestry practices that produce greenhouse gases, it will also drive widespread innovations in managing the land. No doubt public investment in technology research will also be needed. But rather than transforming public behavior exclusively through law or regulation, this measure uses the market to counteract the harm it previously reinforced. Furthermore, if it truly is an untax, rather than a tax—if the federal government distributes all of the proceeds equally among the nation's taxpayers—then it innovates in a further way: it makes protecting the future into collective property, giving each taxpayer a stake in social change. The more citizens get attached to their share of the money, the more they will identify their self-interest with the good of the whole.[86]

This proposal thus represents an important innovation in the American understanding of the market. On one level, the untax apparently accepts without question the market's dominion over the Earth, creating that strange beast, the notion of profit-driven ecological change. But in fact, by using the terms of the market, this solution subordinates the market's workings to a common goal. It suggests that even if the market is a set of mechanisms that usually create cheapness and efficiency, the public can appropriate it for a collective purpose, turning it into a straightforward, low-maintenance, and effective means to create a greenhouse-free economy. In effect, this strategy makes market society into a transformative machine that would generate incredible momentum toward undoing the causes of climate change. When that common goal finds expression within the terms of the market, individual choice can do the rest. The result would be neither capitalism nor socialism, strictly speaking, for it would rely on an alternative to both, using an aspect of capitalism to achieve a socially designated purpose.

This strategy accords well with other aspects of an innovative solution. The shift to sustainable energy technologies, as well as ecologically sound management of farmlands and forests, will rely heavily on scientific research, experimentation, and know-how. This approach thus hopes to use science to reconfigure the fossil-fuel-driven world it has created over the past two centuries. Here again the proposed measures would make possible a fusion of apparently opposed political traditions; it would blend technological innovation with environmental responsibility, making good use of engineering skills to ecological ends. Just as we can use the market to transform itself, we can rely on science to do the same—to find ways of sustaining our lives that are far less destructive than those it has provided so far.

In effect, this measure ultimately proposes a Grand Compromise between free-market ideology and an inescapable environmental imperative. It accepts the bedrock American love of economic freedom and uses it for a cause in which the vast majority of Americans also believe. The nation has used a roughly similar approach on previous occasions, as Social Security and Medicare demonstrate. Those measures blended economic individualism and public protection in ways that were initially attacked as socialist but that eventually received nearly unanimous public support, suggesting that hybrid solutions of this kind are possible in America.

Nevertheless, this proposal has not yet been adopted by our legislative bodies. (In 2010, the Senate rejected a bill without a vote, perhaps because the cap-and-trade mechanism in the bill was riddled with flaws, but more likely because it would have indirectly raised the price of fossil fuel.)[87] It does not seem likely that any legislation increasing the cost of fossil fuel, whether through a cap-and-trade mechanism, a tax, an untax, or a rationing system, will ever receive Congressional blessing—at least not in the foreseeable future. Those opposed to action insist either that climate change does not exist or that the government should not intrude into the market in this way. The first objection is tacitly a stand-in for the second; it signals the fear that if climate change happens to be true, it will give the government an excuse to take too much control over our lives.

The ultimate basis for these objections is the belief that each person has the right to do whatever he or she pleases—as long as such action does not harm the interest of another. This belief is the core of "liberal" philosophy, that is, the strand of political philosophy that places its highest priority on safeguarding individual liberty. (Here our terminology has it exactly backwards; those who place liberty above our future are "liberals," strictly speaking, while those who wish to sustain the biosphere into the future are in a key sense "conservatives.")

The problem with this objection is that it falls flat, right on its face. When we decide to use fossil fuels, we *are* harming each other, as well as the biosphere and all future generations. If there were ever a public imperative that passed this test *better*, I'd like to know what it is. All governments have the right to protect the viability of the biosphere for future generations; otherwise, it's not clear why we bother to let such governments exist. Our Constitution recognizes this right in its Preamble, which states that the purpose of government is to "promote the general Welfare, and secure the Blessings of Liberty to ourselves and our Posterity." Take note: its purpose is to secure liberty for us *and posterity, too*. Since emitting greenhouse gases today will lead to more severe climate change, which will in turn seriously hamper the liberties of our descendants, the only way to safeguard the rights of posterity is to change our own practices today. The liberal tradition is absolutely on the side of changing our society, and doing so *now*. The trick is to find a solution to the problem that also respects the liberal tradition, that draws on individual decision-making, foresight, and creativity. The greenhouse gas untax fits the bill, for it creates the market incentives for all of us to bring about the changes we need.

The obstacle, then, is not present in any feature of the proposed solution, which accords well with our Constitution and our respect for the free market. We can only conclude that the opposition stems from an objection that has no legitimacy and cannot even be spoken: the belief that *no possible public good* can justify an intrusion of this kind into individual liberty, that in protecting freedom we should not take the interest even of posterity into account. Such a belief objects to the very idea of a greater good or a collective purpose. Ever since the "Reagan revolution," many Republicans have strongly resisted the notion that the government is capable of solving *any* social problem, for by definition government itself is the greatest problem of all. In consequence, since that "revolution," these Republicans—by no means all—tend to vilify progressive uses of government as socialist, communist, or fascist, and on occasion, as all three. In the new version of the free-market ideology, it seems, *nothing can ever be more important than the market itself.*

In practical terms, then, the nation's response to climate change must now be debated on entirely different grounds, that of "energy independence"—the goal of weaning America from dependency on "foreign oil." But any legislation adopted on these premises will not be enough. Funding research into new energy technologies is essential, but this step will not in itself make those technologies attractive to individual consumers. Giving tax breaks to help people convert to renewable energy is good, too, but it will be insufficient, since the vast majority of the public will have little incentive to give up cheap fossil fuel. Perhaps the only event that will truly change individual habits is a dramatic hike in the price of oil. In that case, the free market might do what the government cannot, inspiring us all to use new sources of energy as soon as we can. One possible scenario is that the government will pass legislation to generate a new round of technological innovation, and a global economic recovery will push the price of oil so high that we'll all begin shifting to a new energy economy on our own. But such developments will still leave too many gaps: they will leave in place the hope that oil prices will decline again, preventing businesses from making the necessary long-term investments; they will keep alive the popular bias for cheap energy, as well as an immense transfer of funds to oil-producing nations; and they won't cover the management of farmland or forest, create a smart grid, or help reduce the cost of electrical cars. Moreover, they will make it very difficult for the United States to accept a binding target for lowering emissions in international negotiations, hindering truly effective worldwide action. In short, this "solution" simply will not do.

The doctrinaire opposition to effective action has more than purely practical consequences. It will force us to adopt half-measures, to be sure. But it's worth contemplating why we must resort to them at all. It's about time we faced the consequences of the "Reagan revolution"—the notion that protecting the free market is more important than any other consideration. If that dogma is true, then creating a business-friendly environment trumps preserving the Earth. Capitalism matters more than the biosphere. No doubt capitalism might have difficulty flourishing if the biosphere begins to suffer; any sane businessperson should be able to admit to that fact. But free-market dogmatists will not do so, because they will not concede that the biosphere is in danger in the first place. Their resistance to action is more subtle: in their view, capitalism is more *real* than the biosphere. The conditions for business are real, as are taxes and government funding, but in their view scientific assessments of climate change are still so speculative and so dependent on unproven models that they do not yet describe reality. Assessments of the business environment, of course, *also* depend on models and estimates, but at least they refer to modes of behavior that we understand. In this view, climate change, if it exists, arises from physical processes we still don't fully comprehend. Adam Smith is good as gold, but the IPCC is still a bit fishy. There is no need to change until the science is more solid—but even then, how could it ever be as solid as the myth of Adam Smith?[88]

This description of market fundamentalism might sound a bit extreme. But in fact the entire public sphere accepts the principle that no political measure can be justified unless it is consistent with the laws of the market. (The only exceptions allowed these days are national security, a handful of moral norms—such as those that forbid selling people, body parts, or sex—and a few government programs too popular to touch.) We've long since gotten used to obeying this principle: it seems we can't truly face any significant public problem (from elevated high-school dropout rates, drug abuse, and worker safety to disaster relief and the protection of endangered species) without considering its impact on the economy and whether it would be cost-efficient to address it. Our ultimate reality is the economy; any other factor that matters to us must make its peace with that principle or be eliminated altogether. In the United States, at least, human beings must abide by the rules of the market, not vice versa. Here, we all live within the free-market bubble; nothing makes it inside that doesn't submit to the logic of the market.

The consequences of living in this bubble are stark. Quickly now, answer this. What's harder for you to imagine: the end of free-market capitalism, or the end of nature? By now, imagining a devastated biosphere comes fairly easily to us all. Imagining life after the end of the market? That's almost impossible. For *all* of us in this society, *the market is more real than nature.*[89]

But is this the core problem? After all, the greenhouse untax translates a shared priority into monetary terms, working with the rules of the market to achieve a common purpose. It respects the rule that no public good in this nation can be accepted until it speaks in the language of cost incentives. But evidently, this gesture is not enough. The untax relies on the principle that the market *must serve something outside itself*, must ultimately not endanger the biosphere and thus our future. In doing so, it says that *nature is more real than the market*. It declares its loyalty to the Earth, not to economic growth. In attempting to dislodge our dependence on cheap energy, it tries to bring about systemic, radical change to our entire frame of mind. In doing so, it violates a basic taboo; it bursts the bubble.

In practical terms, the greenhouse untax (or its alternative versions) is a fairly innocuous proposal. It would raise the cost of energy, leading to a host of further changes, but it otherwise respects our traditions and habits in every way. Nevertheless, it represents an immense *symbolic* shift. If the "Reagan revolution" sought to limit the government's right to intervene into the market, *this* shift constitutes an *ecological revolution*, one that limits the market's right to intervene into nature. Addressing climate change, it seems, requires nothing less than a radical transformation— one akin to the industrial revolution, the sexual revolution, the Reagan revolution, or all three, for it calls for a transformation in specific aspects of our understanding of government, our physical infrastructure, and our daily life all at once. Its effects are so widespread, in fact, that it may be the most consequential revolution of them all.

Why does such a simple measure have such big consequences? In the past, American movements for social change have taken two paths:

at times they have inspired Constitutional amendments, Supreme Court decisions, new legal protections, and other revisions in our basic understanding of individual rights, and at other moments they have led to the creation of public agencies to oversee and enforce protections for workers, previous targets of discrimination, or aspects of the environment. Although passing Social Security and Medicare required fighting back against charges of socialism, even those battles pale in comparison to what is required today. Seldom have we attempted to change our society by intervening so directly into the market itself, by changing the price of goods necessary to all categories of economic activity for the sake of a collective purpose. The last time we did anything on this order of magnitude, we removed an entire category of goods from the market—namely, human beings—and it took a Civil War to do so. In this country, whenever injustice is woven into the fabric of our economy, change is very difficult indeed, and the current case is no different.

One sign of how much this revolution will require of us may be found in what it shares with "deep ecology," which argued around three decades ago that because the Earth is not here to serve human purposes, we need to repudiate modest protections for the environment and change our societies far more radically.[90] Deep ecology has never become a mainstream movement; it has been regarded, and has regarded itself, as a marginal if fierce presence. But today, climate change is making its central point more clearly than ever: by now, it's crystal clear that we cannot use the Earth in whatever way we see fit, for if we do so, we endanger our own future. We are a part of the Earth, rather than the other way around.

But this insight in itself is not enough. Deep ecology uses misleading terms; by using the term "deep," it implies that depth of awareness on these matters is its own reward, that seeing past gradualist measures is sufficient. That view distracts us from a much more crucial contrast, embedded in nineteenth-century radical traditions, between reform and revolution. At its heart, by opposing reformist measures, deep ecology is *revolutionary* ecology. In that case, merely thinking through a critique of modern society is only the first step. Much more crucial is the task of figuring out how to *change* modern society so that it will no longer destroy the biosphere. Climate change forces us to convert this particular strand of ecological thinking into a political force that can advocate for actual legislation and practical, real-world solutions.

And how, exactly, might we do so? So far, the major activist strategies have not worked. Popularizing climate change science only goes so far, since a good share of the public is dogmatically committed to a "skeptical" stance. A more overt attempt to educate the public would only be perceived as condescending or worse. Direct political action on climate change has tended to follow the two tracks familiar within American activist traditions: either it uses the tactics of reformist pressure politics, which ultimately relies on fundraising and lobbying Congress, or of decentralized, community-centered activism. But both of these efforts have failed and will continue to fail. Lobbying Congress has gradually built support for action, but not enough to get a strong bill through a Democratic House, much less a Democratic Senate. Many activists, having given up on federal leadership, have put their energy into organizing local efforts; such efforts have led to good results, especially in city, state, and regional compacts to reduce emissions. But ultimately none of these local efforts is enough; without concerted, tough federal action, we will simply not reduce our emissions as greatly as we must.

What political strategy is available to us that we have not tried? Perhaps it is worth mentioning in passing that the moral case for violent intervention is strong. If we can justify a nationalist revolt for liberty, as our ancestors did, or a war to defeat fascism, we can easily defend an intervention to save the life of the entire biosphere, whose decline represents a threat on a far greater scale than any crisis in the past. The murder of tens of millions of people during World War II pales in comparison to the potential harm to more than seven *billion* people on the planet in the coming decades.[91]

Yet even discussing the possibility of resorting to violence seems to go too far; by now, in developed countries the mere hint of violent revolution is enough to delegitimize any movement for change. As a result, in the postwar era, the United States has evolved a gentler alternative to violent social change, one that fits the gradualist pace of American politics: the massive, nonviolent rally in Washington to make specific demands for action. Perhaps the key event in this regard is the civil rights march in August, 1963, when Martin Luther King, Jr., gave his famous "I have a dream" speech. That rally has served as the template for virtually every later rally in the nation's capital, each of which has implicitly invoked the civil rights movement as the model of its own seriousness.

But because such rallies are symbolic—because they express certain demands without forcing immediate action—they hit their mark only if the government is willing to listen, only if pressure reaches an official audience that accepts the legitimacy of popular demands. When officials believe that they have already responded to those demands or that the new moral claims are illegitimate, the mass rally does not make a great deal of difference; the crowd will assemble and disband, the press will give it passing attention, and the life of the nation will go on, relatively undisturbed. In that case, the rally ultimately constitutes a feel-good occasion, a day for collective self-expression that has no real consequence. This much, at least, is true of rallies concerning ecology and climate change; the various rallies, protest marches, and other events in recent years have not budged Congressional sentiment a single inch.

What about the strategies tried by the Occupy Wall Street demonstrations beginning in the autumn of 2011? Would the more aggressive attempt not just to demonstrate but to *occupy* public space have a greater impact? For better or worse, however, that protest movement, while addressing real concerns, did not provide a list of demands to which those in power might respond. The movement succeeded in putting certain ideas into the overall political debate and changing the dynamic in the nation's capital and elsewhere, but it did not have a powerful, immediate impact.

Would it be possible for activism to pursue a more courageous, creative tactic to break out of this impasse? Many nations have undergone nonviolent revolutions over the past several decades when vast numbers of ordinary citizens took over public space, demanded a change in government, and succeeded. The actions of immense, persistent, disciplined crowds in the Philippines and Indonesia, Berlin and the Ukraine, Tunisia and Egypt—and elsewhere in the Arab Spring—are excellent cases in point, even if the transformations they helped bring about have not necessarily endured. Could such an event take place in the United States, though for a different purpose? Could an immense rally in the public spaces of the nation's capital—a rally that begins on the premise that it *will not cease until its specific demands regarding climate change are met*—transform our political idiom, crack open our encrusted collective discourse, and force a decision of *some* kind on climate change, whatever it might be?

The answer, I think, is no. Activists have not attempted to organize a protest on this basis, or even considered it, for several reasons. For one thing, doing so does not respect the principle that political demands in this country must be moderate, respectful, and measured—that even if voices for change may not be heard at first, they will be listened to eventually. A massive crowd that demands change *before it disbands* implies that the duly elected government is so neglectful of the collective interest that *it cannot be trusted to act on that interest in its own good time*. That crowd, in short, would attempt to usurp the popular legitimacy of the government itself. Such a tactic cuts deeply against the American grain; at least over the past century, we have accepted the notion that a constitutionally legitimate government is legitimate in other ways as well, that in the end it will serve the common good. To suggest otherwise would come across as the height of arrogance, for it would seem to attack democracy itself. As a result, no one who believes in the urgency of action contemplates a tough, uncompromising rally of this kind; we all in practice accept the authority of this government, come what may—even if its policies endorse market activities that are destroying the Earth.

But the consequences of that loyalty are stark. In effect, we put the viability of our political system above the viability of the biosphere; *our political systems are more real to us than the Earth itself.* In effect, we live in a political, as well as an economic, bubble. If climate change increasingly reveals that our policies do not make sense, we *still* accept the authority of this government and continue to pursue a moderate kind of activism, as if the biosphere can wait while our officials dither.

As a nation, then, we have two overpowering reasons why we have not acted. First, we do not wish to burst the free-market bubble, our belief that the Earth is here to sustain economic growth. Giving up this belief is very difficult for a good portion of the American public. But even those who give it up accept the habits of moderate protest because they do not wish to burst the political bubble, the nearly unanimous belief that this government will in time represent the best interests of us all. Even if the climate transforms before our very eyes, we will hesitate to act, because for virtually all of us, our ultimate homeland, the domain that counts as real for us, is not the Earth, but the political and social traditions in which we live. No natural events are strong enough by themselves to dislodge our unthinking loyalties.

Why can climate change not get us to budge out of these fidelities? What about the ecological revolution of our time simply does not compute? The answer can only be that it goes against the nation's traditions so directly that it can hardly be understood in familiar terms. As a truly *ecological* revolution, it creates a number of unprecedented challenges.

For one thing, every previous revolution in the classic sense (such as the Puritan Revolution, the American Revolution, or the French Revolution) has promised some degree of liberation—from a monarchy or aristocracy, a foreign government, or a system of exploitation or enslavement. In all these cases, people fought hoping that victory would give them much greater liberty and happiness. An ecological revolution promises no such reward. It seeks the liberation of the Earth's ecosystems, and ultimately of human beings as well, from climate change. But it undoubtedly goes against the stream of modern culture. It requires us to *renounce* what we thought we had gained from those previous successes. It tells us that we do *not* have certain rights—that we live within an intricate web of mutual relations that are not subject to our control. Rather than promising us a wonderful expansion of our lives, it offers us something altogether more subtle: it tells us that if we give up a certain kind of abundance, or a certain way of securing it, we will safeguard what we thought we could take for granted, our opportunity to have a livable future.

Similar reflections apply to a social change that, unlike violent revolution, follows the rules of American political culture—a change that takes place through compromise, over many generations. For most of the history of this nation, the great movements for emancipation have taken place within the context of economic growth, industrialization, increasing population, and a greatly expanding use of natural resources. Expanding individual rights is difficult—it has taken generations and is still ongoing—yet it is somewhat easier when economic growth holds out the promise that if relatively privileged groups recognize the rights of others, their own future happiness will not be harmed. Furthermore, this expansion of rights is only one element within the wider effect of industrialization itself, which liberated people from the endless drudgery of preindustrial labor. Released in this way, people had time for education and leisure activities, money for a vast range of consumer items, and an opportunity to extend to their fellow citizens a chance for happiness like their own.

An ecological movement does not follow these rules: it forces us to consider whether economic growth, which inevitably involves a greater use of natural resources, is even viable in the long term, and if so, what it might look like;[92] it demands that we reconstruct our entire industrial infrastructure and potentially deindustrialize many of our practices; it forces us to give up our assumption that we can continue to "develop" previously undisturbed natural spaces; and as a result, it asks us to relinquish, or at least consider relinquishing, the idea that our collective abundance will forever increase. To demand change without the promise of greater plenty would require making an appeal on pure principle. Few previous attempts of this kind have succeeded; as I mentioned in the introduction, the movement to abolish slavery was fought on the same basis, came up against the realities of an entire economic system, and did not succeed until the nation endured a Civil War. Needless to say, that is not a good precedent. Even worse, such an appeal would go further than merely doing *without* the help of the trends in production, population, and settlement that, broadly speaking, enabled previous movements to gain general acceptance; it would potentially argue *against* them. An ecological movement worth its salt asks for more, and seems to offer less, than any previous social cause—even if its ultimate purpose is to safeguard the happiness of human beings. Here again, the demands of the Earth and of our own better selves conflict with our traditions.

The revolution of our time cuts against the grain in these ways in part because it does not have what most people would recognize as an immediate human constituency. Every previous revolution had a discernible protagonist, a group of people who would truly benefit from social change. This time, the immediate constituency is the Earth itself, all its ecosystems, and the human race as a whole. But it turns out that getting the concerns of *that* constituency recognized within our political system is no easy task. Those parties have no direct political representatives; no one speaks for them other than those who volunteer to do so. But the public treats those volunteers with suspicion: who are *they* to represent the natural world or to speak for the human race? Is their knowledge of climate change thorough and sound? Is their demand to put the viability of the biosphere above immediate human satisfaction acceptable? Yet without such representation, we would hardly be able to take the environmental consequences of our actions into account. No one gives ecosystems the vote, nor can the dying coral reefs or melting permafrost make political demands. Of course, inhabitants of islands that are about to be submerged can raise their voices. But they are so few, and their lands so distant, that people in the developed world act as if they do not exist.

The result is an impasse that marks out as clearly as possible the limitations of our political institutions. They take for granted that all matters that pertain to human affairs must arise from within the human community and can be resolved within that domain. But it turns out that *some* matters, at least, are relevant to all American citizens, even if none of us is seeking relief from an oppression that immediately afflicts us. Taking action to prevent severe climate change is indeed in the interest of us all. But to make the natural world feature in our calculation of our own interest is unusual, and on this scale unprecedented: our institutions simply do not know how to respond.

This impasse may also stem from the fact that this potential revolution necessarily sustains an unusual relation to the future. Social movements have typically fought to create a better future; the revolution of our time, however, fights to prevent the arrival of a devastating one. Previous revolutions could attempt to shatter tradition, cut off the relationship to the past, and invent an entirely new world; the French Revolution even created a new calendar, attempting to start time over again. Since the Enlightenment, modern societies have taken this link between revolution and radicalism for granted. But our time is different. The quintessential aim of radicalism—the utopian hope for a transformed future—now requires that we first attempt to conserve as much of the Earth's environment as possible before trying to reconstruct our societies in any other way. *Today, radicalism must first be conservative:* even if its ultimate aim is to open up an entirely new era, it must first make possible a sustainable, ecologically responsible continuity over many generations, a continuity without which it could not even fight for further social and political transformation. This conservatism, of course, also requires radical change to our energy economies, but in the name of making it possible for the biosphere, and thus our societies themselves, to survive.

Because the focus of this movement is to sustain the biosphere, it differs sharply from prior revolutions in yet another way. Climate change waits for no one: if we do not transform our practices *today*, we will feel the heat in years to come. Never before has there been a *deadline* for revolution, a claim on us to bring about social change before it's too late. No doubt previous revolutionaries seized opportunities that would never again arise, certain that it was impossible to endure oppression for another moment. In that sense, they too felt a supreme urgency. But that urgency arose from within the historical situation itself, from the interplay of social and political forces. Now the imperative emerges from the purely physical consequences of actions that a short time ago we may not have considered politically significant. Suddenly, material reality obtrudes into our history, making felt an absolutely urgent demand that we cannot ignore.

There is no mistake about it: we must act, and we must act now. Some might argue that the urgency of the challenge will at last motivate us all to participate in a movement that will transform the world in which we live. But any sense that acknowledging the potentially catastrophic dimensions of what we face will in itself help create an ecological revolution is almost certain to fail.[93] The contrary possibility is much more likely to come true. The revolution we must bring about goes against our traditions again and again. It is endlessly inconvenient: it has no constituency, promises no liberation for us, and imposes its own timeline. It intrudes into our history implacably, utterly indifferent to the normal political calculations. It demands that we change our material practices immediately, whatever our apparent interests at the moment might be.

Because the obstacles to action are formidable, indeed overwhelming, the odds are very strong that we as a nation will not act in time. As I suggested in the previous chapter, the current political realities in Washington make it almost impossible for our government to take the necessary steps in the coming few years—during the crucial interval when we *must* act. In this situation, what should sane and responsible citizens do?

Should we simply give up and go with the flow? Should we accept an intolerable reality because it is so difficult to fight against it, and more strangely, because even a victory would come too late? Not at all. Looking back at the era of slavery, how tolerant are we of a hypothetical slaveholder who argued that because liberating his slaves wouldn't change the system overall, there would be no point in doing so? Or looking back at Nazi Germany, would we accept the plea of a citizen who claimed she cooperated with the policy of extermination because it was not in her power to buck the system? Do we accept excuses like this? No, we don't. The American refusal of the Nuremberg defense during the war trials shortly after World War II says it all: evil action, even when committed under orders, is not acceptable.

Our thoughts in this regard say a lot about what we value. We affirm the necessity to act justly even if doing so requires us to risk our lives. We also affirm that we must do so even if there are no guarantees that our action will lead to the results we desire. The same is especially true in a situation of dire extremity, when the future of civilization seems to be at stake, when nobody knows whether the future for which we sacrifice ourselves will even come to pass. Judging by our response in these examples, it's clear that for us, just action is never about calculating the consequences, but about doing the right thing, *just because it is right.*

If that is the case, we don't really follow Aristotle at all. For us, politics is really the art of the *im*possible. If we do not wish to use the equivalent of the Nuremberg defense, we have to admit that *even if a revolution against the current system seems to be impossible, we must fight for it anyway. We must act, and we must act now.* We owe the Earth and future generations far too much to pursue only reasonable actions, only strategies that have a high probability of success. Instead of complying with conventional wisdom, we must transform it, reconceiving as well of familiar understandings of self-interest. *The crisis of our time is unprecedented; our response must be so too.* We must have the courage to break our society's taboos, to crack open the conventions of our political life, to expose the fundamental illegitimacy of any government that belittles the future of the biosphere. If this demand requires us to gather in vast crowds to hold our nations hostage, thereby defying the complacent assumptions of modern democracies, so be it: only through this or any similarly forceful gesture will we at last place the biosphere above our belief in familiar political traditions. Even if we fail miserably, even if the conventions of public debate are too rigid to accept our intervention, we should not hold back. We will never again face a crisis in which more is at stake; we have no excuse but to salvage at least the possibility of future action. We have no choice but to redefine what is politically feasible—*even if it is too late*.[94] For us, *only the impossible is worthwhile*.

Notes

85. Mike Hulme, *Why We Disagree About Climate Change: Understanding Controversy, Inaction and Opportunity* (Cambridge, England: Cambridge University Press, 2009), especially 173–176. Hulme's argument runs aground on another key fact: social change never takes place through reconciliation, only through the gradual adoption of a new concept of justice that eventually wins out in the face of persistent opposition. The overall acceptance of that change comes about only a generation or two after the change itself has taken place. It follows that disagreement over climate change is inevitable over the period when actions matter most.

86. See Steven Stoft, *Carbonomics: How to Fix the Climate and Charge It to OPEC* Nantucket, Massachusetts: Diamond Press, 2008). Stoft focuses on an untax on the supply of fossil fuels; I've added the suggestion that there be a similar untax on the greenhouse-gas producing management of farmland and forest, and thus have substituted my own term, "greenhouse untax," for his, "carbon untax."

87. See John M. Broder, "White House Energy Session Changes No Minds," *New York Times*, June 29, 2010, http://www.nytimes.com/2010/06/30/science/earth/30energy.html; Peter Baker and David M. Herszenhorn, "Senate Democrats to Pursue a Smaller Energy Bill," *New York Times*, July 15, 2010, http://www.nytimes.com/2010/07/15/us/politics/15energy.html; and Carl Hulse and Herszenhorn, "Democrats Call Off Climate Bill Effort," *New York Times*, July 22, 2010, http://www.nytimes.com/2010/07/23/us/politics/23cong.html.

88. Despite the claims of free-market fundamentalists, Adam Smith was by no means an advocate for an unfettered market, as many scholars have long since argued. For representative statements in this regard, see Salim Rashid, *The Myth of Adam Smith* (Northampton, Massachusetts: Edward Elgar, 1998); Athol Fitzgibbons, *Adam Smith's System of Liberty, Wealth and Virtue: The Moral*

and Political Foundations of The Wealth of Nations (Oxford: Clarendon Press, 1995), especially chapter 10; and Heinz Lubasz, "Adam Smith and the 'Free Market,'" in *Adam Smith's* Wealth of Nations: *New Interdisciplinary Essays,* edited by Stephen Copley and Kathryn Sutherland (New York: Manchester University Press, 1995), 45–69.

89. Compare a statement often attributed to Fredric Jameson: "It's easier to imagine the end of the world than the end of capitalism." But he did not make this remark himself; he attributes it to an anonymous other in his essay, "Future City," *New Left Review,* volume 21 (2003), 65–79; see page 76. Many commentators on our current political dilemmas have invoked this insight; for a book-length discussion see Joel Kovel, *The Enemy of Nature: The End of Capitalism or the End of the World?* (New York, Zed Books, 2002).

90. See Bill Devall and George Sessions, *Deep Ecology: Living as if Nature Mattered* (Salt Lake City: G. M. Smith, 1985), and George Sessions, editor, *Deep Ecology for the 21st Century: Readings on the Philosophy and Practice of the New Environmentalism* (Boston: Shambhala, 1995).

91. On the moral case for the use of violence in response to ecological crisis, see Derrick Jensen, *Endgame: Volume I, The Problem of Civilization,* and *Volume II, Resistance* (New York: Seven Stories Press, 2006).

92. For discussions of capitalism without growth, see Tim Jackson, *Prosperity Without Growth: Economics for a Finite Planet* (Sterling, Virginia: Earthscan, 2009), and Bill McKibben, *Deep Economy: The Wealth of Communities and the Durable Future* (New York: Henry Holt, 2007). For related discussions of transforming capitalism, see Vandana Shiva, *Earth Democracy: Justice, Sustainability, and Peace* (Cambridge, Massachusetts: South End Press, 2005), and William Greider, *The Soul of Capitalism: Opening Paths to a Moral Economy* (New York: Simon & Schuster, 2003).

93. See Sasha Lilley and others, *Catastrophism: The Apocalyptic Politics of Collapse and Rebirth* (Oakland: PM Press, 2012).

94. On politics as the art of the impossible, see Slavoj Žižek, *The Ticklish Subject: The Absent Centre of Political Ontology* (New York: Verso, 1999), 199. In a related vein, Žižek has often commented on the apparently impossible act that reframes the entire political context; for a recent, representative discussion, see *In Defense of Lost Causes* (New York: Verso, 2008), 304–316.

Chapter 5

The Stolen Future

Because our economy and political traditions are more real to us than the biosphere itself, the ecological revolution we need is not likely to take place until climate change itself becomes much more persuasive, until the biosphere tells us in unmistakable terms that it will truly decimate us if we don't change. At that point we will finally understand what it requires of us and will modify our societies in ways still possible for us. The fact that a damaged biosphere will eventually coerce us into action tells us that we face a basic choice: either we carry out an ecological revolution today in a manner that conserves what we know best—or climate change will devastate our society later on and force us to adapt to conditions we did not choose. Here again, our situation is unprecedented: the necessary ecological revolution, however inconvenient, is the product of a forced choice, a decision to prevent a later, much more intrusive and chaotic event.

If we do act too late, it won't be for the first time. Many observers would point out that in this respect, the ecological crisis of our day parallels many others we have already experienced. Hunters on the American high plains decimated millions of buffalo and nearly eradicated the species without much of a public outcry; only a few small herds remained after the great slaughter. Developed nations injected DDT into the food chain long enough for that molecule to drive some species to near extinction before Rachel Carson's call to action finally led to a ban on the product in the United States. In the 1970s, trawlers on the high seas wiped out a substantial share of desirable fish populations by the time nations finally took action. We could add almost indefinitely to this list, each item of which would demonstrate very clearly that in countless cases, we act *after* the damage has been done.

This time around, however, acting too late will be even worse, thanks to yet another strange aspect of our present dilemma. Because the carbon dioxide we emit today will endure in the atmosphere for over a century, and our actions today will have consequences over generations, a failure to act will perpetually undermine and possibly erase any *future* action to address climate change. Modern history is rife with revolutions that led to counter-revolutions, movements to restore the prior state of things. Today, our own inaction would constitute a *perpetual* counter-revolution, a heavy hand destroying the inventiveness of future generations. It's as if the minutemen of the future would endlessly be defeated by King George III, no matter how resourcefully they fought on.

If that is so, we are simultaneously harming the future of the biosphere *and deliberately stealing from future humanity's ability to respond effectively to that fact.* Our emissions are not only harming the biosphere; they are destroying the *future history* of humanity and the biosphere both. Carbon dioxide, it turns out, is not only a molecule that can persist well into the future, contributing to global warming for generations; it is also a *historical* pollutant, fogging up the future with past events, smothering potential brilliance with the stupidity of earlier generations. It's as if our own moment, by some strange wrinkle in time, will come *after* the generation that follows us. The more carbon dioxide we emit, the more contempt we show for the agency of our own descendants. In giving birth to them and raising them, we may to some degree be showing them love and care, but at the same time we hand down to them an inheritance of future disaster, a legacy of the ashes to come.

Our situation is thus utterly bizarre. We have no real clue how to act in time, yet our inaction will severely restrict the benefit of action when it finally does take place. The revolution is not only going to come too late; when it comes, *it will be defeated in advance.* Thanks to us, it will be far less effective than it should be, *even when it does come.* We are the thieves of the future.

Faced with this haunting realization, we might be inclined to pause and listen to a viewpoint steeped in a cynical acceptance of human folly and ecological destruction. Some people might remark, for example, that our present inaction is nothing to lament. In their view, if we act against our own long-term self-interest we will bear the consequences, as we so often have in the past. Nothing in human affairs guarantees wisdom or foresight; our failure to act in the present case is no exception. What is there to regret? After all, they might go on to argue, the value we give to the natural world is not intrinsic within it; it speaks of what we as human beings enjoy and love. Nature itself has no consciousness of harm; it will not protest if we destroy it. In wounding nature, we only wound what we project onto it and no more—unless we harm ourselves, in which case we will ultimately learn our lesson and apply it as well as we can. There is no need for anyone to try to speak for the biosphere; what happens to it matters only insofar as it bears on humankind in a manner evident to all.

This attitude cannot withstand a quick reality check. Do we really believe that the world's ecosystems exist only for us—simply because we possess a certain kind of consciousness? If so, we value the power to know above the power to exist. Yet in one account of our formation as human beings, our ability to know results from God's creating us in his image, in which case we are responsible for preserving his creation. In another, that ability came about through our evolution within specific ecosystems, in competition with other species and in response to many environmental pressures; it links us directly to thousands of other forms of life. In either version, we owe whatever ability we have to something outside ourselves.

Moreover, our ability to "know" is limited; we have mastered very little about our own existence, much less about the lives of other creatures, and even less about their possible forms of consciousness. Rather than making us the sole arbiter of value, this ability speaks of a fallible echo of divine powers or emerges from a particular mode of evolutionary adaptation. Human consciousness is remarkable, to be sure, but it is not a feature that gives us unlimited sovereignty to do what we wish with the biosphere. Few of us, I dare say, would accept existence merely as forms of consciousness without the pleasures of embodied life. We would not wish to sacrifice our existence as natural beings and become purely mental entities. But in that case, we are natural creatures among the rest, and our wish to live well reflects the basic drive of all life to do the same. If we respect these dimensions of human existence, we must respect other forms of life as well and do what we can not to destroy them.

Nevertheless, this objection does have one great merit: it makes explicit the profound anthropocentrism on which all our institutions are based. That attitude, as I have argued, is quite visible in our economic systems, which take for granted that ecosystems are "natural resources" for human beings to use. It is inherent in our political traditions as well, which find it difficult to take a perspective other than the human into account. In fact, it speaks for nearly every dimension of modern, industrial society, which everywhere takes human sovereignty for granted.

Climate change refutes that attitude, and it refutes it for good. Because we regard nature merely as the backdrop for human activities and continue to live as we please, we threaten the conditions of life as we know it and thus undermine modern society itself. We are in the process of demonstrating, once and for all, that without a flourishing biosphere, human life on its own cannot flourish in the least.

But if that is so, climate change tells us that much more is amiss than climate change alone. It is only one consequence of a broad array of anthropocentric activities, each of which threatens the biosphere. From an ecological perspective, we have already intruded into countless landscapes to make space for our own activities, spewed pollutants into innumerable ecosystems on land and sea, and driven a vast number of species to extinction. In the last three or four decades, we have begun to take steps to curb these practices, but we have far to go.

All these problems, including climate change, arise from the enormous increase of productive power that came with advanced industrialization. Drawing on the energy provided by fossil fuels, industry could produce goods more cheaply and abundantly than ever before and generate chemical fertilizers that allowed modern agriculture to be much more productive. Together, the industry and agriculture powered in this fashion sustained a much greater population. That population, with its highly developed way of life, now expects a similar standard of living in the future, as do in some measure the people living in the developing world. Although advanced societies are getting better at producing goods and services with less energy each passing year, providing an advanced standard of living for all the world's people would still require using far more resources than are available on this planet. There is not even the shadow of a chance that the developed way of life under existing energy technology can be shared with all or even most of the world's people.

Nevertheless, in these and many other ways, we continue to treat the biosphere as if it is an inexhaustible resource for human beings.

How much would we change this situation if we managed to convert to entirely renewable sources of energy? It's worth trying another thought experiment: suppose that we *did* decide to do whatever we could to change our energy economy as soon as possible. What would follow? David MacKay's book on what it would take to energize the island of Britain (England, Scotland, and Wales) without emitting any greenhouse gases provides an excellent starting point. Late in his book, MacKay provides several different ways to achieve that goal, leaving the choice to the reader. One scenario relies heavily on nuclear power; others use clean coal; still others avoid both of those sources and rely heavily on wind power. When he puts a representative plan on the map of the island, the real implications of such a shift become clear. Major swaths of the countryside are converted into biofuel or wood-generating systems; eleven nuclear power plants spring up around the nation; several wave and tide farms appear off the coasts; waste incinerators appear all over the map near populated areas; wind farms arise in likely locations around the island's periphery; large quantities of energy from solar power, derived from installations located in the Sahara Desert, arrive through long-distance power lines; and a few clean coal mines appear as well.[95]

MacKay's exemplary work applies indirectly to any other densely populated nation or region, including a good portion of the United States. If we starkly reduce our use of fossil fuels, we will have to intrude into our environment in other ways. We'll need to install wind turbines wherever there is enough wind to justify the expense, put in thousands of square miles of solar panels in sun-friendly locations, gather the energy of wave and tide wherever feasible, harvest every bit of the energy of plants and trees we can on a sustainable basis, and much more. In short, we'll need to exploit the Earth in every way we can imagine *except* by emitting the exhaust from fossil fuels into the atmosphere. Ironically, taking our lesson to heart and trying to ward off climate change would force us to shift our exploitation of the Earth's systems from one mode to another, causing us to *increase* our imprint on the visible surface of the land and sea by a good margin.

This thought experiment suggests that our energy-dependent large populations require so much energy we cannot supply them without a huge imprint on the planet of some kind. We now borrow from the previous history of life by burning fossilized creatures—in the form of oil, coal, or gas. We mine uranium, refine it, and use its radiative energy in nuclear power stations, but that process leaves behind nuclear waste, whose half-life is on the scale of thousands of years. It seems we must either colonize the planet's past or its future. If we wish to avoid these options, we could set up millions of energy farms on land and sea to extract the energy of sun, wind, and wave, of grasslands and forests. But doing so will inevitably intrude into all those ecosystems in ways we do not yet fully understand. How much of the deserts of the Southwest do we wish to cover in solar panels if we respect the ecosystems there? What happens to the Earth's dynamic flows if we harvest a good share of the movement of wind and tide for our benefit? In effect, we would end up colonizing the Earth's *present* in a style that would be novel even for us.

One innovation might be an exception to this pattern: we could try to capture and store carbon dioxide underground. In that case, we would appropriate relatively hidden and unused parts of the Earth, though we'd have to make sure that the stored gas would not escape someday far into the future and do its damage then. Outside this single instance, it seems that our sheer numbers make it necessary to colonize the Earth, and time itself, for our own benefit.

The simple fact is that if we look at the present situation from a non-anthropocentric viewpoint, there are too many of us. If we wished to avoid sucking up the resources of the planet on this scale, we would have to reduce our population by a serious fraction—perhaps to preindustrial levels. *The single greatest legacy of the era of unlimited growth is very close to home: it is us.* No doubt the rate of population increase in industrialized nations has greatly declined over the past few decades. But that fact does not cancel out the reality that the process of modernization since the mid-eighteenth century has made possible a staggering increase in human lives. We have by now far surpassed what William R. Catton, Jr., described several generations ago as the planet's "carrying capacity," the number of people that the Earth's ecosystems could credibly support.[96] The fact that modern agriculture can feed the billions only by using immense quantities of fossil fuel, overusing the available water, and befouling the groundwater and seas with the effluent of nitrogen fertilizers tells us that under sustainable methods it would be much more difficult to keep us all alive. Like climate change, we ourselves are symptoms of an immense excess that has been going on for generations.

If that is so, then we, too, live in a future created by a particular past. We did not choose to exist in these numbers; we are in our own bodies the heirs of decisions not our own. Furthermore, the very fact of our presence in these numbers is a huge constraint on our action today. Much as we are stealing the future from our descendants, our own present actions are seriously undercut by the actions of our ancestors.

But it hardly works to suggest that in retrospect, we would repudiate their decisions—for if we did so, we'd be choosing not to exist. We're caught in a tragic contradiction between our own love of life and an awareness of what that life costs the biosphere. We are the agents of a new future and a danger to it at the same time. This contradiction appears as well in our relation to the modern, industrial era: we are grateful for past revolutions, happy to have been liberated in more ways than we can remember, amazed at the abundance of knowledge and enjoyment that have been made available to us. Whatever we may say, we are inevitably the products of the modern world. But we also know that this world is killing the biosphere and cannot continue. The modern way of life *is* our life, our own breath and blood, yet if we stick with it, we will destroy the Earth.

Insofar as our dilemma comes from our sheer numbers, we cannot help but realize that *our future, too, has been stolen from us.* We already overtax the Earth, whatever we do. Even now, the revolution is far past its time. From an ecological perspective, that event should have taken place long ago—simultaneous with the adoption of large quantities of fossil fuels to power the modern economy. In liberating us from an ancient scarcity, the coming of cheap fossil fuels also set into motion the ecological destruction to which we must now respond. Our task is thus in part to bring about a transformation that is long overdue. Yet in doing so we cannot denounce our ancestors; they could not have known the ultimate consequences of their actions. They stole the future from us without meaning to do so in the least. We are immersed in an immense historical irony, whereby the actions of our ancestors, meant to liberate us, have without their intention also cursed us.

It is no wonder, then, that we find it so difficult to face the current crisis. Inheritors of a vast abundance, and in our vast numbers an instance of that abundance, we cannot easily undo the legacy of generations. In the previous chapter I listed a series of reasons why the ecological revolution of our time has gone missing. Here I can add a further reason to that list: in the end, that revolution asks us to undo certain consequences of a demographic explosion that has lasted for several centuries. It demands that we catch up with an event that should have happened long ago—and that, thanks to our ignorance, could not happen at its proper time. We were born too late and are emerging from our stupidity later yet. We are only beginning to grasp our situation now, at this far edge of time, awakening as it were after our own end.

Where are we, then, in this strange moment on this planet, which is not quite, or not yet, our real home? As I argued in the previous chapter, this hour cries out for a revolution—but one that promises us no familiar liberation, no release. We must act, yet we will not; we must reply to something greater than we are, yet we can barely hear its voice. Now, when we work within our political traditions, they thwart our actions, rather than enabling them. In doing what we must, we discover that we are also asked to give what we do not have. The measures we could take to forestall the coming horror are relatively simple, their purpose clear, yet enacting them seems impossibly difficult.

Yet as I have been suggesting in this chapter, if we did so, we would discover that despite our best efforts, we would still be using the planet for our own purposes. Even as we attempt to forestall the coming crisis, we must recognize that we ourselves, in our great numbers and excessive demands, are already a crisis too great for the planet to bear. We are lost where we are found, ignorant in our knowledge, poor in our wealth, inheriting a blessing that curses us. Here at the crossroads, we are already beyond them, already inhabiting a future we did not choose. Stealing the future from our descendants, we also discover that in some degree ours is missing as well. In retrospect, we might conclude that the whole history of the modern world is shadowed by another future that is not to be— one promised by an ecological revolution that, whenever it takes place, will come too late. We are the heirs, in short, of a tragic contradiction, an impasse no one chose. The challenge of our time is not only to fight against this impasse, to bring about that necessary, impossible revolution; it is also to discover how to live in a world with a disappearing future. To this last, devastating challenge, we now turn.

Notes

95. For the five energy plans, see MacKay, *Sustainable Energy*, 203–213; for the map illustrating one plan, see 215.

96. William R. Catton, Jr., *Overshoot: The Ecological Basis of Revolutionary Change* (Urbana: University of Illinois Press, 1982).

Chapter 6

The Ruins to Come

If we face the reality of climate change honestly, taking into account how urgent a task lies before us and how dim is any hope we will act in time, we must acknowledge that a great shadow darkens our present moment. The biosphere changes apace; the land dries, the ice cap melts, the forests burn; those who lead our public institutions debate, stutter, and go silent; the prospect on which we rely throughout our daily activities erodes and falters; and the hope that inspires our political lives flickers and goes dark. We have always taken for granted that a livable future lies before us, that whatever happens to us now, tomorrow is another day. But we can no longer be so sure.

Human societies have always had a strong image of the future. Traditional societies have assumed that the future will be much like the present—that the tribe, kingdom, or nation will continue to replicate itself, generation by generation, sustaining the link to the gods, the legacy of the ancestors, and the fundamental human ways in perpetuity. Modern societies, in contrast, have held forth the image of the general liberation of the human race, so that at some point in the future no oppression or poverty, no ignorance or violence would afflict the Earth.

These images of the future, however, have relied on the even more basic assumption, never previously called into question, that the planet's ecosystems would remain intact and flourishing forever. The seemingly indestructible continuity of the living systems that surround us has made all our imaginings possible. But what happens if that continuity is in question—when we begin to realize that the Earth's ecosystems are vulnerable to destruction or decay?

Our first task in confronting this question is simply to absorb the significance of putting that continuity in doubt. How do our most basic assumptions change when we begin to imagine the future differently? What, for example, takes place when we take the scenarios of general climate change, social dislocation, and perpetual adaptation seriously?

When scientists imagine what the world might look like in a century if we continue with business as usual or alter our energy economies a few years from now (and thus too late), providing details about changes to familiar landscapes and the consequences for the places we know best, they ultimately depict for us the ruins of our own culture. The best science available to us requires us to imagine an America with damaged coastlines, decaying forests, and drying soils, with countless trees, plants, and animals under severe distress—and to envision parts of coastal cities standing in the water of elevated seas, as well as the cities of the heartland crouching beneath the dust storms rising from parched fields.

These images capture for us the ruins of our own future. If we continue to live in the way we do today, we will eventually find ourselves in strange, almost unrecognizable places. Our own lives will change as well: because they will be at once something like what we know today and very different, with major elements missing and other elements adapted to new conditions, they too will be in ruins.

To think of ruins in this way provokes a new emotion. We are all familiar with images of ruins—of human structures, built long ago, that have survived the disappearance of the cultures that created them, have fallen into partial decay, and remain in the landscape as reminders of a distant era and as symbols of what time will inevitably do to all human enterprise. In the presence of the ruin, whatever it may be—from the Roman Colosseum to an abandoned farm down the road—one contemplates not merely one's own mortality but the mortality of cultures or historical eras; one senses a great gap between the intensity with which we pursue our goals and the indifferent flow of time.

But now, we contemplate the prospect of *future* ruins, conceiving of a cultural decline that has not yet taken place. Indeed, the thought of these ruins is so fascinating to us that we have long enjoyed depicting them fictionally in science fiction stories and movies. (Think *Planet of the Apes* or *Waterworld*.) More recently, however, those fictional scenarios have given way to sober forecasts of what *will* take place if we continue to live as we do. Reading the IPCC reports, we can find utterly serious, detailed analyses of what is likely to happen if greenhouse gas emissions rise to a certain level. We no longer need science fiction to help us imagine future ruins: a generation of scientists is now analyzing our prospects while attempting to remove every trace of fiction from its scrupulous estimates. We can now absorb professional assessments of how dry central Africa and eastern Australia will become, how much the water levels in the Great Lakes will recede, how much of Bangladesh or Florida will be submerged, how much of the grain of northern China or the American Midwest will die under the greater heat of the sun. As we begin to think of adapting to these and other possibilities, what was once science fiction has become the reality of our world, the ruins in which we must prepare to live.

Those ruins are not terribly picturesque. Contemplating the remains of Mayan temples, we might take pleasure in the surviving structures of a distant culture. Contemplating the ruins of our *own* cities and landscapes is entirely different, if only because we still live in them. While we take in a fictional scenario, we might enjoy putting ourselves in a distant future to look back at the present with wonder or regret. But in reality, we take the ongoing viability of our lives for granted. To think about our future ruins, then, is ultimately to confront the fact that the world in which we now live is about to transform into something else—something we may not wish to live through at all. Those future ruins, in short, bear upon our *present*, casting a shadow over who we are.

Those future ruins are strange in another respect. In them, the idea of ruins will extend from buildings to landscapes, from landscapes to continents and seas, and then to the Earth itself. Today we can easily imagine that an observer a century hence, viewing a pine forest in Colorado, will see a good share of its trees browned and dying, others already fallen and in decay. Such an observer, having experienced part of the previous century and having learned about the rest, will see in that landscape the ruins of a forest. To think in this way of an ecosystem in ruins also provokes a new emotion. Where a visitor to the Colosseum might ponder the decline and fall of Rome, and thus the mortality even of the mightiest empires, this observer of the pines will contemplate something quite different. The inevitable mortality of nature? Not exactly: those pines stood there for millennia and presumably could have stood much longer. The

end of a civilization? Not quite: that civilization will no doubt be enduring in some form nearby, most likely in the observer herself. What, then,
will these ruins speak of? The power of fossil-fuel civilization to put that
forest into irreversible decline.

It might work, then, to say that the forest speaks of the ruins of a civilization. In that scene, then, a cultural disaster will be made visible in a
wounded ecosystem. But even that unusual feature does not fully capture
the strangeness of our future ruins. Normally when we think of ruins, we
do not imagine that the people who built them still live on in them; those
sites are abandoned and empty. No Caesars visit the Colosseum today
to witness gladiatorial contests; somewhere along the way, the inhabitants of Rome gave up such spectacles and failed to maintain that ancient
structure. No soldiers now patrol along Hadrian's Wall; it lost its original function, fell into disuse, and some of its stones were plundered for
other purposes. A certain cultural continuity was lost, but the physical
object remained. In contrast, we must imagine ourselves or our descendants actually living in the ruins of the cities we built—or perhaps in
the less difficult regions nearby. In some sense, then, those future ruins
will be the opposite of the picturesque ruins of the past: *we will outlive
the environments we have destroyed.* The buildings we use will still serve
important cultural functions, we will still live in their vicinity, and yet
we face the prospect that eventually our use of them will no longer be
tenable. We would *like* to stay in our cities; we would *hope* to maintain
our traditions—yet our way of life will erode nevertheless. Strangely, that
way of life, thanks to the ecological consequences of its very "success,"
will end up interrupting *itself*, making itself unlivable and obsolete. After
we realize as much, however, we or those who follow us will still live on,
scrounging in the shadows of those ruins for habitation and sustenance.
We will be part of the ruins, eking out a damaged way of life.

No doubt others in the past have lived through something like this
experience. When enemies took over a city, burned it, and destroyed its
sacred places, those who lived there know they witnessed the passing of
their way of life. But they never doubted that the lives at least of their enemies would go on. When civilizations exhausted their surrounding environments, outliving the resources available to them—whether in ancient
Mesopotamia or the Yucatan—people certainly lamented the passing

of their civilizations, but they could still assume that they might survive elsewhere and that they or their progeny could build anew.[97] The passing of a civilization, however enormous an event, is never definitive; everybody knows that something else will happen, another round of history will begin. And all these changes are paltry in comparison to the endurance of the natural environment that human beings take for granted. Rome falls, the Holocene endures, and thus Rome can be built again.

Not anymore. If anything, Rome still flourishes, only more successfully than ever. No previous generations have experienced anything approaching the abundance of modern life. Modern, industrial civilization is being replicated around the world, "developing" nations seek to join the club of wealthy countries, and the reckless consumption of the Earth goes on unchecked. Yet that fossil-fuel abundance is threatening the Holocene, the complex, relatively stable state of the Earth we have enjoyed over the last 10,000 years. Now, Rome flourishes so extravagantly that the Holocene will fall—and as a result, so too will Rome. We cannot be confident that other societies will flourish in place of our own; what will befall us will happen in some other way to all the world's cultures. Nor can we assume we will build anew. We may not yet know how to build anything that will endure on this transformed Earth; finding a way to do so will be a perpetual challenge. At least in one respect, the eclipse of our future will be *definitive*: it admits of no escape, for it will apply to the human species as a whole.

A defeat on this scale may still place us in a dilemma that others have faced. Other societies, after all, have been faced with even bleaker prospects, barred from sustaining their former traditions on their own terms. Consider the aboriginal Tasmanians. After they were colonized on their native island, decimated by disease and violence, and imprisoned by their European masters on a small portion of their former land, they found themselves so spiritually destroyed that they merely waited for death and within a few years disappeared entirely.[98] A less devastating version of this defeat happened in the recent past, not long after the fall of the Berlin wall. When capitalism swept over the Soviet Union, shattering the remnants of communism's promises, the life expectancy among men dramatically declined, as if the loss of that society's foundations gave them little reason to go on.[99] Neither society was especially heartened that another culture would endure, for the world that mattered to them, the world that supplied them with their core system of beliefs and concerns, had vanished.

Our dilemma is a little like theirs: eventually, when we realize that no one can escape the future we have created, we too will have to doubt our core system of beliefs. But this time, no one will have defeated us; we will not be imprisoned, nor will we be the losers of the Cold War. We will have defeated *ourselves*. That event will at once distress us, since we will indeed be stuck on an Earth we never hoped to see, but it will also give us *some* hope, since as the agents of our own undoing, we would still presumably have the chance to do something about it. At once perpetrators and victims, we'll endure a crisis, to be sure, but we will still be confident we can face the crisis on our own terms, find means of adaptation, or discover some style of living on.

But too much confidence in this respect will be illusory. Until this point in our histories, we could take for granted that if we foresaw a danger to our collective lives, we could take action and ward it off. If we *did* something, we would see *results*. But if our societies fail to act soon and those positive feedback loops kick in, we will enter a truly bizarre condition. At that moment, if it has not already taken place, we will discover that the future we dread will arrive *no matter what we do in the present*. In that strange hour, the future will become at once inevitable and alien; it will bring about devastating events *even if* we attempt to prevent them.

Where we could once shape the future in some fashion, in that moment we will discover that the future has become estranged: *that* future, as well, will be in ruins. Of course, our actions even in that moment will continue to have an effect: they might prevent an even more devastating future from taking place or might save various aspects of the planet for later generations. But they will be too little and too late to prevent a wrenching change for all the world's cultures.

The possibility that we might cross those tipping points without knowing it makes our situation uncanny. If we do make that transition, it will take place silently, without notice—as if we are on board a ship that has been struck and will eventually sink even though we heard nothing of that blow and the band plays on. In a case like that, the events determining the future will have arrived already, while we carried on, oblivious.

Although our cultures will already be stricken, we will continue to participate in them as if they still thrive. Several recent movies imagine that ghosts are dead people who have not yet learned that they are dead; they haunt the living because they are ignorant of their true condition.[100] In a similar fashion, the world's societies, unaware of their actual state, may soon become phantoms, enduring in a posthumous condition.

But this depiction of ghostly cultures may still not do justice to our dilemma. For the most part, we tend to place these ruins in the future, whether we are enjoying fictional tales or pondering scientific assessments. We mostly assume that the major cultural dislocations caused by climate change are yet to come. But in fact those changes are already taking place. Some observers suggest that the dryer, hotter conditions in the Darfur region of the Sudan helped create the conditions for conflict and crimes against humanity there.[101] Alaskan towns built on permafrost are tilting, their foundations cracking.[102] Countless farmers around the world, including in the United States, are discovering that the seasonal rhythms on which they once relied are being suspended.

We are *already* living in a ruined future, already enduring changes in the biosphere for which we are not prepared. But why are we not ready? Why should the arrival of this future surprise us? Evidently, even though we are highly entertained with the *thought* of strange futures, projecting them endlessly in our fictions, we do not ultimately expect them to *arrive*: when they do, they seem premature, catching us by surprise. The very category of the future, it seems, floats in the distance; even if we are oriented to it as the basis of our present actions, we keep it on the other side of a conceptual wall, safeguarding the present from its arrival. The same is true of the scientific study of what climate change might do: while we may absorb what researchers tell us, their findings often remain mere information to us, not a vivid reality in our ordinary lives. Even if we *know* that climate change is happening and may devastate our homes, we might not truly *acknowledge* this fact to ourselves. The arrival of that future deprives us of the security and pleasure we take in contemplating it in the distance, throwing the conceptual map of our lives into disarray. When it arrives, it short-circuits what we thought we understood. Never having lived through such a change before, we cannot know what it will be like to experience it. We are inevitably unprepared for this event; it can only take place when we are unaware.

Our tendency to keep the ruined future at a distance forces us into a contradiction: if its arrival has not taken place, then evidently we still have time (to argue about it in Congress, to negotiate new treaties, to prepare to alter our technologies), as if it is still years away; if it has occurred, then it's too late, and we need do nothing. Either way, we believe we don't really have to do a thing. Perhaps here again we live in the ruins of the future: modern culture has long since prided itself on its capacity to control its conditions, to plan for contingencies, to predict trends, to provide for long-term safety and security. The future, you could say, was its specialty. But this time around, those who manage the future are in over their heads. The future has been their specialty, just not *this* future. This version, it seems, is by *definition* too much to handle: we caused it, yet it eludes us, primarily because it contradicts our basic assumptions. We've been making life *much better*, not *worse*; the thought of a devastated future profoundly conflicts with everything we've been trying to do. If the future is in ruins, so also is our expertise in the future. But then the most basic premises of modern culture are in ruins as well.

At first glance, our way of enduring the prospect of these future ruins may share much with how we respond to our own mortality. We cannot know when our deaths may arrive; we might know that they will take place eventually without taking that prospect seriously; we might even have contracted a terminal disease without suspecting a thing. But does it follow that pondering the ruins is something like contemplating our own deaths? Are these meditations on dire events to come in some ways the same? In an older religious tradition, believers once meditated on the *memento mori*, a reminder of death such as a skull, to teach themselves that they would die, that all their passionate attachments and fierce longings would pass, that everything melts away, so as to set their sights on eternity instead. More recently, philosophers such as Martin Heidegger argued that the most authentic mode of being for us is *being-toward-death*, the direct encounter with our mortality.[103]

But this analogy ultimately fails. Climate change is absolutely vaster than any individual's passing—even one's own. It is of another order of business entirely. We all know that individuals will die in the ordinary course of things. But for a *species* to die is another matter altogether. An individual's death arises from the same process as its birth, its participation in reproduction, its maintaining a certain adaptive behavior within a particular ecological niche. Similarly, in the context of the biosphere's dynamic life, the passing of a species arises from the same process as its emergence, its flourishing, and its participation in the relationships of symbiosis or competition. Its extinction fits within the pattern of a wonderfully complex but coherent interaction. What we face, however, is not extinction of this kind, but the *murder* of species, ecosystems, oceans— purely as a result of the biologically unnecessary indulgence of our species. This is not death, nor even extinction, but a destructive intervention into the web of life.

Climate change, in short, does far more than mortality could ever do: it harms the lifeworld that sustains our species, and in consequence damages the societies in which our deaths have meaning, the cultural context for our own aspirations and achievements. It imposes an extra level of difficulty on each species, each society, each life—one that none previously had to bear. As a result, all will face something more than mortality, something altogether unanticipated and more strange.

This bizarre future differs from mortality in yet another way. Two centuries ago, in one passage of his elegy to John Keats, *Adonais*, Percy Bysshe Shelley wrote that when nature revives in the spring and the dead do not return, we are reminded that the circle of the year differs sharply from the shape of an individual human life. Spring cannot bring back the dead; ultimately, then, it cannot console us but instead revives our grief. He concludes this portion of the poem with these lines: "As long as skies are blue, and fields are green / Evening must usher night, night urge the morrow, / Month follow month with woe, and year wake year to sorrow."[104] For the speaker of these words, human beings pass while nature endures. Today, however, we face virtually the opposite emotion. Under climate change, you, or I, or a friend may live on *beyond* the death of a local forest, the silencing of a nearby stream, or the browning of a neighboring green. The years will return, no doubt, and night will still urge the morrow, but whether nature will revive is another question. Where we once thought we would die and nature endure, we may instead survive after the passing of an ecosystem we know. Our response to the land-scapes surrounding us alters irreversibly.

In that case, our relationship to many other aspects of experience changes as well. Even in a nation as industrialized as the United States, the movement of the seasons serves as the basis of the ritual year, anchoring Easter and Christmas, Passover and Yom Kippur, Independence Day and Thanksgiving; as the seasons drift to new regions of the calendar, plants blossom or decay at other times, and the natural world becomes more confused, the significance of these ritual events changes too, speaking less of the deep turning of the world and more of sheer convention. Our association of youth with spring, of age with fall, begins to falter if spring comes too soon, if fall extends into winter; our metaphors start to melt away, even though youth and age remain to us. Our lives are cut adrift from the seasons, our span of time knocked askew from nature's rhythms, our mythic associations made threadbare.

We may in consequence find ourselves grieving more for the vulnerability of the biosphere than for our own. That emotion might lead us also to grieve for our excessive *in*vulnerability, our capacity in these latter, hi-tech days to defeat disease, master the body's ills, and generally ward off aging and death—and for that matter to protect ourselves from cold or heat, reduce hunger and thirst, shrink every distance, and master further reaches of the unknown. We may end up wishing for a return of *greater* vulnerability, a more open acceptance of weakness and mortality, for only with that return might we release other forms of life from the devastating effects of our dominance.

Such thoughts, however, will ultimately demonstrate that our own mortality fades in comparison to something altogether more harrowing—the possible mortality of our societies, the natural systems we know, and to some extent the biosphere itself. In our world, the temporal coherence of a future into which our individual lives vanish—the coherence, in short, of mortality itself—is falling into decay. What once served as an instance of the ultimate contemplation is now dwarfed by a much more difficult thought, the prospect that our very metaphor of what endures and what is timeless has itself fallen into ruin.

Notes

97. On ancient Mesopotamia, see Clive Ponting, *A Green History of the World: The Environment and the Collapse of Great Civilizations* (New York: Penguin, 1991), 68–73; on the Maya in the Yucatan, see Ponting, 78–83 and Jared Diamond, *Collapse: How Societies Choose to Fail or Succeed* (New York: Penguin, 2006), 157–177.

98. I refer to the fate of the Tasmanians after being rounded up and imprisoned on Flinders Island; see Robert Hughes, *The Fatal Shore: The Epic of Australia's Founding,* (New York: Knopf, 1987), 423.

99. Michael Wines, "An Ailing Russia Lives a Tough Life That's Getting Shorter," *New York Times,* December 3, 2000, http://www.nytimes.com/2000/12/03/world/an-ailing-russia-lives-a-tough-life-that-s-getting-shorter.html?pagewanted=all&src=pm.

100. See, for example, *The Others,* directed by Alejandro Amenábar, 2001.

101. See Stephan Faris, *Forecast: The Consequences of Climate Change, from the Amazon to the Arctic, from Darfur to Napa Valley* (New York: Holt, 2009), 5–29.

102. Elizabeth Kolbert, *Field Notes from a Catastrophe: Man, Nature, and Climate Change* (New York: Bloomsbury, 2006), 13–17.

103. Martin Heidegger, *Being and Time,* translated by John Macquarrie and Edward Robinson (London: SCM Press, 1962), 279–311.

104. Percy Bysshe Shelley, *Adonais,* lines 187–189. See Donald H. Reiman and Neil Fraistat, editors, *Shelley's Poetry and Prose,* second edition (New York: Norton, 2002), 417.

Chapter 7

The Broken Present

Many of us contemplating these possibilities might answer quite simply, "Why should I care? The events you describe, if they take place at all, will change human life on Earth after I am gone. Besides, the problem is so vast, and the actions we must take are so difficult, that I can make very little difference on my own. I'll just live out my life in the best way I can and let history take its course."

There is a kind of sanity in this response: in many circumstances of life, repression may be a fine thing indeed. But is it truly possible to set aside the reality of what might take place to us all in the future? Can we simply divorce our present actions from their consequences?

If, as I suggested in the previous chapter, every human society has cultivated a strong image of the future, it has done so because such an image is necessary to justify its activities in the present. Some kind of future, some orientation to a goal or destination, is intrinsic to all of our intentional activity as individuals and as members of groups. Whether or not we care in a deep or heartfelt way about what will take place to our society, or for that matter about the human race or the Earth itself, *some* kind of investment in the future is implicit in our situation as human beings. Even if we repudiate the significance of that future for us on a conscious level, the fact that we are purpose-driven beings implies that our actions will betray us, endlessly demonstrating that in fact we *do* care, that we are everywhere and always invested in creating a livable future.

So there is no way for us to evade some difficult questions. If *that* kind of future is in store for us, what happens to the goals we have set for ourselves and that we seek through our various efforts? Everything we do in our ordinary lives is based on the assumption that we will have a future—that our houses will remain standing, that we will continue to have a home in the nations in which we live, that the skills we have acquired will be useful in some fashion, that we will be able to participate in the cultural activities we care about, and that we will have some chance to achieve our goals. Our businesses run on credit, borrowing their very capital from the financial resources of the future; our governments staff and equip standing armies to defend against attacks that may come to pass; and we insure our properties, bodies, and lives against harm that may befall us. Many of our daily activities are directly oriented toward ensuring that the future will be livable. Sustaining our loving and erotic relationships, cultivating our family ties and our friendships, raising children, giving or getting an education, giving or getting preventative and acute medical care, and building and maintaining the physical structures in which we live and work: all these, and countless further activities, reveal how greatly we wish to sustain the lives we already know, to hand them down to further generations, and to maintain something like our current level of abundance and happiness. Our orientation to the future, in short, provides the very pith and substance of our present.

Individual lives take for granted that they are shaped by narratives with a past, present, and future—that they are oriented to satisfactions, achievements, or realizations that will reward lifelong commitments. Only through such narratives can we live our lives ethically, for only through them can we establish a context for intentional action, whatever it may be, in relation to everyone and everything that matters to us.[105] Such narratives also shape the collective life of families, communities, and nations, as well as political groups, commercial enterprises, and religious faiths. Without such narratives, it is hard to imagine that modern, democratic societies could legitimate themselves at all, for from the start they are founded on the principles of liberation and progress. This orientation is so deeply embedded in our activities that even an outright nihilist who repudiates all notions of a collective good nevertheless assumes he will be able to sustain that identity and share that perspective in the future. Merely speaking of that viewpoint to others takes for granted the timeline of persuasion, the long-term contexts of argument and debate.

At times, of course, people sacrifice too much of their present lives for the sake of the future: they too eagerly practice the well-known art of deferred gratification, working so hard in the present that they almost forget what all the effort is for. We often tell such people that they should stop living for the future and enjoy the present. No doubt we are giving them good advice. But we should not assume that it is truly possible to live *only* for the present. Even the most dedicated contrarian, one who rejects a job and ignores her friends, will still turn off the water after taking a shower, knowing it would be nice not to flood the bathroom. Our practical actions constantly speak of our knowledge that the next hour and next day will come, even if at times and for specific purposes we might not wish to emphasize that fact.

But what happens when, in reviewing the narratives of our lives, looking ahead to the futures we hope to have, we realize that climate change will damage our world in ways that will directly and permanently affect us? What happens to our orientation to the future when its livability is cast into doubt and begins to dissolve? What if the place we choose for our abode becomes unlivable, the profession for which we have been trained is no longer needed, or the income we hoped would support us threatens to disappear? What if we realize that the life we wanted to lead is ecologically outrageous, that the children we've been raising have no chance to live as well as we have, and that the political causes for which we've been fighting may never succeed?

The answer, I think, is clear: all our practical activities, our human relationships, our professions and goals, are harmed in their very substance. The value of our ordinary activities begins to fray, and the entire framework of our lives becomes suspect. Climate change does not just melt the ice caps and glaciers; it melts the narrative in which we still participate, the purpose of the present day. In this sense, too, we are already living in the ruins of the future.[106]

Climate change devastates the future and the present alike. But that is not all. Most of us hope to transmit to new generations something of the values, achievements, and joys we inherited from our forebears. When our future is cast into doubt, so also is the transmission of that past. In much the same way, the memory of our own pasts, which we may still regard as strongly continuous with our present, shifts more emphatically into the past tense, as if it now speaks clearly of something that is gone. At certain moments, perhaps, we might almost sense that our very present should be rendered in the past tense—as if, like those on board the ship I mentioned above, we live in a society that is already dead without knowing it.

This bizarre possibility extends well beyond the framework of our own lives. We live in cultures that have long and storied histories, that have produced and been shaped by the deeds of monarchs and rebels, the achievements of statesmen and engineers, the thoughts of theologians and philosophers, the works of poets, playwrights, and intellectuals, and the discoveries of scientists. But without a future, these heritages, while still crucial and precious, subtly change, as if they endure after their foundations have disappeared. Suddenly, all these legacies belong to a planetary era that is passing away, for they were built on the security of ecological foundations that have collapsed. When the future goes, so do the present and the past. The entire framework of human time tilts, decays, disappears.

Does our situation leave us without hope? On one level, it does: we can no longer hope that the civilization we inherited will thrive or that future political changes will give all human beings a chance to participate in the abundance we have known. If that hope came true, the Earth would perish very quickly. As Robert Jensen says, hope of that kind is lazy, and the traditions it relies on are dead.[107] As long as we stick within the framework of what we have known, we will no longer envision great things, only the prevention of the worst. We will imagine no utopia, only the best dystopia we can get.

But if we change our perspective and abandon the premises of fossil-fuel culture, another kind of hope may be given to us: we could hope for a post-carbon culture that could thrive even on a greatly wounded Earth. *That* kind of hope, however, is far more than the bare emotion, for it can arise only out of the activity of reinventing who we are and becoming uncharacteristically honest about the difficulty we face. Yet even that hope cannot come without its shadow: as I argued earlier, converting to renewable energy sources for everyone on this overpopulated planet would *still* do great harm. The hope we now have, it seems, will always be mixed with a certain dread. Rebecca Solnit, writing about the challenges that will always face political activism, calls this "hope in the dark." In our moment, that darkness is darker yet.[108] In our broken present, however, this may be the best we can do.

I have been suggesting that an awareness of our future ruins harms the very substance of our present activities. Does it follow that we should simply give up, abandon all our efforts, renounce the world, and live in a kind of catatonic despair? Why not just stop all our labors and lie passively on the sofa? *That* would hardly be a solution; before long, the guy on the sofa would wonder how to get food to eat, how to keep the roof over his head, and how to satisfy other basic physical needs. If he *truly* gave up taking care of himself, eventually his friends would have to do so for him. He'd become a pain to everybody he knew. However great our awareness of what may come, the basic imperatives of life demand that we carry on. In fact, the more we deny those imperatives, the more we tacitly acknowledge them: you can't *deliberately* ignore something unless you already know it is there. Even the guy on the sofa has to acknowledge that life goes on.

Would it work, then, to embrace our everyday lives with a vengeance, as if to escape our knowledge in doing so? Why not respond to our dilemma by saying, "I'll just keep working until the waters rise up and carry me away"? But if a person makes this declaration, she would show that she values activity for its own sake, not for any purpose it might serve. She might hope to prove that she will not submit, that she can conquer any despair. While such a choice reveals a certain courage, it too is ultimately desperate, for rather than truly responding to the conditions around her and adjusting her life accordingly, she would attempt to value what she knows is futile. Although ignoring climate change might seem to protect her from it, the uselessness of her efforts would necessarily strike her from time to time, especially when she relaxes from her heroic strain, and since she had not created a viable response to it other than sheer stubborn effort, it would hit her with special force. Pure stubbornness is no better a response than passive despair.

The difficulty of our situation only becomes clear if we realize that the future is in ruins *and* that life goes on. As a result, even if we are aware that the blow has been struck, even if we live in knowledge instead of ignorance, we find ourselves having to live on as if nothing has changed: that knowledge, it seems, does not alter the basic challenges of everyday life, the ordinary tasks of doing our work, taking care of our loved ones, and planning for the future. The contradiction is stark, inconquerable.

Our orientation to the future inevitably remains, but for us it is directed toward what is no longer entirely there. We are caught between two imperatives: we must lead our lives, but we must also recognize that our life narratives are no longer credible. Neither renunciation nor stubbornness, neither reckless grief nor furious assertion, can finally erase the eerie quality of persisting within a narrative whose conclusion is slowly being erased. No plausible course of action is open to us. The ruined future forces us to endure in a broken present.

Is it even possible to live in full awareness of this contradiction? Can we at once perform our ordinary activities and be conscious that the narrative they imply may be in ruins? Our first option is to do everything we can to prevent entering this contradiction at all: the prospect of life in these terms should be enough to motivate our unreserved participation in a movement to change our societies and to change them *now*. But as I have been suggesting, the time available for action is so short it has virtually disappeared. We may have little choice, then, but to live in a mode that might seem impossible for us, to endure a life that will go on, even though it has been damaged fundamentally. We who are alive at this strange moment may end up having to reckon with its strangeness by enduring in this impossibility. If the Earth passes the turning point and we still endure, we will discover that the ruins of the future have thrown us off the track of our personal narratives and disjoined us from who we think we are. In that moment, if we are sane and aware, we will be off-kilter, out of balance.

The ruins of the future inevitably undo any coherent way to live. If events force us to construct new strategies for surviving in an altered world, we will also have to face this more intimate challenge: how to endure this incoherence, how to live on in the ruins of the lives we thought we would lead, in the ruins of who we thought we might be. All our basic emotions will be up for grabs, for none will remain unchanged: desire and grief, joy and sorrow, hope and despair. Living in the physical ruins of the Earth will be tough. But doing so will also symbolize living in the ruins of another sort, the broken language of the heart.

Notes

105. For an exemplary discussion of this point, see Alasdair MacIntyre, *After Virtue: A Study in Moral Theory*, third edition (Notre Dame: University of Notre Dame Press, 2007), 204–225.

106. For a related argument on how we might respond to the possibility that terrible things may happen to others *after* we die, see Samuel Scheffler, *Death and the Afterlife* (New York: Oxford University Press, 2013).

107. Robert Jensen, "Hope is for the Lazy: The Challenge of Our Dead World," *Counterpunch*, July 9, 2012, http://www.counterpunch.org/2012/07/09/hope-is-for-the-lazy/.

108. Rebecca Solnit, *Hope in the Dark: Untold Histories, Wild Possibilities* (New York: Nation Books, 2004).

Chapter 8

A Slow and Endless Horror

So far I have been suggesting that our situation of facing the consequences of climate change for our future is unprecedented. We've never before contemplated the possibility that the life we know might be altered beyond recognition in quite this way. But it's worth pausing to consider whether this relation to the future is really all that new. Are we in fact experiencing as strange a moment as all that? Aren't people in modern cultures used to facing these kinds of uncertainties as a matter of course by now? What is really new in our current situation?

We are, after all, the heirs of a long history of devastation. Over the past several centuries our societies have engendered and endured systemic, irreversible transformation in its various forms, including those in which expansion and liberation evolved into devastation and genocide. For half a millennium we have had to accept the possibility that the invasive power of modern economic and political regimes could destroy entire traditions, cultures, and peoples. This history is so long, difficult, and bloody—and so convenient to ignore—that it may be useful to review it for a moment.

The European encounter with the New World led to an era of colonization on nearly every continent, a pattern that in turn frequently decimated native populations and drew upon the murderous enslavement of Africans to provide labor for the new world. The scientific and industrial revolutions, in their turn, made possible the creation of modern industrial capitalism, which superseded traditional trades and handicrafts, forced a long demographic shift from the countryside to the city, and subordinated national economies to global trade and financial networks, forever altering the preindustrial way of life. At times, that process had brutal effects. The British application of a particular theory of the free market in countries across its far-flung empire led to the Irish famine of the 1840s, the devastating famines in India in the late 1800s, and ultimately to what Mike Davis has called the "making of the Third World."[109] Eventually, the bureaucratic power of the modern state, coupled with military and imperial ambitions, nationalism, or racism, created the concentration camps in South Africa during the Boer War, the little-known genocide of the Herero and Nama peoples in Namibia (then South West Africa) under German control in 1904 through 1907, and the Armenian genocide of 1915–1923.[110]

This history has only intensified over the decades since. World War I shattered the complacency of Europe and destroyed a generation of young men; a decade or so after the war ended, the Depression began; that long ordeal ended with World War II, which in turn introduced the nuclear bomb and the Holocaust. The changed geopolitical conditions after the war led to the foundation of the state of Israel and the displacement of the Palestinian people; it also opened the way for the independence of India, which came to pass with the Partition of India and Pakistan, an event accompanied with the slaughter of around one million people. Shortly thereafter began the Cold War, the arms race between the superpowers, and the proliferation of nuclear weapons, which in limited ways continues to this day. Over this period, the legacy of the Enlightenment took on a darker hue; the example of the American and French Revolutions, which had initially opened the way for nations around the world to intervene in their traditions and reinvent themselves, inspired the Russian and Chinese Revolutions, whose leaders eventually sought such systemic, wholesale change that they plunged their nations into famine or worse (under Stalin in the 1930s and Mao in 1958–1962). In the wake of the Holocaust, which inspired the world to vow that it would "never again" tolerate the attempt to destroy a people, we instead witnessed genocide and the massive destruction of human life in Burundi, Cambodia, the former Yugoslavia, East Timor, Rwanda, Darfur, and elsewhere, as well as the murder of roughly five million people, still ongoing, in Congo. In the early years of the present century, 9/11 brought to the fore international, stateless terrorism and its counterpart, the "war on terror"; these developments, along with events in Rwanda and Congo, suggest that in the coming decades this history of violence will continue outside of state control, becoming an endemic feature in failed states around the world.

Throughout the past several centuries, then, human beings have never been assured that the life they know will endure; on the contrary, the prospect of global violence, the attempted decimation of whole peoples, and in recent decades, the destruction of the entire human race have loomed large as distinct possibilities. We have been living with disaster for a long time. By now we may have become used to the possibility that the entire lifeworld in which we live is terribly fragile and that humanity itself may disappear. In response, however, we have attempted to beat back the forces of destruction in the hope we can put the worst behind us and enter an era of peace. In the United States, for example, we have tended to assume that the emancipation of the slaves put the most egregious forms of oppression safely in the past. The international community, having founded the United Nations, warded off a nuclear war, survived the Cold War, and prevented the outbreak of many other conflicts, may also believe that it has finally marked out the boundary of disaster's kingdom.

How well does climate change fit within this history? In her remarkable Earthseed series, composed of the novels *Parable of the Sower* and *Parable of the Talents*, Octavia Butler depicts a future United States wracked by the consequences of climate change, speculating that in a society torn by violence, insecurity, poverty, and lawlessness, slavery will return. The form of slavery she envisions is more sexual and economic than racial, based in the exploitation of individuals rather than a visible category of persons. Nevertheless, her work suggests that if things go awry, the forms of injustice we Americans think we have surpassed will return.

While we have not often contemplated these possibilities in the debate about climate change, her suggestion has the ring of truth. If a crisis is deep enough and lasts long enough, all bets will be off; the guarantees of the Constitution will not protect the poor from the rich or the weak from the strong. After all, they have never done so completely, and even now the battle to guarantee civil rights for all continues. Butler's novels remind us that we have not eradicated inequality and exploitation from our society; the endurance of class privilege and deep poverty, as well as the resegregation of public education and the neglect of inner-city communities, tell us that we have used the fact of our previous abolition of slavery and other open abuses to justify tolerating a host of social ills today. The persistence of these profound inequalities creates the conditions for harsher practices to return. This point extends to the international context as well. If we consider the inevitability that under the pressure of climate change millions of people will attempt to migrate across national boundaries, that societies will clash over resources, and that various states, weakened by perpetual crisis, may not be able to prevent conflict, we must admit that conditions will be ripe for the return or proliferation of many forms of injustice.

In that case, climate change may create the conditions for reversing the guarantees established by democratic societies and the modest achievements of the United Nations. Going forward into the ruined future, we may instead recede into a version of the past. The major difference is that this time, we would not be able to escape from that past so easily through establishing individual rights or creating economic growth. That future will have discredited such possibilities, showing that they could not deliver on what they promised, for the societies that protected individual rights will have been the same that created planetary distress. Moreover, because we will retain the memory of less woeful days, we may experience such injustice with greater pain than did our ancestors, many of whom had no memory, and no notion, of human rights. Used to being treated fairly, we will resent the opposite fiercely. The return to certain abuses will not merely take us back to the past; it will cancel what we thought were permanent guarantees and thus traumatize us intimately. We may then learn that the notions of liberty and individual rights are only fictions, resting within a network of exploitative social relations we never fully attempted to dismantle.

Inspired by reflections like these, we may wish to denounce those who keep alive the structures of inequality. But climate change undercuts such an attempt at moral clarity. A look at the international consequences of climate change tells us this much. On one level, the fact that the world's industrial nations have emitted and will eventually emit far more greenhouse gases than other nations is already a sign that we live in a world shaped by yet another form of oppression, a greenhouse gas imperialism.

We who live in the developed world are clearly perpetrators of a great violence. Yet it is not as if we will escape the consequences of our actions. We are immersed in a society that continues to emit greenhouse gases at a ridiculous pace, and most of us will also live long enough to endure the consequences of those emissions. We, too, will endure great difficulties; our societies will be wrenched as well. As a result, we will become our own victims. Some of today's wealthy may assume that their money will enable them to survive relatively unscathed through a dystopian future. But no individual should be complacent; economic disarray and internecine violence have a way of shattering any smug arrangements, destroying businesses and households, and leaving individuals stranded in the midst of chaos. The return of injustice and violence potentially extends to *all* of us; we cannot be sure we are not enslaving ourselves, creating a prison that neither we nor others can escape.

If we take these scenarios just one step further, we can place the potential consequences of climate change within the history of collective destruction. In a previous chapter I mentioned that climate change most likely created the conditions for the brutal violence in Darfur.[111] In itself, of course, climate change does not actually take human lives; it creates the miserable matrix for that violence. By destroying ecosystems, depriving people of their livelihoods, and forcing them to migrate, climate change vastly increases the opportunity for conflict. The events of Darfur illustrate that fact well. Once climate change increases in its severity, further violence of this kind is nearly inevitable—and not only in areas far removed from the developed nations. Because the modern state often takes unintelligent, corrupt, and oppressive forms, because several versions of violent stateless entities (insurgent armies, separatist organizations, or jihadist movements) have emerged and are likely to arise in many regions of the world, because absolutist ideologies of various kinds still have armed adherents, and because ethnic rivalry and prejudice thrive as well, all the ingredients for international conflict, civil war, and systemic murder remain in place. Now that we're adding climate change to the mix, those ingredients are more combustible than ever before.

The prospect of this future violence takes shape against the background of our greater awareness of its costs. In recent decades, many interpreters have become increasingly conscious of the psychological consequences of surviving war, genocide, sexual violence, domestic abuse, and other horrific events. As they have argued, trauma is devastating because its severity breaks into consciousness before the mind can adequately prepare itself—or, more precisely, in a way for which it could never prepare itself; as a result, the mind bears the wounds of events it cannot absorb or understand. Because traumatic experiences in some sense never fully *take place* for their victims, they can never move on, never entirely live after those events.[112] In the era of the Vietnam war and after, we in the United States have called this "post-traumatic stress disorder," and in the wake of the wars in Iraq and Afghanistan, we recognize that this syndrome continues to afflict soldiers and civilians alike.

But if we take the possibility of severe, global climate change seriously, and thus acknowledge the near inevitability of the genocides to come, what happens then? Can we be traumatized by events that have not yet taken place? If trauma is characterized by an inability to absorb experience into the ordinary realities of life, could envisioning the horrors of the future have a similar effect? For a modern Cassandra, such a trauma would be possible: she would behold events to come with an intensity that would devastate her. Perhaps a modern version of a biblical prophet would endure the same. But it is instructive that such figures, announcing what they see, are never believed; those who hear their warnings melt away, unmoved. That indifference makes clear that for the rest of us, anticipatory trauma does not seem possible. After all, if we are *imagining* trauma, we are not truly living it, nor is it shattering our minds in a way for which we are not prepared. Perhaps future events can never be as real to us as past or present ones. In that case, climate change simply cannot be as vivid for us as the horrors of a certain past.

What, then, is the status of a violence to come? An awareness of the immense consequences of our ordinary acts today for the lives of ourselves and others will shadow those acts, giving them a haunting depth. A truthful look at our current practices—especially at the exceptionally high rate with which we burn fossil fuels in the United States—should give us pause. Are we perpetrating a kind of genocide ourselves, just one that will take place later? Are we participants in a systemic violence that will work itself out only over the coming decades? Part of the answer must be no; as I suggested above, climate change is not itself genocidal, for it provides no more than the matrix for conflict. But since it does that much—and can therefore generate a perpetual *series* of horrific events— it is actually much *larger* than any single genocide. It is at once less and more than the violence in Darfur.

In fact, since we cannot know precisely what form of climate change our present use of energy will create in the future, the *specific* implications of our acts remain out of reach. The problem here is not an experience that is too vivid, so shattering we simply cannot absorb it, but one that is too removed, too difficult to capture. Climate change works on tape delay: someone acts in a harmful manner, and the results might emerge soon, perhaps decades later. It also works in the aggregate; any single act can contribute to an overall disorientation of the climate, which in turn causes a series of further physical processes to kick in. Climate change is caused by a systemic violence that is cut off from any direct tie to its consequences.

As a result, our actions as participants in a fossil-fuel economy are accompanied, not by trauma, but by its photographic negative, as it were, its equally devastating counterpart—a violence we can infer but not actually see. Our actions thus take on an unknowable extra dimension, an imprecise but palpable edge, for they are inevitably shadowed by the horror to come. For trauma in its original sense, events are too vivid and specific for the mind to handle; in contrast, for the anticipatory trauma of our time, the mind conceives of a real violence that is not yet vivid or specific enough. If trauma is the result of an experience that is too intense, too heavy, we live an experience that is too light. But in this way, we too participate in events we cannot absorb, a horror we cannot assimilate.

These reflections may clarify the place of climate change within the history of enslavement, war, and genocide. But what about its effect on a world now used to the prospect of global nuclear war? That threat, far more encompassing even than genocide, threatened to destroy the entire human reality in a moment, almost without warning, wiping out everything we cherish in a single blow. Without a doubt, it endangered our individual and collective lives on a fundamental level. The fact that a head of state in the United States or the Soviet Union, and to a lesser degree in other nations, could in a single gesture threaten the viability of the human race was unprecedented. In the nuclear era, the existence of

humanity as a whole ceased to be guaranteed; it was no longer as definitive a reality as nature itself.[113] No longer could we be confident that a
divine force was protecting us or that our cultural values might in some
way prevent our annihilation. Indeed, for a time it seemed possible that
the contest over those values might *lead* to our annihilation. The things
we held sacred and the things that threatened our reality were potentially
one and the same.

But in contrast to climate change, nuclear annihilation, however horrifying, seems almost comforting. We imagined that event as an *interruption* of our everyday lives. What made it truly terrible was the prospect
that it would suddenly destroy billions of lives that would otherwise continue and possibly flourish. As a result, for virtually everyone the threat
of nuclear war inspired an immense desire that ordinary life itself would
endure. The absolutely horrifying thought of the world's end autho-
rized an absolute affirmation of the familiar. That emotion was typical
not only of anti-nuclear activists but of heads of state as well: the doctrine of mutually assured destruction, propagated by the U.S. Secretary
of Defense Robert McNamara, drew on this emotion, claiming that the
Soviets would not destroy us if they knew we would destroy them in turn,
and vice versa. The idea was that our affection for the lives we led and
our hope for the future would make it impossible to push the button. The
prospect of total destruction could paradoxically lead ordinary citizens as
well as heads of state back to their primary loyalty to the familiar world,
perhaps even intensifying that loyalty in a manner not known to any prior
generation. If anything, the nuclear era inspired us to regard ordinary life
as fragile and so to value it all the more. The threat could somehow give
the everyday a stunning intensity.

Climate change, however, is another matter. As I suggested in the
introduction, this time around, the prospect of future ruins *arises from*
our way of life, rather than threatening to interrupt it. Virtually everything we do in advanced industrial societies is powered by the burning
of fossil fuels in a process that directly contributes to global warming.
The implications of this threat are thus truly unprecedented. If we wish
to ward off a globally traumatic event, our task is not simply to *avoid* a
certain course of action, to refrain from hitting the button. We face the
much more difficult challenge of *undoing and transforming* a fundamental

aspect of our societies on a massive scale. This time, *we* are the threat, and if we wish to preserve anything like the lives we lead today, we must change those lives as soon as we can.

As a result, this threat has a very different impact on our attitude toward everyday life. Under the pressure of climate change, the everyday is at once precious and a threat: it is split at its core. Where the nuclear led us to affirm ordinary life virtually without reserve, climate change forces us to imagine how it can be transformed so it will no longer undermine itself. This affection for our way of life paradoxically does opposite things: it at once motivates us to sustain *and* to change it, to cherish *and* transform what we know. Our way of life speaks at once of what we wish to protect from trauma—*and* of the trauma it will create. In that case, we are *even today* both perpetrators and victims, slowly destroying our lives and surviving that destruction at the same time. Thus even the relative clarity of trauma dissolves into a contradictory, paradoxical state that blends the imposition and endurance of disaster.

The moral clarity of the threat and the necessity of responding to it are different this time as well. If severe climate change takes place, it will not happen in a single, annihilating event. An all-out nuclear war truly would have decimated the conditions for human life; even if a few victims struggled on briefly, in the end no one would have survived. Climate change, however, has its impact over decades and centuries. In contrast to the single event, its pace seems incredibly slow—so slow that we might decide simply to ignore it. If it seems slow, it is also sure; if we ignore it, it will destroy what we take for granted. It is thus a truly insidious threat, almost creepy in its persistent force. But it is also less absolute in its potential devastation; because it is comparatively slow in human terms (though not on the evolutionary time scale), we can well imagine that it would never truly annihilate us, never actually bring our world to an end; on the contrary, given its pace, we might guess that a good share of the human race would survive it, though with lives quite different from what we know today.

This contrast between nuclear war and climate change may explain why we do not yet take the latter very seriously. In the nuclear era, we got used to an all-or-nothing scenario. Either the world would end, truly and for good, or it would go on without a hindrance. Climate change doesn't give us either ending to the story. It doesn't destroy us outright, nor does it let us live on as we are. It combines devastation and survival. It doesn't give us apocalypse, nor does it give us the satisfaction of having avoided the world's end. It is something altogether different, as if it is at once sinister and benign. It's as if climate change tells us that the world ends, yet it goes on—or that it ends, gradually, *as* it goes on. It gives us that unprecedented experience: a slow and endless horror.

This dimension of climate change compounds its already paradoxical effect on everyday life. Because the consequences of climate change are neither immediate nor absolute, we can surmise, if we wish, that it imposes far less of a moral imperative on us than the nuclear threat did. Our society so far hardly wishes to embark on the necessary effort to comply with that imperative, for it is still thwarted by those who protest against taking action, and the rest of us have not yet demanded a revolutionary transformation strongly enough. We delay and hesitate while crucial decades go by. Such recalcitrance would have been impossible in the nuclear era: nobody seriously attempted to deny that the bombing of Hiroshima had taken place or that the Soviet Union existed. Today, however, in the United States, negating reality has become the profession of many and the hobby of millions, and a general indifference or passivity characterizes many more.

In consequence, for Americans reality is split once again: the physical fact of climate change has not yet achieved the status of a social or political fact. At the moment, we Americans live in a society that fails to acknowledge the crisis of the biosphere. The climate tells us one thing, our politics another. In consequence, we endure a state of radical dissociation. For us in the United States, things are truly confusing: not only is the world ending as it goes on, we also hear that it is not ending at all. Because we cannot defeat that false message, we sense that our everyday lives devastate our own future—and present—while also being asked to pretend they are doing nothing of the sort. The contrast between our knowledge of the consequences of our actions and a collective, deadening indifference continues to grow, making the incoherence of our experience even worse.

Here again, in retrospect the nuclear doesn't look so bad. The nuclear threat almost seemed to take care of itself: the doctrine of mutually assured destruction captured the situation well, making it plausible that no one would ever push the button. Furthermore, once technicians installed various fail-safe devices to forestall accidental nuclear war, we could assume that massive annihilation would take place only if a person actually *chose* to authorize it for some purpose. That notion of human control gave us hope that the moment of destruction would never arrive. We could believe that this choice came with a certain moral clarity, a deliberate decision to destroy or preserve the world.

With climate change, however, we can have no such illusion. If anyone is in control of *this* threat, all of us are. But it would be foolish to imagine we actually *are* in control. The physical complexity of climate change dramatically undermines the moral clarity we might bring to bear on preventing it. The limits of our knowledge, the immense difficulty of communicating what we *do* know to all the world's citizens, and the huge challenge of altering our material practices in midstream make it very likely that many of the world's people, including ourselves, might help bring about severe climate change without knowing it and without intending to do so. The physical processes at stake will work themselves out even if we do not fully grasp them or if we deny that they exist at all.

That possibility points to another instructive contrast to the nuclear threat. In the height of the nuclear era, observers sometimes rated the degree of danger by estimating how many minutes remained before "midnight"—before the dread hour of nuclear conflagration. Today, the same metaphor would work well—up to a point. But this time around, it's quite conceivable we could live *past* midnight and not notice a thing. As I suggested earlier, the dread hour of triggering a series of positive feedback loops could arrive while no one lifted a finger. What then? We have no common language for describing what the world looks like when it survives such a moment. Our nuclear fictions, of course, constantly imagined not the nuclear event itself but a post-nuclear landscape—as if it were even remotely possible that something like human life could go on for very long after that event. Those fairy tales have little relevance to our situation today. Now we must confront the possibility that all of us will live in a world that seems unchanged after it has been fundamentally harmed.

How do we describe that world? We could use the metaphor of the ship already struck by the iceberg and about to sink, as I did in the previous chapter. But even that notion only goes so far. That ship might keep going for a few more *decades*, sinking very slowly into the depths while the years pass. We simply do not know how to understand a world that lives after the disastrous moment has passed and finally becomes aware of its situation—but *too late*.

One type of story provides an inventive response to this situation. The back-to-the-future scenario, especially in the *Terminator* movies, imagines that in a disastrous future we might come back to this present and avoid doing anything to cause that future. This scenario does at least imagine a life *after* the disastrous event. But it does so in order to convey the urgency of acting *now*—as if all of us in the present have been sent back from that future to make sure it doesn't happen. This type of story is perfect for the era of climate change: indeed, nearly all of the warnings that scientists give us about the effects of our fossil-fuel economy could be told in that way. But what happens if we discover that the event has already taken place—and we have no machine to help us go back in time and make things right?

Our inability to know when that moment will take place or if it has already happened, as well as our relative lack of control over whether it will happen, stems in part from the radical limits in our knowledge of climate change. In the nuclear era, everyone knew well enough what pushing the button would lead to. But with climate change, things are utterly different. If scientists had not begun to calibrate the levels of carbon dioxide in the atmosphere in the mid-twentieth century, and if they had not become attentive a couple decades later to the possible consequences of introducing greenhouse gases in novel quantities into the atmosphere, none of us would have had more than a vague sense of what was taking place. Without the ongoing work of hundreds of scientists around the world, we wouldn't have a ballpark estimate of our situation even today. Yet despite that effort, nobody knows how climate change works in all its permutations. One reason for this contrast may be that human beings created nuclear bombs, could test them, witness their results, and contemplate their possible use. Nobody planned and implemented climate change.

But we could plan and implement a planetary *response* to climate change. Some observers are fond of saying that if America once embarked on the Manhattan Project to create the nuclear bomb, why couldn't it do the same to create a new energy economy? One problem with this comparison is that today the United States, or more likely the international community, would need to create *several* equivalents of that project, invent a range of new technologies, and implement them on a wide scale. We need a Manhattan, a Brooklyn, a Queens, a Bronx, *and* a Staten Island Project, just to get started. But the further irony is that the goal of that earlier project was to create a devastating weapon; the goal this time— and a far more difficult one—is to *prevent* destruction. Of course, in that era American government officials argued that they needed a weapon to prevent the Nazis, and then the Soviets, from destroying the nation. They hoped to use destruction to ward off destruction. This time around, we have no convenient weapon we could use to blow up climate change.

This demand for a different kind of national—or more likely, international—project will require us to alter our relation to the technological breakthroughs of the modern era. In the Manhattan Project and thereafter, the United States hoped to secure its dominance by taking the logic of destruction to its limit and becoming the supreme master of annihilation. Although the development of a nuclear weapon was certainly new, it nevertheless operated within the general flow of history, toward the ever-greater capacity to destroy. It arose as well from within that broader historical dynamic, the creation of many technological innovations—the production of the automobile and the airplane, radio and television, digital systems and the Internet—which took for granted another version of the power to destroy, to use the Earth's resources without reserve for human benefit. Climate change will not allow us to go with this flow, for it demands that we make technological breakthroughs that will roll *back* the pattern of destruction. It demands that we *contest* the entire momentum of the modern era, indeed the celebration of the "modern" itself.

On many different counts, then, climate change represents a major shift from a danger that has become quite familiar to us. In retrospect, the nuclear era seems positively saturated with moral clarity—with a clear and present threat, the prospect of an instantaneous and absolute end, a public that readily agreed that such a threat existed, a specific technological project that could be completed to respond to that threat, and a presumably sane and rational figure who could be relied upon not to choose annihilation. Climate change undercuts these certainties at every turn. It gives us a scenario loaded with paradoxes and contradictions, one that seems to complicate the necessary urgency several times over.

If this quick, cursory look at our place within the history of the modern world teaches us much, it tells us at least that the terrors of the past few centuries, along with their apparent moral certitudes, have not prepared us for the present moment. Climate change ushers us into a truly new era. Living with climate change throws us out of our familiar narratives: it tells us that we have not surpassed the violence of the past and that the apparent guarantees under which we live may be illusions. As we live in the shadow of future devastation, the bitter taste of what may eventually transpire invades our daily lives, giving us the uncanny sense that our ordinary actions are accompanied by the trauma to come. Climate change also cracks open the tale of the willed, instantaneous death of nuclear annihilation, for it constitutes an event that finishes off one way of life while letting us live on in a disaster that takes generations, if not centuries, to unfold. It is as grave a threat to the Earth and its people as any before it, yet it is less understood, less amenable to our control, and more difficult to prevent. As this prospect weighs on us, it splits our reality to the core, forcing us to live at once with and against our ordinary lives, to cherish what we must also change. Our challenge today is to bear up under all these difficulties nevertheless, to do what must be done, and in defiance of the long odds, to sustain as habitable a planet as we can for ourselves and for those to follow.

Notes

109. Mike Davis, *Late Victorian Holocausts: El Niño Famines and the Making of the Third World* (New York: Verso, 2001).

110. On the genocide in South West Africa, see David Olusoga and Casper W. Erichsen, *The Kaiser's Holocaust: Germany's Forgotten Genocide* (London: Faber and Faber, 2010).

111. Although many observers use the word "genocide" regarding the events in Darfur, it may not be the best term to capture the complexity of the violence

there. "Genocide" is now our term of choice to designate collective murder, even though it technically refers to an attempt to decimate members of a particular race or ethnic group. We need another term to specify violence that arises from different motives or spills over particular ethnic boundaries. For a reliable guide to the recent history of Darfur, see Julie Flint and Alex De Waal, *Darfur: A New History of a Long War*, revised (New York: Zed Books, 2008).

112. For a classic discussion of these themes, see Shoshana Feldman and Dori Laub, *Testimony: Crises of Witnessing in Literature, Psychoanalysis and History* (New York: Routledge, 1992). For a broader history of constructions of trauma, see Ruth Leys, *Trauma: A Genealogy* (Chicago: University of Chicago Press, 2000).

113. The "nuclear era," of course, is by no means over, since technically the possibility still remains that one or more powers could use nuclear weapons. Nevertheless, the fear of nuclear war between the great powers no longer defines our moment (although the international community continues to worry about nuclear proliferation and nuclear terror), and accordingly I will describe the "nuclear era" using the past tense.

Chapter 9

Infinite Responsibility

If what I have been suggesting is true, our present failure to do what is necessary to ward off severe climate change constitutes a grave threat not only to Earth's living systems but also to fundamental aspects of our ordinary lives. As I have argued, it endangers the future that shapes the narratives by which we live, undermining the significance of everything we do. The reality of that threat calls upon us to value the lives we know and to see them as destructive at the same time, as a result splitting our response to ordinary experience.

The ethical implications of our inaction are equally divided. Our failure will ultimately steal the future from those who follow us, depriving them of a full opportunity to address the problems that will afflict them. But our ineptitude, in turn, arises in part from the decisions of our ancestors; over several recent generations, they expanded the world economy exponentially and produced us in staggering profusion, greatly limiting the options available to us.

Heirs of a discredited past, haunted by a disappearing future, we meet our present moment in dismay. Yet we cannot simply surrender to despair, for the demands of ordinary life perpetually call us to orient ourselves to a future, even if it is disappearing. We are thus caught beyond reprieve between the demand to act and a great difficulty in doing so, shackled and stumbling at the crossroads of history.

If we truly experienced in full the haunted, broken qualities of the present, we would yearn for an emotional and spiritual resource through which we could gain consolation. Yet our situation already undermines nearly every version of comfort and hope familiar to us. As long as we work hard to provide for a better future, as long as we depend upon hope that the world we know will endure, and as long as we grieve in a mode that still promises eventual recovery, we are caught within an emotional dynamic whose foundations are disappearing.

We thus find ourselves in a situation where we cannot help but seek some other basis for ethical action, another resource for endurance. Once we recognize that the future is in ruins and our present is shattered, the task of encountering the human significance of climate change is not yet complete, for we must still discover *some* foundation on which we can build, a foundation that can stand no matter what may come. Finding that foundation is the task of this chapter.

The first step in doing so is simply for us to accept the present horror in full. Doing so is surprisingly rare. One would think that our highly contradictory, almost impossible position would inspire consternation or outrage. Instead, we have in general responded in a very different tone. Nearly everyone endures this crisis in distraction, mild dismay, ambivalent passivity, indifference—or in a sort of baffled indignation. This very absence of a passionate response from the great majority of us is striking. What could possibly explain our reluctance to acknowledge the nightmare qualities of our ethical dilemma—or what is worse, our tendency to accept it in a mode of quiet desperation?

The answer may well lie within the history I outlined in the previous chapter. We've been living with disaster so long that we're used to it. For generations now we have accepted the shattering of tradition, the decimation of native peoples, enslavement, economic displacement and exploitation, genocide, and the threat of nuclear annihilation as inevitable aspects of our world. Such violence is so interwoven into the very fabric of modern culture that we cannot imagine a world after it has ceased. In consequence, we do not truly attempt to move beyond what we know. We seem to have surrendered ourselves to the prospect not only of our mortality, but of the potential destruction of our societies, our ecosystems, and the biosphere itself. Although we protest against these prospects, in the end we consider any concerted attempt to overcome them as delusional.

We might at times suggest that we disapprove of this violence, but at every turn we take it for granted, accept its results, and flourish on the wealth it produces. We often treat those who protest as moralizing annoyances, as partisans of a simplistic and ultimately failed viewpoint.

We incorporate their denunciations of contemporary society into our own thinking without giving up our love of what we possess, ending up in a partly ambivalent, partly celebratory mood, uneasily aware of what our history has cost but not finally regretful. When we do acknowledge some dimension of that cost, we usually turn it into the pretext for partial, narrowly construed resentment, a demand that our particular group be invited more openly to the party and given a greater share of wealth and respect—as if that broader world, despite the systemic violence on which it is based, remains legitimate. In short, although we know that the world in which we participate emerges from a history of devastation, we ultimately accept its violence because of its benefit to ourselves.

Our response to genocide, however, suggests that on occasion certain events do give us pause. Shocked and appalled by the Holocaust, we vowed never to let murder on that scale happen again. But we have not yet made good on this vow. Although we created the United Nations to help adjudicate conflict, that body places too great a trust on the powers of the modern state to intervene into its affairs and accordingly to this day often allows nations to commit grievous violence against their own citizens. Neither the destruction of a third of the world's Jews nor the long series of genocides in the last four decades has inspired us to act with sufficient resolve. Although we decry the consequences of state violence, we have not dared to shift our loyalty to any alternative that would be powerful enough to curb it.[114]

Our inability to realize the goals stated in that vow may arise from an even greater inability to understand violence on that scale. Yet such incalculable violence should not disable our resolve but make it incalculably strong in its turn, elevating mourning into an even more powerful emotion that demands resolution. Our failure in this regard in the six decades since the Holocaust suggests either that we did not mourn those deaths or, more likely, that we have learned to dissociate mourning and action, emotion and institution.

The response to genocide thus exposes a fundamental impasse in our culture: a vast gap between our vows and our actions, our confidence we can build new institutions and our ability to do so. We have so far not passed from intention to fulfillment, from horror to resolution. The failure to act in one regard exposes a much broader, long-standing failure

to recognize and address the destructive consequences of modernization for the world's people. Our response to the Holocaust foregrounds
what is true virtually across the board: however great our private grief,
we live within a public sphere that on ultimate matters remains largely
disabled and bankrupt, that operates from within a legacy of uneasy,
haunted denial.

This legacy is intensified even further in the era of climate change. If
we cannot grieve for those destroyed by genocide, we are even less likely
to grieve for those we have not yet lost. Yet the potential violence to
come, as I have suggested, dwarfs the destruction of any genocide, indeed
of many more genocides than we have yet seen. Our present moment is
thus characterized with a dissociation more striking than ever before—a
strange compound of horror and complacency, resolution and indifference. It is as if in our halting way we wish to explore the ultimate reaches
of disorientation and self-estrangement.

As I suggested a moment ago, our inability may stem from a continued
fidelity to the very thing genocide already discredited: the unchallenged
rule of the modern state. The United Nations has not yet found a way to
supersede the claims of its member nations to govern their internal affairs
without interference. This collective failure to curb the powers of the state
is especially harmful today as negotiations over an international treaty to
address the causes of climate change frequently run aground on competi-
tive assertions of state interest. Such assertions arise from developed and
developing nations alike, even from the world's wealthiest nation that can
best afford to be generous. Recently many commentators have blamed
international inaction on the resistance of nations such as China or India.
But we should not forget that in response to the Kyoto accords, in July
1997, the United States Senate voted 95-0 not to agree to any protocol
that did not apply as well to developing nations or that would harm the
American economy.[115] States clearly assume that their priorities are more
important than any potential threat to the biosphere, just as their interests are more crucial than protecting human beings from mass slaughter.
The rule of the state, it seems, can brook no interference, except from limits the state freely accepts on its own terms.

Our tolerance for the power of the state finds its equal, in the American
political sphere, in our respect for the abstract liberty of the individual.

As I suggested in an earlier chapter, the harsh resistance to a carbon tax or untax expresses the wish to protect individual liberty even from the overriding demand to transmit a living biosphere to posterity. The fierce defense of liberty defined in this way—a liberty free of obligations to others or responsibility to the future—ultimately protects *ir*responsibility and a refusal of obligation, much as the tolerance of state power in the abstract authorizes a potential abuse of power. The international inability to respond to genocide is echoed in our general endorsement of the right to drive SUVs, build excessively large homes, apply nitrogen-based fertilizers to crops, or engage in mountaintop removal coal-mining. Taken seriously, the perpetual complaint about environmental regulation voices a demand that one have *the right to use or abuse the Earth's resources as one pleases*, or more directly, *the right to destroy*. Such an insistence, I would suggest, applies in one domain what the murderous abuse of state power enacts in another.

This insistence on the rights of states or individuals makes clear what is at stake in the habits of indifference and self-estrangement. We refuse to mourn the violence of modern history primarily because we are its beneficiaries—because it exemplifies, on a much broader scale, the right to destroy that we claim for ourselves. We ultimately do not wish to take responsibility for the violence that sustains us because our belief in a certain liberty requires us to value that liberty more than responsibility itself. Although we may deplore the exploitation that pervades the world economy, we do not finally lament it, for we do not allow it to crack open the notion of individual liberty or the reality of our relative economic privilege.

The most direct way to overcome this flawed legacy is to renounce the notion of an abstract, purely formal liberty—a right in the end to destroy—and affirm instead our place in a web of relationships with family, friends, neighbors, and partners at the workplace, with fellow citizens in our locality, state, region, and nation, with the living beings who share our habitats, with those who make the goods we use or who consume what we produce, with those who share our humanity, with the dead and the unborn, and with the Earth's dynamic, living systems. An abstract liberty is as nothing compared to our power to respond and be responded to in turn—that is, our power to be responsible for others, to others, to all others, and indeed to the very domain in which all others can flourish.

The interpretation of the world as a scene of countless relationships, familiar in archaic cultures but gradually marginalized in recent centuries, provides the ground for a much more coherent approach to the challenges of our time. Our ambivalent acceptance of the legacy of violence, for example, stems in part from our inability to conceive of strangers as related to ourselves. Marooned in the past or future, in another country, in a reality we consider too far removed from our own, they do not have enough substance in our minds to merit serious attention. They exist within that vast abstraction, our world, which in its incalculable complexity cannot move us. When a great evil such as the Holocaust takes place, we may experience astonishment, horror, and pain, responding with enough interest, perhaps, to learn something of its history. But without recognizing its implication for our ordinary lives, its power to arise from within institutions familiar to us, we enact only an empty grief, a formal attentiveness without consequence. We could instead allow our relationship to strangers to have a practical effect on our lives or on the practices of which we are a part; if we did so, we would actually complete the process of grief by identifying the cause of the horror and dealing with it directly. The point, in short, would be to consider ourselves responsible for the event and its possible reappearance and to act accordingly.

The same applies to our situation in the era of climate change: we must not simply mourn the victims of the future, nor merely comprehend the problem and its potential solutions, but above all consider ourselves responsible for whatever damage will take place—responsible, in short, to coming generations—and thus by definition *to respond*. Only if we regard ourselves as participants in a web of mutual obligation will we have the motivation necessary to overcome indifference and shatter our unthinking, psychotic belief in our right to destroy. Others have given to us and made our lives possible; let us give to others in return.

To live our moment fully, to feel the horror without reserve, is to be given fierce motive for ethical action. If we were truly to accept our place within a web of relationships and thus attempt to respond, what would follow? Let's imagine that we were to face what Al Gore calls *our choice*, decide wisely, and thus reduce greenhouse gas emissions, use more energy-efficient techniques, minimize the environmental harm from our management of forests and farmland, create market-driven incentives for everyone to take these steps, fund a wide array of new technology projects and implement them as soon as possible, and reach international agreements that would enable nations around the world to undertake similar efforts of their own.[116] As I have suggested, to do so would require that we act in a truly revolutionary manner—that we would defy the assumptions and habits of generations for the sake of a common end.

By acting in that decisive way, however, we would also do much more. We would demonstrate that we are free in a sense scarcely ever mentioned by the pretended partisans of liberty—that we are not merely puppets of our cultural traditions but are still capable of making the right choice despite all odds. For much of this book, I have outlined a series of tough obstacles in our path, including the short timeline for action, the difficult technical challenges, the limits of our political institutions, our addiction to economic growth, the self-interested calculus of state interest, and the belief in a false version of freedom. But it does not follow that these factors ultimately determine what we will do; we are still capable of surpassing what we have so far achieved.

But acting in this way would ultimately go much further than showing our power to alter our common history. If we truly enacted the necessary ecological revolution, we would finally bring about what our forebears barely envisioned and scarcely ever attempted. In doing so we would also address the systemic violence and excess of modern culture, that vast legacy of exploitation and devastation that still defines our time. Choosing justice would not only enable us to transform our historical circumstance; it would also take responsibility for that history. It would say that in our freedom, we are capable of making that history our own, *placing it to our charge*, and judging it in the clear light of its consequences. Most crucially of all, it would show that we can make reparation, do justice to those we have harmed and would otherwise still harm, and fight against the motivating force of this history. By taking up this task, we need not admit to an inherited guilt; we are not automatically accountable for the actions of our forebears, any more than those who follow us will be accountable for ours. Our act would thus be free in yet another sense, for it would be freely chosen rather than demanded; it would suggest that we are capable of shouldering a burden that should never have fallen to us, but that in taking up that burden we can at last pass beyond enduring the weight of our history and move to a new phase, into a world we have not merely inherited, but made.

But that is not all. Because this ecological revolution would salvage something of the future of the biosphere, as well as of all human societies, it would demonstrate our capacity to assume responsibility for the encompassing ecological context of humanity's future as well. Insofar as *not* acting would deprive people in the future of a full opportunity to respond to climate change, as I argued earlier, an ecological revolution would do precisely the opposite: it would protect the very possibility that in the future we or others could act on humanity's behalf.

Acting in this way would, in short, go far toward restoring some dimension of the stolen future and thus mending in some degree our own broken present. It would salvage something from the ruins, piecing together a remnant of the human despite the shattering effects of climate change I have been describing over the last four chapters.

In doing so, however, we would take on a task breathtaking in its scope and significance, for we would necessarily assume the ethical burden of generations not our own—the weight of a violent history, on the one hand, and of the potentially devastated generations to come. But even this is not all. Between these two domains, of course, lies our present, which in its almost insurmountable momentum, its ambivalent indifference to the violence it still causes, and its refusal to accept genuine transformation imposes still another burden on us—one that we can instantly recognize as our own. In our free choice to save the biosphere from further destruction, in our attempt to salvage something from the ruins of our shared history, *we must ultimately assume responsibility for addressing the violence enacted throughout the entire sweep of modern history*, from the past through the present and into the future, and thus for many centuries of human endeavor.[117] Strangely enough, to act justly we would *in our single generation* bear the weight of that *entire* development, discharging an immense debt on behalf of the dead, the living, and the unborn. Although we did not choose this moment, we might still freely choose to accept its challenge, to make at last a full reckoning with modernity itself.

Yet even this description does not capture the full dimensions of our moment. We would hardly grasp the implications of this choice if we did not extend our view further into the past. With Jared Diamond, for example, we should trace the chronicle of civilizations that pushed their environments beyond the breaking point and eventually collapsed—or those that through foresight avoided that fate.[118] A decisive moment has occurred on many previous occasions to civilizations around the world; our version of that moment is unique only because it encompasses the fate of the biosphere itself.

We could extend this view even further back. Contemplating the whole sweep of human evolutionary history, we could attribute its disastrous effects to an inherent fault in the species. After all, the story might go, over the millennia we have wiped out most of the large mammals, destroyed many ecosystems, learned how to exploit nearly every living thing for our benefit, multiplied our numbers seemingly without limit, and now are about to torch the climate itself. If we continue with our ways, consuming the biosphere to our heart's content, we will make survival for a good portion of living things difficult if not impossible.

Such stories could justify utter despair; if we have depleted the planet's resources so systematically for millennia and have pushed the logic of civilization beyond natural limits time and time again, there can surely be no hope we will depart from this pattern today. But such a despair would hardly take into account how often we have acted wisely, or—as Diamond's examples of the New Guinea highlands, Tikopia Island, and Tokugawa-era Japan indicate—how often we have lived within our means.[119] Nor would it recognize that we are neither simply a biological species nor directly determined by our long history; we are also capable of recognizing our status as animals whose actions threaten the other forms of life on this planet and therefore are capable as well of surpassing our selfishness for the sake of all life. Evolutionary and historical knowledge should *count* for something; the *awareness* of that long legacy, unique to our era, necessarily alters what it means to be human, transforming our relationship to the conditions of our existence. It is surpassingly strange that we as a species, arising from within the complex web of living forms, would ultimately prove capable of damaging that web itself. But if that is so, we have exceeded purely evolutionary determinations and become *un*natural in a precise sense. Facing that legacy, our challenge is to step outside biological determinations in a further and opposite sense, *to accept responsibility for addressing the ecological violence endemic throughout our history as a species*, to make reparation as greatly as we can to the web of life from which we evolved and in which we live.

Taking responsibility for that history may not be the first course of action that many observers would consider. Contemplating this long history of ecological destruction, some might simply wish that human beings would cease to exist: only that prospect, they might argue, could protect the further flourishing of life. But this profoundly misanthropic wish, which could never come true in any case, denies that we, too, are part of the life whose future we wish to protect; eradicating ourselves, if only in thought, is to partake in a version of ecological destruction and genocide multiplied many times over. It is to imagine the kind of devastation that our ethical action is aiming to prevent.

The point is not to destroy humanity, but to undo what Stephen Jay Gould called our "cosmic arrogance," the anthropocentric attitude that imagined we were the pinnacle of evolution, its ultimate goal.[120] The best strategy in defeating that arrogance is not to negate human history but paradoxically *to affirm it and transform it as a result*—to make our presence on the Earth into a presence *for* the Earth, as an agent charged with protecting all its forms of life. Choosing to do justice to the life of which we are a part, we would freely accept a task that no other species has attempted to perform: to deny our impulse to thrive and reproduce without limit. By taking this unnatural step, we would finally become the stewards of that realm to which we owe our existence and which, thanks to us, can no longer flourish of itself. Paradoxically, by fully assuming our unnatural status as stewards, we would at last do justice to the biosphere, making the thriving of all life an *ethical*, not merely biological, good. If we set out to do so, we might set as our goal the challenge of becoming genuinely indigenous again, of truly *inhabiting* the ecosystems where we live with intelligence, modesty, and foresight, and thus prove ourselves capable at last of joining that long counter-tradition, also evident throughout our history as a species, of human generosity to the ecosystems of which we are a part.

Considering the full dimensions of this decision, then, teaches us that enacting an ecological revolution is a world-historical act, immense in its implications, for through it we would accept responsibility for the ecological costs of human evolutionary and cultural history across the past, present, and future, and as a result would ultimately accept our role as stewards of the biosphere itself. But such a massive act is not a further example of cosmic arrogance. On the contrary, that act has these dimensions only because *any* act we commit today will ramify backwards and forwards across our whole history; in its physical consequences for the biosphere our decision will reveal the overall significance of that history for better or for worse, showing that human beings are in the end agents of reparation or disaster. The enormous, overbearing import of our current moment arises not from our ambition but from our position at the crucial moment of the Earth's climate history. We are at the crossroads, and we simply must choose.

But this act may seem far too immense in another sense. How can we turn against the longstanding historical patterns that have produced our current ease and convenience? Why would we relinquish the unprecedented abundance that meshes so well with our wishes? No doubt doing so will be very difficult. But we need not act out of purely altruistic motives. We now know that business as usual will condemn us to a miserable fate, dissolving the future that anchors the narratives of our lives. To retain the value of our *own* present actions, to maintain the possibility that *we* can live intentionally, we must intervene. Acting wisely, in short, is in our own self-interest. This fact should give us some comfort. It is not so difficult, after all, to set aside immediate whim in the name of long-term self-interest; we learn to do so as soon as we go to school in childhood and in various ways continue to do so throughout adulthood. Delaying some portion of gratification is a necessary part of modern life. A smart decision would simply take such prudence one more crucial step, extending it to the fate of the biosphere itself. Acting responsibly does not require us to become exemplars of stunning virtue, moral heroes of some kind; it only demands that we step up our prudential thinking, applying it to a part of our experience that once seemed exempt from such concerns.

Because acting in this way serves our interests, the fact that it would also conserve a future for others seems less of a burden than a bonus. In this case, the usual contrast between selfishness and altruism disappears. As it turns out, if we take our own interest seriously, we will fight to preserve a future for a whole range of others as well. Protecting ourselves, we would also save the prospects for Earth's living systems. Our single decision, then, would operate on several levels, saving the future for ourselves, humanity, and the biosphere, all at once.

One way to imagine the full dimensions of the present choice is to incorporate into our present activity the possible experience of those to come, ultimately making them into the guardians of our own future as well. We would see the present through their eyes, judging it as we imagine they will judge it. We might even fancifully imagine ourselves to be the emissaries of the ruined future, its embodiment in the present. We might see ourselves as people out of time, terribly inconvenient to our contemporaries—ambassadors charged with interrupting our moment with bad news, cracking open today's complacencies with a dire message from coming generations. We would warn our compatriots of the disaster to come.

If we saw ourselves in this light, some might suggest that we would be the secular counterparts of the biblical prophets, who warned their hearers of what would follow in the absence of repentance. But we would also have to extend that scenario to contemplate the failure of our warnings. In the biblical world, when prophecy failed, the hope for apocalypse followed; the redemption that did not come to pass in history could only take place through a divine decision to bring history to an end, pass judgment on the living and the dead, separate the elect from the damned, and create a new heaven and earth. (Apocalypse in the biblical sense does not refer to a cataclysmic, final event, but to a final *redemptive* event, one that liberates the redeemed from the horrors of history. The book of Revelation, or of Apocalypse, is after all full of *good* news for true believers.)

In our time, however, we face the possibility that redemption will not come in any form, neither from within history nor from its end, leaving us without divine guarantees, without a judgment day that could impose a moral significance on all time. In that case, we endure in a post-biblical landscape, abandoned to a history that provides no ultimate justice, no final consolation. Our willingness to serve as emissaries of the future would make us nothing like the biblical prophets; we would instead simply serve as messengers from our own future selves, spokespeople for those whom we will otherwise have damned. We would merely be fallible citizens who wish to do the least harm to those who will follow.[121]

Yet even the prospect of acting in that way is now disappearing. Although the case for action is extremely compelling, indeed definitive, our society is now taking the opposite course. As I have argued above, the odds of our taking the necessary action in time are slender indeed and are virtually gone. We are thus in the position of outlining the overall implications of the right choice primarily to grasp its opposite. Understanding responsibility at this late hour may be most useful in helping us comprehend the full force of a radical *ir*responsibility.

What might that irresponsibility look like? Today, although the effects of climate change are already quite visible around the world, we still hesitate to act. It thus seems very likely that those effects will get our serious attention only when they are more widespread, continuous, and severe—only when they are significantly worse. In short, it seems we will act only when the consequences of climate change have become much harsher than today.

A concerted effort in a decade or two, of course, would come far too late; it would not counteract the climate patterns that will have already set in. As a result, in the years after we do act, people will soon notice that their efforts will seem to have accomplished nothing. They will ask, "Why are all the eco-friendly measures not working? Why are we not seeing the results we hoped for?" The usual relation between action and result will be suspended, raising tough questions about the value of addressing the problem at all. Only then, perhaps, will we finally experience the nightmare of enduring in a world that is much more difficult to inhabit, whatever we do.

At that point, we might be tempted to abandon ethical action altogether. Because we will be living in wounded ecosystems, shrinking economies, and distressed societies, we might well cast aside the attempt to live responsibly, choosing instead to hunker down and weather it out on our own terms. For many, only the promise that ethical action might alleviate *further* suffering later on, by ourselves or others, could sustain a choice for ecologically responsible living. But because by then we will already be enduring the partial collapse of the civilization we know, surviving social conflicts, natural disasters, and food shortages that are unprecedented for us, we may not even have the luxury of worrying about our future fate. We may discover that we are living in the ruins of ethical action itself. Our position might be akin to that of a person who has endured an amputation but must nevertheless save someone from drowning, or a person who has had a lung removed but still must help carry the wounded. In such a situation, acting to help others might be possible, but it is far more difficult and may not occur much at all.[122]

It is thus all the more astonishing that we will not act today, when doing so might actually prevent that nightmare scenario from coming to pass. The possibility that we might act freely to save the Earth, however, helps clarify that a failure to act is also a choice: a choice to destroy. The ecological revolution is missing today, and will be missing tomorrow, not because it is impossible for us to carry it out but because we *will* not; it speaks of our *decision* to remain relatively indifferent to the destructive aspects of modern culture, to sustain that destruction well into the future, and thus to remain caught by the habits of our common history. This decision, too, we should regard as freely given, as an instance of moral assertion—this time, however, *for* inertia, ineptitude, and ultimately for disaster. It would freely allow our traditions and the bounds of circumstance to define us without limit, to saturate us through and through, and to make us exemplars of what could well be judged as idiocy, mendacity, and moral cowardice. If we made this choice in full awareness of its consequences, we would do so with a certain negative dignity, perhaps, as if we were intent on displaying willful blindness and self-destruction, in embracing intoxication, excess, conflict, and death. But it is far more likely that we will make this decision without noticing it, without truly asserting ourselves at all, lapsing into self-destruction as if it came over us in our sleep.

So far, at least, we may go if we adhere to that slight possibility that acting *now* will enable us to salvage a bit of the stolen future. But if we are honest about the lateness of the hour, we must acknowledge that we may well have *already* decided for calamity without consciously choosing a thing. That numbed decision for disaster grows stronger every day;

irreversible climate change draws nigh; the world we dread is upon us, for it will be almost impossible for us to ward it off now.

What does responsibility look like in the midst of this surrender, as our ecosystems and societies undergo a slow and irreversible collapse? How can we remain responsible in the midst of this general indifference, as the benefits of action are continually superseded, cancelled, or ignored? In these circumstances, the case for responsibility becomes even more difficult; the paradoxes of climate change hit home with terrible force. If we try to sustain an ecological ethics today we would face the stunningly difficult, if not impossible, prospect of *deciding to preserve a future even after it has been largely destroyed*. Even further, we would find ourselves *living forward into the very disaster we are fighting to prevent*. If we take such action, the momentum of history would still carry us directly into the fate we did not and do not choose. In our moment, history not only fails to reply to such efforts; it directly *contradicts* such efforts, as if to mock us for believing in the purpose of action at all. In effect, we would attempt to sustain responsibility amidst its ruins, to remain just when the frameworks in which justice is effective have dissolved.

To sustain an intentional sense of human life in this context takes a supreme moral effort, a belief in human freedom that can defy nearly all odds, a sense of integrity that insists on justice even where it retreats beyond virtually every horizon of possibility. All the overtones of free responsibility I outlined above would be tested to the breaking point, for in our new setting we would be asked to take up a *responsibility seemingly without purpose*.

The difficulty of that moment would come home to us in other ways as well. Once severe climate change kicks in for good, the Earth's temperatures will not return to their former levels, nor will the climate restore itself; on the human time scale, the loss will be permanent. Moreover, the harsher the climate, the greater harm it will do to the communities and people we know, and the more we will grieve for the climate's impact on our lives as well as on the Earth itself. But our grief will have few effective outlets, little space for meaningful resolution. Instead of embarking on a process of mourning that will absorb what we have experienced and renew us, we will find that *there is nothing beyond this loss to move on to*.

Many observers have written about the experience of environmental grief, of mourning for ruined ecosystems. In ordinary circumstances, grief enables us to accept the loss, to acknowledge a new absence within the reality in which we must live, and to face the future having integrated that past into our lives. Through this process of recovery, in some sense we recover our sense of reality, regaining a future through absorbing that loss.[123]

But grief in the era of climate change can no longer operate in this way. Grieving for those we have lost, we will move forward into *more* loss, into a generalized experience of even *greater* mourning. In effect, because we will face those losses and absorb further devastation *without end*, we will *never fully recover* from them. The process of mourning, which will become inevitable for virtually everyone, will lead to little healing at all. Furthermore, if we acknowledge the prospect that we are not likely to act in time, our emotional situation today transforms as well. Facing a stolen future, mindful of the immense social crises to blossom around the world, already enduring the traumas to come, we have little choice but to mourn *forward*, to mourn *into* the very disaster we grieve. Even the specific emotional future promised by the process of grieving disappears, replaced by nothing that grief can overcome. Already today, and to a greater degree in the years to come, we will have to take on a kind of second-order process of grieving *for the future and for grief itself*, for the very *possibility* of integrating such losses into our lives and surviving.

Because of that fact, we cannot rely on grief, or indeed on any other emotional process, to carry us through this moment. However devastating the crisis for longing, hope, grief, and despair, however harrowing our emotional lives may be at this moment, we cannot salvage them on any familiar terms; we simply must find *another basis* on which to build any prospect of ethical integrity.

The same difficulty confronts us if we contemplate our responsibility to the generations to come. In our era, as the future is disappearing, any ethics that grounds itself in a future good is in danger of shattering beyond repair. Abandoned to history, living without guarantees, we may soon discover that the basis of our efforts to safeguard the biosphere for ourselves and others to come will fail. A purely secular description of our moment may falter as much as a purely religious one; both dissolve when we attempt to do justice in the midst of the ruins. Once irreversible, severe climate change arrives, once the domain of indifferent events sweep away nearly every positive consequence that might arise from our actions, what could possibly inspire us to be just?

Our only choice in that case would be to abandon all reference to the future—a future for ourselves, for others, or for the biosphere itself. Although I argued earlier in this book that nearly every action we take is grounded on our orientation to the future, under the unrelenting pressure of severe climate change we would have to construct an ethics that has no such orientation, that takes its inspiration from a radically different resource. We would have to adopt an ethics that would no longer have for its ultimate basis a belief that just action would necessarily lead to an eventual good for ourselves or others or a material benefit that might actually arrive. Adopting such an ethics, we would enact justice for another purpose entirely—one realized in the act itself. We would respond to others without calculating whether our action would pay off in the long run, without measuring our action according to the demands of a realistic common sense, accepting the possibility that our actions may have no results that would ever be visible to us or to others. In effect, we would accept a responsibility that would be infinite in still another sense—one that would bear upon us beyond all pragmatic, finite considerations, aiming for a good that is valuable in itself—a good visible, perhaps, only in our intention, in our sense of a justice without which the value of *all* action disappears.[124]

An ethics of this kind—an ethics *in extremis*—can endure nearly any circumstance. In the midst of disaster, where pragmatic action may fail us, where grief itself must run aground, when all the familiar scenarios of daily life and of human emotion decay, we can still enact justice for its own sake. If we act on these terms, we accept a world without redemption, whether religious *or* secular; giving up any appeal for a transcendental solution, by the same token we release ourselves from a purely material history, discovering instead our ability to do justice beyond all calculation. From a certain point of view, it might seem that this mode of justice would enact a caring that could not heal, a politics that could not liberate, a hope that could not come to pass. Yet in fact, if we take action whose benefits we cannot know, giving ourselves to what may never come to pass, we discover a integrity in the very act of doing justice and show respect for a sanity that may endure even in the ruins.

It might seem that anyone who could adopt such a practice would truly have exceeded the limits of self-interest and become something other than human. But acting in that manner, while exceptional, is not outside ordinary human experience. Today if someone we love contracts a terminal illness, we do not abandon that person; on the contrary, we care and love that person to the bitter end. Love's purpose is the person, not the future. Does it follow that love is somehow religious, that it aims for transcendental ends? Not at all: love ignores transcendence, too, realizing nothing but itself, and as a result constitutes a form of action that aims beyond the religious *or* the secular, one that beyond all others realizes itself through its own acts. However strange it may sound, then, it follows that those who practice an apparently impossible ethics enact a version of this love on another scale.

But even these reflections do not bring us face to face with the most difficult challenge of all. If we found ourselves in the midst of disaster, how would we take responsibility for that disaster itself? Since it would have arrived thanks to human activity as well as human indifference about the harm our activity has been doing to the biosphere, we would have to take the final and unbearable step of accepting the burden of that failure itself.

Some might do almost anything to avoid taking this step. After all, they might say, we have done all we could to save the environment, reducing the harm we do in our own lives and fighting for years to bring about the necessary actions. No doubt for certain people such a protest could ring true. Nevertheless, none of us can claim innocence; all of us in developed societies are implicated in the harm wrought by modern industrial culture. Our very knowledge of climate change depends on the technological infrastructure available to contemporary scientists as they do their research; our very ability to converse about it, to organize activism against it, relies on modern publishing, communication technology, and forms of mobility. We couldn't even participate in a movement to save the Earth without inhabiting the structures we fight against. No doubt it is entirely understandable that we who endure a horror created by human beings might be tempted to sink into resentment and anger against others. Such a gesture might be bitterly pleasurable and even be partly accurate, but it would enable us to evade the fact that we benefited from and participated in the practices that brought about such devastation.

We would thus do far better to take this failure as our own, to wear the mantle of defeat, to take responsibility for the collective decision not to do the right thing—in short, to accept untold loss as a consequence of our own collective history. Such a step might seem almost impossible to contemplate, so directly does it name our futility and humiliation. Yet by taking that step, we would achieve a certain integrity in our power to assume the full measure of our defeat, to name as our own what would then be visible as the true contours of human being: its ultimate inhumanity. In that bleakest moment, we would accept responsibility even for the fact that our attempts at responsibility fail, taking to our charge what would then be revealed as the nullity of our entire history.[125]

Here is the ultimate, most unbearable level of responsibility: the task of *owning* disaster, putting it to our charge, taking its burden on ourselves as human beings. At first such a step might seem to take us to the furthest, most bitter reach of self-contempt and humiliation; here at last, it might appear, we truly give up, collapse, dissolve into ruin ourselves. But such is not the case. Here, at last, we would move beyond our horror at our inhumanity as well as our grief for the passing of the societies and ecosystems we knew. By taking responsibility for a vast failure, we would in that same gesture accept absolute loss without nostalgia and without condemnation. Giving up the temptation to dismiss humanity as a mere evolutionary anomaly or to cling to some faint idealization of our kind, we would accept humanity in all its inhumanity and thus find ourselves in a space of radical openness, capable of affirming the entire process that brought us into being. Marooned on the junk heap of history, facing no prospect of redemption, we might attain a great serenity, broken and destroyed though we may be.

So it seems that the baffled, broken life I described in the past four chapters can ultimately lead to something more, to a basis for a renewed integrity even in the midst of the ruins. That basis is not a new hope, but the capacity to affirm and endure the worst. To find our way beyond the trauma of our time, to push beyond a scenario of endless grief, we can abandon anything that might heal us and instead *embrace trauma and grief themselves without reserve*—and discover that by doing so they subtly change: through embracing trauma more fully we can accept the broken world without being haunted and distressed by it; and through submitting fully to grief, even a grief for grief itself, we might find how to relinquish our attachment to recovery, accepting instead a serenity in destitution. By owning disaster in these and other ways, we might relinquish that fidelity to a sense of our innocence and that belief in the validity of our culture which made the shattering of both so painful. Through that process, we may at last lay hold of a new foundation—one so radical that on its basis we may endure whatever may come. On the other side of a mutilated happiness we might discover vaster possibilities, including a capacity for affirmation without limit and a power to love without the hope of return.

In discovering that we may persist in doing justice even in the ruins, we can find the basis for an *ethical* optimism that can survive even in the midst of utter defeat. We need not fear, now or later, that political or climatological realities will cancel our capacity to follow through on our responsibility to others and to the forms of life that have sustained us. By working through the series of potential ethical challenges to the bitter end, by imagining the worst that may befall—and finding that we can survive even *that* horror with integrity—we discover an indestructible ethical agency we may never have known we possessed, discerning hints of possibility that lie unremarked within the impossible challenges of our era, sources of strength that will remain to us even if the future disappears. Through that same encounter with the worst, we learn how to dwell with the full range, however painful, of emotions that arise in response to the dilemmas of our time, at last overcoming the dissociation habitual to our culture.

Bringing these discoveries with us back from this hypothetical future to our own moment, when we cannot yet be certain that all action is futile or that the future has utterly disappeared, we may realize that we can make good *even now* on the agency we have gained through this foray into the future and as a result can face our present difficulties with a surprising authority. Moreover, by returning to the present in this way, we expand the significance of that future ethical decision outward, to include our own present as well. But by assuming responsibility *today* for the disaster that may come, we necessarily accept the demand to renounce any further participation in the practices that are leading to catastrophe and to make reparation, as far as is possible, for the harm we have done. No doubt our ability to do either is severely constrained; for most of us, simply living our lives does far more harm than we wish, and the task of reparation requires far more of us than we will ever achieve. We who are the inheritors of a disastrous history were never meant to carry that entire history on our backs; it is only understandable that as we try to do so, we may stagger under the load. We will have to develop new reserves of humility, new levels of resilience, new styles of dark comedy to endure. The task we accept seems well-nigh impossible. Yet by taking it as our own we become the agents, and not merely the heirs, of our shared history—even if, as agents, we necessarily have in our hands a truly horrific power to destroy as well as save. In accepting this task, we finally acknowledge what would be true in any case, that at this juncture, as in no other, ours is an infinite responsibility.

What does that power mean for us today in our ordinary lives, as we inevitably face a wide array of decisions about our everyday practices? We cannot do better than to take the most transformative, constructive steps available to us. Because our task is to reduce those practices that do the greatest *physical* harm to the biosphere, the ultimate measure of our willingness to do justice is not purity of heart or intensity of spirit but the practical, measurable effect of our actions. Yet to bring about those concrete results requires a real ethical commitment. As a result, we find ourselves today in what might seem to be a paradox: we accept an incalculable responsibility best when we calculate with great rigor exactly what we can do to make the most difference in our ordinary practices—and carry through on that calculation as well as we can. In short, we must cultivate nothing other than a *pragmatism of infinite responsibility*, one that is endlessly resourceful in discovering and implementing the most sophisticated ideas for salvaging a future. To that task I now turn.

Notes

114. For a harrowing discussion of a recent failure to halt genocide, see Roméo Dallaire and Brent Beardsley, *Shake Hands with the Devil: The Failure of Humanity in Rwanda* (New York: Carroll & Graf, 2004).

115. Library of Congress, Bill Summary and Status, 105th Congress (1997–1998), S. Res 98, http://thomas.loc.gov/cgi-bin/bdquery/z?d105:S.RES.98:.

116. Al Gore, *Our Choice: A Plan to Solve the Climate Crisis* (Emmaus, Pennsylvania: Rodale, 2009).

117. For classic discussions of infinite responsibility, see Emmanuel Levinas, *Totality and Infinity: An Essay on Exteriority*, translated by Alphonso Lingis (Pittsburgh: Duquesne University Press, 1969), especially 220–247, and Levinas, *Otherwise Than Being: Beyond Essence*, translated by Alphonso Lingis (Pittsburgh: Duquesne University Press, 1998), especially 131–162. For a recent meditation on similar themes as they bear on our current ethical and political dilemmas, see Simon Critchley, *Infinitely Demanding: Ethics of Commitment, Politics of Resistance* (New York: Verso, 2007).

118. Jared Diamond, *Collapse: How Societies Choose to Fail or Succeed* (New York: Penguin, 2006).

119. Diamond, *Collapse*, 277–308.

120. Stephen Jay Gould, *Ever Since Darwin: Reflections in Natural History* (New York: Norton, 1977), 14; see also 38, 62.

121. For further reflections on biblical religion and its relevance for our response to climate change, see chapter twelve.

122. In the midst of disaster, people can demonstrate an amazing capacity for generosity; see Rebecca Solnit, *A Paradise Built in Hell: The Extraordinary Communities that Arise in Disaster* (New York: Penguin, 2009). But if climate change becomes truly severe, it will constitute an ongoing, endless disaster, in contrast to the specific, local events Solnit describes, stretching the human capacity for generosity much further.

123. For discussions of grieving for environmental devastation and loss, see Phyllis Whindle, "The Ecology of Grief," in *Ecopsychology: Restoring the Earth, Healing the Mind*, edited by Thomas Roszak, Mary Gomes, and Allen Kanner (New York: Sierra Club Books, 1995), 136–149; Kristine Kevorkian, "Environmental Grief," *Ecology Global Network*, February 15, 2012, http://www.ecology.com/2012/02/15/environmental-grief/; and Marie Eaton, "Environmental Trauma and Grief," Curriculum for the Bioregion Initiative, Science Education Resource Center at Carleton College, August 2012, http://serc.carleton.edu/bioregion/sustain_contemp_lc/essays/67207.html.

124. For related arguments in recent critical theory, see Jacques Derrida, *The Gift of Death*, second edition, and *Literature in Secret*, translated by David Wills (Chicago: University of Chicago Press, 2008), 82–116; the essays by Slavoj Žižek, Eric L. Santner, and Kenneth Reinhard collected in *The Neighbor: Three Inquiries in Political Theology* (Chicago: University of Chicago Press, 2006); and Simon Critchley, *Infinitely Demanding*. Such discussions emphasize the demand to love others beyond all thought of merit or return, but they do not consider the unprecedented ethical challenges posed by climate change, including that of enacting justice even without a future. On the need to extend Derrida's thinking in response to climate change, see Tom Cohen, "Anecographics: Climate Change and 'Late' Deconstruction," in *Impasses of the Post-Global: Theory in the Era of Climate Change*, volume 2, edited by Henry Sussman (MPublishing, University of Michigan Library; Open Humanities Press, 2012), http://quod.lib.umich.edu/o/ohp/10803281.0001.001/1:3/--impasses-of-the-post-global-theory-in-the-era-of-climate?rgn=div1;view=fulltext.

125. Compare the account of how the subject can assume responsibility for state of things, thereby converting substance into subject, in Slavoj Žižek, *The Sublime Object of Ideology* (New York: Verso, 1989), 217, and how, by working through the fundamental fantasy that sustains one's being, "the subject accepts the void of his [sic] nonexistence," Žižek, *The Ticklish Subject: The Absent Centre of Political Ontology* (New York: Verso, 1999), 281.

Chapter 10

Making Reparation: Offset Your Life

If, as I have just suggested, owning disaster is also to own the demand for reparation, even where reparation is impossible, then our way of surviving the slow horror of our time does not relieve us of the task of practicing justice in everyday life. On the contrary, given the enormity of the disaster we now take to our own account, the task becomes enormous as well. All our pragmatic actions in consequence thus become small indications of a reparation we will never and can never complete, a task as incalculable as the disaster it is meant to repair.

But if we commit ourselves to doing justice in our daily lives, we immediately face a series of skeptical responses from ourselves or others. What can we do as individuals in the face of such an enormous crisis? Individual action can do very little in comparison to concerted national and international measures to address the key causes of climate change. But this is not in fact an objection to a renewed ethics; it is rather a description of our first, overriding, and most pressing task: fighting hard for an ecological revolution. All other actions we might take pale in comparison. When our political institutions pose obstacles to the necessary transformation, we should become more creative, change tactics, and try new angles on the problem. If we fail again, we should persist with still further efforts. Nothing should ever intimidate us.

But it does not follow that we need do nothing to change our behavior in our own lives. If we are to do justice no matter what comes, we must commit ourselves to making a difference however we can. Doing so may be difficult if it's clear that we are still caught within a society that refuses to alter its ways. Yet we cannot use that fact as an excuse. As I asked above, how tolerant are we toward a slaveholder who refused to liberate his "property" on the excuse that his doing so would not by itself liberate all slaves? How well do we accept the plea of a woman living in Nazi Germany that she cooperated with the system of extermination because she did not have the power on her own to bring it to an end? If we are not likely to let such people off the hook, we must believe that people should do justice whatever the odds, even in the face of impoverishment, punishment, or death. Since living in an environmentally responsible fashion would provoke no such threat against us today, we have even fewer excuses; our criteria in those other cases make our judgment about our current behavior quite clear.

We may hesitate to go further than we already do because we are not convinced it is necessary or all that helpful to do so. We might conclude, for example, that statistically speaking, our personal actions will have only a miniscule effect on the overall situation. But even if such action may be statistically insignificant, it is still necessary. Our ordinary moral compass tells us as much. If one of us kills someone we hate, statistically speaking we would have reduced the human population by an almost infinitesimal amount. Similarly, if we break into someone's home to steal an object we coveted, we do virtually nothing to harm the gross national product. Yet we refuse to commit such actions for good reason. The same applies to environmental ethics: it's silly to imagine that driving a gas-guzzling vehicle is acceptable simply because that machine is only one of millions on the road. If we're destroying the biosphere, we're destroying it—and statistics is no excuse.

Other factors may enter into our thinking as well. Even if collective efforts to change our societies are weak or tardy, individual action can still make at least a minimal difference. For one thing, it will help realize, if only on a small scale, some aspect of the society we are demanding. For another, it will relieve us of a certain kind of hypocrisy, helping us close the gap between what we demand and how we actually live. Finally, if enough of us act, and encourage others to do so, together we may build momentum for a much more widespread transformation.

Such considerations may already motivate us to do a great deal. Already millions have learned that we should use renewable energy in place of fossil fuels, rely on energy-efficient forms of transportation, save energy in our households, consume less, reuse and recycle as much as we can, buy local and organic food, and compost our waste. Over the past four decades or so, these practices have gradually become a familiar part of developed societies, at least in many locations, and now sound like basic common sense for many of us.

But because even now the greenhouse gas footprint of the average American citizen remains sharply higher than that of people elsewhere in the world, in this nation we have far to go. Moreover, as I suggested in chapter five, even if humanity as a whole shifts to renewable energy soon, our imprint on the Earth's surface will still be enormous in part because of the immensity of the global human population.

To address these challenges, we must go significantly further than we already have. We may be forced to examine aspects of our habits or assumptions that we do not want to think about at all, to tackle serious difficulties not only in the public sphere but in our own lives as well. If we are to see our own moment through the eyes of the future, we may have to endure changes to our intimate lives that we can hardly bear, to do what seems at first impossible. Our dilemma forces us toward radical thinking and action on every level—political and cultural, social and ethical, collective and personal. It demands that we cut to the root in every domain, including in our own individual lives.

In the end, we have no serious reason to hesitate applying a pragmatic environmental ethics to our own lives. Refusing to do so cannot withstand close scrutiny. Living by such an ethics will be no easy matter; we will inevitably meet resistance from that part of us still caught in the familiar habits of our culture. As a result, we might be tempted to alter our practices only when it is most convenient to do so, when it intrudes least into our lives. We might attempt to combine ease and responsibility, blending our current habits with new ways, as if changing our lives a little bit will be enough. Most dangerously, we might bargain with the future, giving up practices that do relatively little harm so that we can keep those that do much more. Renouncing the disastrous habits of our culture can be surprisingly difficult. The toughest and most essential task is to overcome this resistance, especially with regard to those truly destructive practices on which we most depend. On this score we should compromise as little as possible.

Accordingly, in this chapter I will focus on one example of damaging activity—travelling by air—to examine how great a harm it causes, why we might resist abandoning it, and what steps we could best take within the actual limits of our lives. Thinking through this single example may provide us with a template for how we can confront other destructive practices. Since air travel eventually will lead to the question about whether to rely on carbon offsets to compensate for our flights, we might also take up whether those offsets could work more broadly, whether they might be a useful strategy in response to all the harm we do. In short, this chapter will attempt to outline one practical approach to the chief ethical challenges of our time.

In most discussions of how we might shift to a new energy economy, the topic eventually turns to air travel. In nearly every other area of greenhouse gas usage, we can imagine a transition to alternative energies and can begin to make reasonable steps in that direction. But not with air travel. As David MacKay points out, "planes are already almost as energy-efficient as they could possibly be."[126] Yet flying by plane has an enormous, negative impact on the atmosphere. George Monbiot, in a representative and remarkably clear discussion of the subject, citing the research of the (British) Royal Commission on Environmental Pollution, writes that "the carbon emissions per passenger mile 'for a fully loaded cruising airliner are comparable to a passenger car carrying three or four people.'" So far so good. But as Monbiot goes on to point out, "while the mean distance travelled by car in the United Kingdom is 9,200 miles per year, in a plane we can beat that in one day." Planes are such an efficient form of travel—they enable us to cover such huge distances so quickly— we forget how much energy is required to move us so far. If the carbon footprint of a given air mile doesn't seem so great, taking the full distance into account expands that footprint very quickly.

But this isn't the half of it. The impact of travelling in airplanes, Monbiot continues, "is not confined to the carbon they produce." Airplanes emit many different particles that have varying effects. The IPCC thus estimates that the overall impact "is a warming effect 2.7 times that of the carbon dioxide alone," due primarily to the mixing of vapor from jet engines with the air in the troposphere, creating the vapor trails we can see from far below. "This means that subsonic aircraft, if all their seats are full, cause roughly the same total warming per passenger mile as cars."[127]

Bringing this analysis home to our own lives can be quite sobering. Let's say you drive a fuel-efficient car, recycle, and live responsibly—except each year you take a single cross-country round-trip flight. According to a representative carbon footprint calculator—the one at terrapass.com—driving a car that gets forty miles per gallon 12,000 miles a year pumps an estimated 5,869 pounds of carbon dioxide—just under three tons—into the atmosphere. In comparison, a round-trip flight from Boston to San Francisco, with one stop along the way each direction, emits 2,553 pounds of carbon dioxide per passenger. But if you multiply that number by 2.7 to reflect the full impact of that flight on global warming, it has a net effect of around 6,893 pounds—a half-ton *more* than the carbon footprint of driving that car *the entire year*.[128]

So would it be better to take short-haul propeller flights? The latter, it turns out, are inefficient because they require planes to spend a greater percentage of the fuel getting aloft. It's far better to use other forms of transportation to reach destinations so close; Monbiot's own estimates suggest that it's about twice as efficient to travel that distance by car (with the British average of 1.56 passengers on board), over ten times more efficient to take the train, and around fifteen times more efficient to travel by bus.[129]

Wouldn't it be possible for airplanes to use renewable sources of energy? Not yet. Ethanol and other biofuels do not burn well at the extremely cold temperatures found in the troposphere, and a hydrogen-fueled plane would contribute thirteen times more to global warming than today's jet airplanes.[130] Amyris, a biofuel company, has created a renewable jet fuel suitable for actual use and is currently testing it for release in a few years.[131] But whether it can be produced cheaply enough and at an appropriate scale without causing too great a damage to current ecosystems is doubtful. So far, there is no available alternative to the kinds of aircraft we fly today.

Facts like these fill a good number of us with outright dismay. Those who live far away from family or friends, whose professions virtually require us to get around by plane, or who simply love to explore the world would do almost anything rather than give up air travel. We might even regard the very thought as a kind of personal affront. But that is the very fact that makes this example so powerful and so instructive. The biosphere doesn't really care all that much about how we feel; the reality is what it is, and we must bear with it.

Our first reaction might be that we should simply stop travelling by air. For many of us, that is no doubt the best option. We may be lucky enough, or smart enough, to live near all those we wish to see. Most of the rest of us should be able to visit with family members or colleagues using phone calls, Internet video links, or videoconferencing. If we do need to travel, we might be able to do so by bus or train. In fact, given the harm that air travel does, we should set this as our default response: we should determine to fly as little as possible, regarding it as a harmful act that we should undertake only when we have no other options.

But for millions of us, adopting such a response seems to ask too much. The most crucial part of this discussion thus arises when we must decide how to adjudicate between the harm of air travel and its apparently necessary place in our lives. It may be useful to pause here to ponder a series of motives for travel and imagine a plausible response to each.

Many of us use air travel as a way to take a break. What happens to the family vacation, the weekend getaway, the mid-winter trip to see sunshine? What about that week in Hawaii or the visit to the Caribbean resort? These outings are pleasant, but scarcely necessary, especially in the midst of the climate crisis; we would be wise to forego them entirely. Changing our habits in this regard will not be easy. It will alter our relationship to the very idea of getting away from it all; we will have to rethink our sense that the biosphere exists in part to assist us in enjoying leisure time.

Cutting back on air travel also raises a number of tougher questions. Should students apply to the best colleges, wherever they may be; should workers relocate to wherever the jobs are good; and should seniors retire to Arizona or Florida—if doing so requires that somebody travel by air to join the family gathering at Thanksgiving and Christmas, if not the summer holidays? What must give way: personal ambition and satisfaction, the notion of family, and the satisfactions of retirement, on the one hand, or the threat of climate change on the other? If we care at all about the survival of the biosphere, the answer over the long term is clear: we must learn how to become a far less mobile society, to abandon our belief that something fabulous will happen to us if we settle hither and yon or venture continually to the far pavilions. Yet because we *inherit* the consequences of that mobility for our own lives, we may find ourselves far removed, and perhaps permanently, from family members.

Perhaps a good compromise is to be honest about what we can do, but also what we cannot give up; perhaps we should accept what has already taken place—such as our moving far away from family members—and thus accept occasional air travel to see them. But such a reason cannot serve us forever. As time goes by, we should take steps, wherever we can, to rejoin those we love and find far more local and settled ways to live. Adopting an environmental ethic will inevitably force us to rethink our improbable attempt to combine distance and intimacy.

Similar pressures abound elsewhere. Should members of various professions attend annual conferences intended to keep them apprised of developments in their fields? How well could they share information without meeting face to face? To cover contemporary events, journalists fly to destinations here or abroad in order to observe developments first-hand. How urgent must developments be to justify such a large environmental footprint? Salespeople, consultants, businesspeople, board members, and executives—to give a partial list—are among the nation's most frequent fliers; how are they to conduct their business?

Insofar as these professions take for granted that flying should be *routine*, that it must become in part a frequent activity over the year, they have accepted what amounts to the perpetual abuse of the biosphere. The assumption that actions of such harm should be ordinary must go. As a result, those professions must evolve very quickly into another form, relying instead on alternative forms of contact, such as videoconferencing, to conduct ordinary business. Such a change is in fact plausible if those in such fields make a concerted effort over the next few years. But calling for an absolute ban on face-to-face encounters might go too far and create a backlash against this entire effort. Here again, one might justify occasional flights on the basis of the most pressing needs or most fruitful encounters.

Even further questions arise when we contemplate our place in the international community. How are we to break out of an insular narrowness if we cannot travel to other countries, learn their languages, and partake in their cultural traditions? Artists, performers, filmmakers, musicians, chefs, cultural critics, and people in the world of fashion cannot remain on the cutting edge without being exposed to cultures elsewhere. Would we welcome the results if they travelled less, if mutual influence took place in another way? Diplomats, workers in nongovernmental organizations, and employees of aid groups travel frequently around the world, but in a severe irony, by doing so they contribute to harming the planet. How are they to do their work without relying on air travel?

The consequences of globalizing trade relations are at stake as well. The increasing volume of goods moving between nations, especially by sea, are inevitably accompanied by an increase in international air travel, at least to support bilateral business arrangements. Globalization is also felt in cultural exchanges of all kinds. Nowadays people who live in large towns or small cities assume that they will have access to good French and Italian food, a nice Mexican place, good Chinese food, a sushi restaurant, Thai and Indian food, and maybe even a tapas place as well. In any large city, we assume that we'll experience some real multiculturalism, too—that there will be sizable ethnic or cultural communities integrated into the mix. In the last several decades, the United States has invited highly skilled or educated immigrants into its society, creating an influx of people from many nations around the world—migrants who may wish to take flights back to their homelands from time to time. All these trade relations, cultural contacts, and family ties rely on a mode of travel that does immense and ongoing harm to the biosphere. Is it possible to maintain anything like this openness to the world without doing further harm?

However greatly we may value these cultural benefits of globalization and the gradual shift from insular to more cosmopolitan attitudes, we cannot give those benefits absolute priority over the survival of the biosphere. Converting the planet into a multicultural ash heap does not serve humanity well. To the extent that we can, we should sustain the vibrancy and creativity associated with these international exchanges while dramatically reducing the number of international flights. And because those flights have a staggering carbon footprint, since they damage the biosphere more than any others, we must consider cutting them back as far as possible. If we do so, however, we will inevitably relinquish many aspects of globalization on which we have come to rely—the easy exchange of goods and fashions included. Our cultures and economies, our sense of multicultural contact, will have to evolve as we do so. We may thus end up in this case as in the compromises above, accepting occasional journeys for truly urgent purposes but otherwise giving pride of place to the planet's survival.

How do things look so far? On the broadest scale, we could pressure governments to adopt a greenhouse gas untax of the sort I described earlier in this book. An increase in the price of fossil fuels would raise the price of air travel and could prompt us all, whatever our sense of the climate crisis, to change our ordinary practices. If necessary, we should also ponder how to change the attitudes that our professions take for granted. Workers could insist that their employers allow them to travel visually rather than in person or to find other workable alternatives to flying. We could all begin to think creatively about how we can meet, exchange information, socialize with professional peers, and forge workable bonds. All these changes will be necessary if our societies take real action; we might as well get a start on that massive cultural shift before it is too late.

Moreover, if the compromises I outlined above sound plausible, we could then commit ourselves to flying only on specific occasions, narrowing the number of flights over a year to one or less, and over a lifetime to a few: to study abroad, to return to an ancestral homeland, or to make a few visits to specific, long-desired destinations. This severe reduction in the number of flights might rightly inspire us to do the most with each one, to make those air miles *count* as much as possible. If our lives allow us, we might for example stay at our destination for several weeks if not months, substantially reducing the climate impact per day of the visit.

Wherever we fly, we could take into consideration research that suggests we could reduce the environmental impact of air travel if we fly when a plane's vapor trail can reflect sunlight back into space—that is, in the daytime and in the relatively bright seasons of the year. (One study suggests that travel from December through February, only one-fourth of the total number of annual flights in southeast Britain, caused one-half of a year's warming effect from contrails; travel at night, around one-fifth of the total there, caused 60 to 80 percent of the effect.) However, because contrails may constitute only a portion of flying's overall impact on the atmosphere, taking this step may have no more than a partial benefit.[132]

Although these compromises might seem sensible, flying to this degree would still contribute to climate change. As a result, the approach I have sketched so far is still inadequate. A key further element, then, is the opportunity to purchase carbon offsets for each of those flights—that is, to contribute to organizations that use the money for projects that reduce greenhouse gas emissions. Surprisingly, such offsets are fairly cheap: you can offset the emission carbon dioxide through a credible and certified organization for around $12 to $15 a ton. Doing so responsibly, however, takes a bit of research. For such offsets to be effective, they must fund efforts that would not otherwise take place, do not merely shift harmful activities to another site, and are not already being counted under an existing environmental policy. Furthermore, such offsets should support interventions that truly make a difference *now*. If you fund projects for planting trees, for example, they may not begin to pull carbon dioxide out of the atmosphere for many years, and already, as I mentioned in earlier chapters, many forests under the pressure of climate change are drying out, decaying, and are thus on the verge of emitting more carbon dioxide than they absorb. It is thus much wiser to fund programs that choose other strategies, that reduce the burning of wood or charcoal for cooking fires, for example, or help construct renewable energy plants whose power local consumers will actually use. (Those cooking fires, by the way, typically produce great quantities of black carbon, which researchers have recently found may be far more harmful than previously thought; funding efforts to reduce that harm may thus be far more helpful than we knew.[133]) Fortunately, others have done careful research on all these concerns and have made the results available online, along with links to those carbon offset companies whose efforts seem to be making the most difference.[134]

If we travel only on occasion *and* purchase offsets when we do so, we would go far toward reducing our overall carbon footprint and do much to fulfill the demand for reparation. What's more, by purchasing offsets we would be contributing in our own small way to efforts that the international community could sponsor wholesale if it so chose; we would in effect begin to bring about the ecological revolution we demand. By living in this way, we would declare our commitment to that revolution and

thus begin to make good on our choice to take responsibility for the ecological disaster now unfolding around us.

One problem with offsets, however, is that they are so cheap and so
easy to purchase that they may become too convenient. If one can afford
that minimal cost, why not simply continue flying as much as one pleases
and offset it all? Such a strategy is certainly better than flying *without* offsets; at least it helps cancel out the harm of one's travel. But the purpose
of offsets is to compensate for those emissions we cannot eliminate, not
to enable us to travel as much as we might wish. Otherwise, it becomes
a tactic to allow people to live in continued extravagance, as if they
can do all the harm they please as long as they buy the sense that they
are doing none.

Offsets are limited in this way because our eventual goal is both to
reduce emissions *we* might cause and help reduce emissions *elsewhere*,
for a *total* reduction much larger than offsets can make possible. While
it does much good to fund projects that decrease environmental harm,
our eventual purpose is to do so while also reducing the harm to which
we *directly* contribute. Our eventual goal, then, must be to eliminate *all*
of our contributions to climate change while also enabling those in other
regions of the world to do the same.

These considerations inspire some people to deplore offsets entirely. If
we can potentially abuse them to excuse doing harm to the biosphere, the
logic goes, then we should avoid them altogether. But those who make
this point almost inevitably still travel by air; the virtue they espouse by
excluding offsets is thus illusory. The only responsible way to avoid using
them is to eliminate one's carbon footprint in the first place.

Nevertheless, we should take this hesitation to rely on offsets seriously. Ultimately, offsets will be of value to us only if we see them as tools
to help us as we construct new practices that will do no direct harm. If
we decide to use offsets, we must commit ourselves to doing so sparingly
over the course of a transition in our actions—*so that eventually we would
reduce our air travel so much we would no longer need those offsets at all.*
Thinking of offsets as a transitional strategy may be our best option.

This is only one example of how we might shift our habits in the era
of climate change. How well does it represent a transformation in all our
activities? How can we build on it to rethink the whole pattern?

It shouldn't be too difficult to apply many aspects of this example to others. Setting a low threshold for a carbon footprint, sorting out whether we should make any exceptions, and offsetting those exceptions carefully—while regarding those offsets as a temporary measure—will enable us to reduce our overall carbon footprint responsibly.

But in that case, this example teaches us that we should begin to offset *every* aspect of our carbon footprint, in effect, to *offset our lives* entirely. Since offsets are relatively inexpensive, most of us could afford to calculate all our greenhouse gas emissions annually and compensate for them. Because most of us use energy in rough proportion to our income, it follows that most of us with more money could afford more offsets, and those who need them the least would need to purchase the fewest. Even then, of course, they might be too expensive for some. Nevertheless, if all of us did our best, and all of us who could afford to do so offset our lives, we would make a real difference for the biosphere even without government action. And because we would be linking this practice to a prior, systematic attempt to reduce our carbon footprints as far as possible, we would be going even further to eliminating the harm we do to the planet.

By taking these steps, we would be following through on our commitment to make reparation. Indeed, that reparation would be visible both in the greatly reduced harm we cause in our own lives and in the active transformation we would make possible here and elsewhere. As people around the world shift to less harmful practices, as renewable energy plants come online, some version, however limited, of undoing harm to the Earth will take place.

But if that is the case, why stop there? We should also contribute to organizations that restore ecosystems where we live, that actively protect wild spaces, waterways, wetlands, and wildlife preserves, and that not only protect but also dare to *restore* damaged landscapes. Even further, if purchasing offsets can do so much good, why shouldn't we contribute money to those organizations quite apart from offsetting per se, enabling them to go much further than they would otherwise? If our lives are truly about reparation, we could commit ourselves to purchasing twice, or even three times, what we would need to do to offset our carbon footprint, doing what we could to decrease the harm brought about by the society in which we live.

Making these compromises and accepting the cost of these offsets may be no easy matter; at first, for people in many professions, taking these actions might pose a tough challenge. But it's pretty clear that our current crisis requires us to change our whole way of life. In these specific ways, it may push us well beyond the comfort zone, demanding what we do not really want to give. Yet we simply must make changes of this kind if we want to tackle the challenges that face us. If we do not, we are no different from those who proclaim against all the evidence that there is no problem at all—or are even worse, since we become far more inconsistent and hypocritical than they. We have no choice but to do all that we can.

Notes

126. MacKay, *Sustainable Energy*, 35.

127. George Monbiot, *Heat*, 173. For the Special Report from the Royal Commission on Environmental Pollution, see *The Environmental Effects of Civil Aircraft in Flight*, 2002, especially paragraph 3.22, available as a pdf document online. For the IPCC estimate, which is drawn from research into the greenhouse gas impact of air travel in 1992, see the Special Report, *Aviation and the Global Atmosphere*, 1999, section 6.6.5, http://www.ipcc.ch/ipccreports/sres/aviation/index.php?idp=86.

128. I calculated these numbers on the Carbon Footprint Calculator at terrapass.com, which, as its name suggests, provides estimates only for the carbon emissions for a given plane flight—not for its overall effect on the environment. In this regard it is typical of most carbon footprint websites. Responsible users of these sites would be well advised to multiply the estimate of footprint for air travel by 2.7. See http://terrapass.com/carbon-footprint-calculator-2/.

129. Monbiot, 180.

130. Monbiot, 180–82; see also MacKay, 35–37.

131. See Krupp and Horn, *Earth: The Sequel*, 88–89; http://www.amyris.com/.

132. See Nicola Stuber and others, "The Importance of the Diurnal and Annual Cycle of Air Traffic for Contrail Radiative Forcing," *Nature* 441 (June 15, 2006), 864–67, doi:10.1038/nature04877.

133. Elisabeth Rosenthal, "Burning Fuel Particles Do More Damage to Climate Than Thought, Study Says," *New York Times*, January 15, 2013, http://www.

nytimes.com/2013/01/16/science/earth/burning-fuel-particles-do-more-damage-to-climate-than-thought-study-says.html?_r=0 and T. C. Bond and others, "Bounding the role of black carbon in the climate system: A scientific assessment," *Journal of Geophysical Research: Atmospheres*, 118 (June 6, 2013), 1-173, doi: 10.1002/jgrd.50171.

134. A good place to get started on such research may be found here: http://www.offsetconsumer.org/providers/.

Chapter 11

Bear No Children

Let's say a person who is already unusually responsible in all the obvious ways—who uses very little gasoline, expends very little energy to heat or cool the home, recycles, and much more—decides to take the seemingly drastic step of no longer flying. Would that be enough? Wouldn't dramatically reducing travel by air make a huge difference? Certainly it would. But thinking about our challenge in these terms, however necessary, still relies on a fairly narrow assumption about the task before us. For the most part, we tend to focus on how we as individuals can lower our greenhouse gas footprint through various practical actions. But that approach leaves out of view another key question—*whether to bring more individuals into the world in the first place*, each of whom will, in turn, contribute a lifetime's worth of emissions to the atmosphere.

Insofar as bearing children is a personal choice, the decision to have a child properly belongs within the domain of one's personal impact on climate change. Yet because our culture regards that decision as in some sense absolutely private, as the very essence of personal liberty, we have so far seldom examined the ethics of reproduction as such. Typically, even the toughest commentators on climate change keep silent on this question or approach it with fear and trembling, as if examining the politics of reproduction would somehow violate a taboo. They have a point: it does. But keeping silent on this question makes a mockery of the pretense to have considered the broader impact of our individual decisions on climate change with any thoroughness. The decision about whether to have children is so enormous in its implications it dwarfs virtually all others; if anything, it is *the* question individuals must face when considering how to lead an ethical life today.

As we consider the full range of what we as individuals can do, then, we cannot remain content with the options I outlined in the previous chapter. We must examine the issue of bearing children as well, for it is central to any serious look at the question of how best we can make reparation.

Even the briefest consideration would tell us what a huge impact bearing a child must have on an individual's contribution to climate change. If you have a child, you've added another entire lifetime's worth of greenhouse gas emissions to the biosphere. You can basically assume that your child's impact on the environment will largely replicate your own, or what yours hypothetically would be over the lifetime of that child. At the very least, then, you will have increased your imprint by half (since you will share the responsibility for conceiving the child with your partner). But because that child might well have further children, who may have further children in turn, that imprint is likely to be much larger still. Under what they call the constant scenario—the assumption that individual greenhouse gas emission rates of the parents will continue indefinitely for their children—Paul Murtaugh and Michael Schlax, in a paper published in 2005, estimate that an American woman (on whom they focus, rather than a man, for technically statistical reasons) who drives a more fuel-efficient car, reduces the number of miles she drives each week, installs energy-efficient windows, uses low-energy light bulbs, installs an energy-efficient refrigerator, and recycles will over her lifetime, using the emissions averages of that year, keep about 486 metric tons of carbon dioxide from entering the atmosphere, but a woman who reduces her offspring by one child will over her lifetime save 9,441 tons. If emission rates rise or fall over the course of the child's life, the picture changes dramatically. But this estimate fairly represents the ethical choice facing a potential parent today. It's worth emphasizing what these researchers have found: an American woman who has two children will add "nearly 40 times" as much carbon dioxide to the atmosphere as she might save through her eco-friendly activities.[135]

All this follows from a fairly straightforward look at an individual's environmental footprint. But if we consider as well the fact that humanity as a whole now vastly exceeds this planet's carrying capacity, the case for not reproducing becomes even stronger. As I argued in an earlier chapter, if we manage to shift to renewable energy sources on a scale vast enough to make a difference, we will greatly expand the presence of our energy infrastructure across the land and sea. As a result, that action will make the sheer overabundance of human beings more visible to us than ever before. Reproducing our current numbers into the foreseeable future—even with zero population growth—simply hands this pattern of devastation down to future generations, who will have many fewer options to solve it well. If we want the life forms of this planet to thrive, we have to reduce our numbers as soon as we can. The only humane way to do so is to reduce our birth rate.

The implications are unmistakable: a person who wishes to forestall severe climate change *should not bear children*. No doubt saying so violates one of the strongest taboos in our culture. But for that very reason, it is all the more necessary to speak the unspeakable, speak it repeatedly, and speak it *now*. If we are to have the slightest chance to reduce the damage our culture causes the environment, we should begin with the activity that causes the most harm, and without question, this is the one.

I freely concede that simply thinking this thought is enormously painful to most of us. The idea that we should not bear and raise children cuts against a host of assumptions we may have about "normal" life. Although American society no longer so openly disapproves of people who remain single or childless and is becoming increasingly tolerant of nontraditional families of all kinds, including those headed by gay and lesbian couples, people still speak about "getting married and starting a family," as if the people in question do not constitute a family in their own right but "start" a family only when they bear or adopt a child. Our society also tends to assume that starting a family in this sense is a sign of maturity, an indication that a participating adult is becoming responsible. Moreover, we also take for granted that parents are somehow more nurturing and unselfish than childless adults, more likely to care about the coming generations, and thus more responsive to humanity's fate. All these assumptions are reinforced by the desire many people feel to bear children. That desire can feel so natural, so self-evident, that they might assume other people feel it as well, and that people in general should have the right to satisfy this desire. Needless to say, that desire is often so profound it can define an entire life.

The environmental consequences of childbearing, however, should inspire us to reverse these assumptions, however difficult and nearly unthinkable it may seem to do so. We need to define our notion of family anew so that the very phrase "start a family" takes on a new meaning. We should contemplate the possibility that *not* reproducing is more nurturing and responsible, more loving to others and to humanity, than bringing more people into the world. Clearly, we should not simply assume that childless people are automatically responsible in these ways: leaping to that conclusion is simply not justified. But we should not only respect but *admire* the decision to remain childless if it is part of an individual's broader effort to reduce harm to the environment. The corollary is true as well: we should seriously consider the possibility that having children is *not* responsible. No matter how strong a person's desire to have children might be, we should not assume that it automatically overrides every other concern.

The absence of any serious discussion about these matters permeates our culture. The leading political and economic theories in the Anglo-American tradition, for example, start from the notion of rational self-interest, an assumption that takes for granted the adult status of all parties. But that sort of analysis does not explain what brings individuals into the world in the first place. Apparently the principle of self-interest includes one's decisions about reproduction, but that possibility is not discussed explicitly in the theories of, say, John Locke or Adam Smith, the people whose ideas shape the American traditions we adhere to even today. Perhaps a child is simply an extension of oneself until coming of age, when she presumably turns into a rational adult (but then Locke and Smith also don't seriously consider the possibility that *women* are rational adults as well). Such theories never examine whether a rational adult should have children in the first place, nor do they ponder how childbearing figures into the consequences of self-interest for society as a whole. This question constitutes an immense blind spot throughout the modern tradition of political and economic reflection.

The consequences are immediately clear in the rather muddled state of our constitutional law. Since *Roe v. Wade*, Americans have typically invoked the right of privacy to defend a woman's decision to have an abortion or attacked that right in the name of the unborn child's right to life. Typically, then, we end up putting one version of individual rights against another. Yet the terms of that debate mask a more honest discussion about whether the principle of equality between men and women should override the woman's traditional role as the bearer of children—whether the principles of modern individualism, now finally applied to women, are more important than the ancient endorsement of reproduction. In this debate as it is currently conducted, the modern notion of individual liberty confronts traditional norms, as it has so often over the past three centuries.

But in our time, that debate is hopelessly outdated. Given the immense pressure of climate change on us all, the abstract liberty of the individual—male or female, born or unborn—cannot take precedence over the basic question as to whether humanity as a whole has any further right to use the Earth for its own purposes. The answer to that question is simple: we do not. But if we as a species have no such right, neither do we as individuals. In that case, the liberty we take for granted—to reproduce or not, more or less as we please—no longer applies. It follows as well that elevating the life of the unborn child over all other considerations is utterly blind to its consequences for the life of the species, as well as the life of the biosphere as a whole. For sexually active people, a "pro-life" position is actually "pro-death," for it favors human reproduction at the expense of all other forms of life, and, in the end, at the expense of human life as well. Neither the "pro-choice" nor the "pro-life" viewpoint can be very persuasive today.

The same blind spot appears as well in discussions about the falling birth rate in the developed world. Demographers, policymakers, and journalists often ponder what it means that women in the industrialized nations seldom bear children at a rate that would replace the current population. That fact leads to questions about how to support increasingly elderly populations on the labor of a diminishing workforce, for example, or how to provide new incentives for women to reproduce. But few participants in this discussion mention that a lower birth rate is a *good* thing ecologically speaking, that it may be a sign that some people are awake to the challenges facing us and are acting responsibly.[136]

This blind spot in our thinking shows up even in contexts that supposedly encourage environmental responsibility. Websites that help you calculate your carbon footprint, for example, include all kinds of details about the gas mileage on your car, how much you travel by air, or how much energy you use to heat your home, but they seldom ask whether or not you have decided to bear children. That concern evidently just doesn't figure into our thinking, even in eco-friendly circles. The neglect of this question permeates our culture from start to finish, from top to bottom. Either we're afraid to raise the question or it just doesn't occur to us.

What will happen when we break this silence is a good question. Although it will no doubt be difficult to do so, we desperately need to reexamine all of our attitudes and theories in this new light, to start *thinking* about our reproductive assumptions for a change. Here, as in so many other areas, facing the consequences of climate change really does require us to revise the most basic elements of our common culture. It's impossible to know in advance what new policies, theories, legal interpretations, or actions that endeavor could lead to. The most fundamental working hypothesis to guide us throughout that work, I would suggest, is that *not* reproducing is the most ethical choice we can make today. The burden of proof, the challenge of providing a clear and thorough justification, falls on those who would take the opposite course of action.

Because this is an immense topic, one that requires an extended and focused public debate, I can only touch on a few themes in this brief discussion. Perhaps the most useful thing I can do here is raise a number of the most likely objections to this argument and reply to each in turn.

The first objection might well be the most basic of all. Let's say a loving couple shares a strong desire to bear children; why should they not satisfy that desire? But can our desire on its own justify a decision that may cause environmental harm? Suppose someone with excellent taste and a large income wishes to build a huge, beautiful, and inspiring home—one that will have an enormous carbon footprint. Do we think that's ethically acceptable? No doubt the wish to bear children is more defensible. But in the end, unless the potential parents have something more than desire to go on, they still haven't explained why their plans are ethical.

Evangelical Christians and conservative Jews (among others) might insist that God himself has commanded us to reproduce. According to the book of Genesis, as soon as God created human beings, he told them, "Be fruitful and multiply, and fill the earth and subdue it; and have dominion over the fish of the sea and over the birds of the air and over every living thing that moves upon the earth."[137] In effect, God wanted human beings to participate in the process of creation, to extend his founding act over generations of procreation. So far, humanity has fulfilled this command very well indeed: have we not filled the earth and subdued everything that moves? In fact, haven't we already *exceeded* the earth's capacity to sustain us? Aren't we in the process of subduing even the climate itself? Should we go right ahead and help *kill* the Earth? Doing so would hardly keep faith with a command that sees us as part of the creation, not the agency of its destruction. To reproduce unthinkingly would hardly do justice to the divine plan.

Some might object that if everyone chose not to reproduce, before long the human race would come to an end. They have a good point. If this practice became truly universal across all humanity and were sustained long enough, it would indeed result in the end of the species. If the ideas outlined here became widespread enough to influence a good part of the human race, we'd obviously need to collaborate intelligently as a species to reduce our numbers while still guaranteeing our survival. Anyone who feels responsibility for the fate of all life must greet the prospect of such a development with joy, not dismay; if we as the human race proved ourselves capable of cooperating for such a purpose, we would at last demonstrate that we had grasped our place within the network of life and were capable of acting accordingly. Until then, individual actions will have a very positive impact in their own right. The point is not to end reproduction forever for the entire species, but to make a difference in humanity's impact on the biosphere now, at a moment when it really counts.

Some people raise a much more mundane objection, arguing that they would like to have kids who could take care of them in old age. One problem with this idea, of course, is that parents cannot know whether their children will live nearby or have the time or inclination to help out. Moreover, having kids for personal convenience scarcely takes into account the situation of other people, much less the good of the biosphere; it places one's own potential interest above the survival of all others. Finally, and most crucially, it takes for granted that there will be a future to worry about in the first place. If everybody reproduces in this way and continues to live this kind of life, the last thing to worry about is how we'll do after we retire; at that rate, having kids will help *destroy* our chances for a peaceful old age. These reflections apply as well to the argument often cited in the United States that we need to raise children so they can pay into Social Security and Medicare. But why would we worry about one version of the future—the financial support for us after we retire—if we will not trouble ourselves about another—the consequences of climate change? It would be far more ethical for us to put the interest of all humanity above our own, not have children, and save up enough money over our working years to support ourselves in old age. If we're truly self-interested, let's do the work ourselves. And if we're looking for personal support as we age, we should build an active, loving community of friends and neighbors where we live.

Ecologically minded parents might insist that *their* kids will grow up as good citizens of the Earth. *They* will use less energy than others, recycle carefully, and do all they can to support the environmental cause. All that may be true, but even responsible adults in the United States still cause more damage to the climate than nearly anyone elsewhere in the world, far more than the biosphere can sustain. Even when we are doing our best, we do very badly indeed. Adding more people to the equation won't help.

But these parents have one more idea. What if one of their kids turns out to be a genius who comes up with the technological invention that will save the world? But this rationale falls apart almost immediately. The very notion that we should wait for such an invention is part of the problem in the first place; it encourages us to keep going with business as usual while engineers come up with clever schemes to get us out of our dilemma. That plan will get us nowhere fast. Moreover, any child born in 2015 won't be ready to reveal her invention until, say, 2040—far too late to prevent serious harm to the planet.

Some potential parents might ask whether it would be ethical not to reproduce but to adopt children. Wouldn't it be fine to raise children that others brought into the world? Judging by basic principles, it might be. But because American couples are increasingly adopting children from around the world, where the average carbon footprint is relatively small, in effect they are greatly increasing the lifetime impact of those children on the environment. Whether we have given birth to children is less crucial than whether we replicate our destructive habits in another generation.

Parents who already have little ones might object that this argument ultimately accuses them of doing wrong. But this argument does not lead to such a conclusion at all. Most people in our society have never given this viewpoint a moment's thought; accordingly, we can't assume that parents have *deliberately* chosen to put their wishes above the future good of humanity. People are not to be accused if they have transgressed a principle of which they are unaware. Once they have heard this argument, however, we might wish to hold them accountable, at least to justify their eventual decision. But doing so is not the same as making parents feel guilty for loving children they already have.

Others might comment that choosing not to reproduce reveals a subtle hatred of humankind, a sneaky sort of misanthropy. In fact, the opposite is true: those who choose not to reproduce place the future interests of humanity—as well as the Earth's living systems—above selfish considerations. Doesn't that sound more like the *love* of humanity? But it's worth pausing to take this objection literally. If we love dogs, for example, does it follow that we'd like to see, say, eight billion dogs roaming the planet? If not, does that make us dog haters? Not likely.

The same response goes for the idea that this ethical position somehow reflects a hatred of children. This objection is no more convincing than the previous one, but it has the great merit of bringing a basic question to our attention. If we are quite sure that the biosphere will be in worse shape over the coming decades, that our society will suffer enormously as a result, and that those in the next generation will face increasing difficulties as time goes by, is it more responsible to bring children into the world to face all these challenges—or not to do so? *Is it an act of love to choose a difficult life for those who have no say in the matter?* Is it better to give kids the gift of life, whatever difficulties they might face, or to protect the unborn from the potential disaster to come? Needless to say, we should bless the life of children who are already with us. We should do everything we can to help our young descendants thrive. But choosing a tough life for people *before* bringing them into the world is an entirely different matter. In fact, it is far more an act of true love for the unborn *not* to force them to accept a difficult life.

What about those who love children but choose not to bear their own? They have many opportunities they might pursue: they can work in professions that allow them to care for infants, the young and growing, the curious and learning, training them to live and thrive responsibly. These adults can heal kids when they are sick, coach them as they play, and include them in a range of adult activities where doing so might be fruitful for all.

No doubt people might object in further ways, but in the end nearly all these replies boil down to the first one I discussed above. I'd like to return to it and ponder a somewhat more aggressive version, one that might reveal the stakes of this discussion even more clearly.

Very well, someone might say. Not reproducing may make sense for most people, but my partner and I are well-educated, well-off, and capable of protecting our children from whatever happens down the road. Why shouldn't we have children if we want to? (Or, conversely, someone might say: My partner and I are quite poor, and the only profound joy in our lives is the opportunity to have children and raise them. Why deny us this joy if we have so little else?) The answer, as I have suggested above, is that our lives do not simply belong to us; whatever we do contributes to our *common* problem or its solution. To think we can do what we like while the rest of the world collapses is to see ourselves as a sublime exception, figures of total privilege. This is at once naive—since no one is truly such an exception—and hopelessly selfish.

Such a response ultimately reveals a willingness to sacrifice the wellbeing of others for the sake of one's children. That attitude is just beneath the surface in much of American life. Occasionally American-produced movies capitalize on this feeling, inviting audiences to adopt as their own the belief that defending one's children justifies very threatening behavior. In *Flightplan*, starring Jodie Foster, a woman does everything she can think of—including releasing the oxygen masks and turning off the lights in the passenger section of the aircraft on which she is flying—to distract the crew while she looks for her lost child. *John Q*, starring Denzel Washington, tells the story of an African American father who invades a hospital demanding an operation for his son. Neither of these movies descends into celebrating aggression for its own sake, but each champions the notion that it is acceptable to frighten or threaten other people for the purpose of caring for one's child.[138]

These movies deserve credit for telling a certain truth about American culture. They cast light on the blind spot in our political thinking, showing that we don't give much credence to the notion that we all benefit from arrangements of mutual self-interest. Self-interest turns into something much uglier when children are at stake: it turns out that the child is so sacred that his or her well-being is more important than the interests of others. In comparison to the child, social relations are so much chaff to be tossed into the wind. In daily life, this attitude is expressed in the willingness of many of us to buy the biggest, baddest SUV we can find to protect our kids from harm. If we get in a crash, it's the *other* guy who will suffer, not us. We may even imagine that we show love for our kids precisely through this willingness to make sure that other people will die first. But because in doing so we are potentially harming others to protect those *we* choose to bring into the world, our attitude reveals that we will give up others for the sake of our own priorities. What's worse, the logic of this sort of selfishness collapses very quickly. When the SUV's emissions help destroy the biosphere, it's not just the *other* guy's biosphere that will go. What then? We may *think* we're looking out for our own interests by driving the biggest, safest vehicle on the roads, but in the long run we're destroying our own lives and those of our children, too. Ultimately, this sort of attitude reveals that strange paradox: a *self-destructive* selfishness. When we insist on our abstract liberties, on our right to destroy, we are also choosing to destroy ourselves and those we love.

This general attitude has taken on a kinder, gentler form in Cormac McCarthy's novel *The Road*.[139] This novel suggests that it is a praiseworthy endeavor for a father to guide his son through a world bereft of any form of life and devoid of any kind of food except for canned goods stored here or there in ruined dwellings—or murdered human beings. Such a world promises no future for any living thing, yet we are asked to admire the effort of raising the son and passing him down to a nonexistent future. Instead of suggesting that it might be acceptable to torch the world for the sake of the son, as violent selfishness would have it, this story suggests that even if the world has already been torched, we should still bear and raise children. But because the world of that novel could never exist—for without other living things, human beings would have little oxygen to breathe—it is finally a metaphor for *our* world, and thus encourages *us* to think that even if the planet is dying, we should bear children just as before. In the world of the novel, such a belief is delusional: it is truly horrific to usher a child into a dead future. In our world, that belief is far more harmful, for it allows us to comfort ourselves that even if we are contributing to the planet's decline, we are still good people—because we are bearing and caring for children. But in that case, having kids helps us avoid facing the real ethics of our choices. In its gentler way, *The Road* also reinforces a mode of ecocidal parenting.

Since we Americans now live in a society everywhere shaped by these ideas, since our destructive impact on the planet's life continues to grow apace even after we have become aware of that fact, we who wish to preserve a future must consider adopting the *opposite* point of view—one that places the interest of the biosphere above our own wishes. Instead of raising a beloved child in a ruined world, our better option is to raise no children at all—on a thriving, beautiful, and beloved planet. It might sound like the basis for that choice is a joyous selflessness, an utterly altruistic commitment to the life of others. No doubt about it, this choice is altruistic. But only this choice preserves a future for ourselves as well. Only in a thriving biosphere can we live out our lives in the way we might imagine. Choosing otherwise might be selfish, but it would also be suicidal—or at least would kill the future.

I admit that it is more than a little paradoxical *not* to have children at the same time as choosing for the future. After all, children have always served as the very emblems of the future, the embodiment of what is coming next, the carrier of what will be. Nevertheless, a choice not to have children today will make it possible for that understanding of children to return someday. Once we actually transform our culture so that we do not eat the Earth as a matter of course, *then* we can restore the ancient alignment between sustainability and reproduction. A choice not to reproduce would make that eventual alignment possible.

What would be the cultural consequences if many Americans took this ethics as their own? It goes without saying that it would transform our basic assumptions and practices almost across the board. We'd end up living through a whole array of odd demographic realities that we would need to consider carefully in advance. For many people, it would be hard to explain what all the effort is for—all that hard work—if they can't come home to their kids. The children are the whole point; they, and the home of which they are a part, constitute a relief from professional stresses, a refuge from the rat race, a haven in a heartless world, and a hope for something more. If that is the case, they already help us endure what we see as unendurable or at least as not terribly delightful. But is it really impossible to think otherwise, to stop splitting our lives between the difficulty of labor and the joy of family? Can't we reimagine our working day so that it, too, can become a source of pleasure and joy? Must the experience of family be private, enclosed, aloof? Or can it be found in collaboration with other adults, in less private settings, and in common endeavors that also speak of a hope for something more?

Similar questions arise around our attitudes toward the communities in which we live. If you ask people why they live where they do, in many cases they'll explain that their town isn't all that interesting or thriving, but it's a nice place to raise kids. This answer says a lot: it suggests that people are capable of putting up with the absence of urban pleasures they might desire so they can raise their children in peace. But if they did not have kids and thus had to face the reality of life in the town more squarely, what might they ask it to become? What kinds of events and activities might they create? How might the entire community be transformed?

Some of our basic attitudes suggest that we merely tolerate our workplaces and communities and give our real love to our partners and children. What would happen if we stopped segregating our lives in this way and expanded the range of our affections? What if we treated *all* the arenas in which we live with love and care, seeing those domains as the carriers of our future, the embodiment of our hopes? What if we extended this care to our local ecosystems, and beyond that to the biosphere itself? Why don't we already do so today?

Taking the climate crisis seriously forces us to rethink our most fundamental attitudes. It asks us to contemplate what might seem impossible—to question the core loyalties by which we live. If we hesitate to go that far, to question that deeply, we show that we finally do not care all that much about the future of the biosphere or indeed about how our own lives may go a couple decades from now. We demonstrate that we think our lives are really about us and are indifferent to the ruins of the future. Most of us would not choose to live that way—but we may not really wish to cast off that attitude entirely, either. Climate change forces us to choose; its potential severity has the power to concentrate our minds. When it does so, it may inspire us to rethink entire areas of our culture, reexamine what family means, imagine a new relationship to place, reinvent our jobs and communities, and sustain a new relation to the biosphere. But how could it be otherwise? If the very context of our lives is at stake, to do it justice demands that we consider reinventing it all, from top to bottom. If we are to begin the task of owning the disaster we are already causing and make reparation to the biosphere as a result, we can do nothing less.

Notes

135. Paul A. Murtaugh and Michael G. Schlax, "Reproduction and the Carbon Legacies of Individuals," *Global Environmental Change* volume 19, issue 1 (February 2009): 14–20, available as a pdf document online. The quoted statement appears on page 18. The authors argue that working through lineages including both men and women is "computationally prohibitive," but that because "the number of genetic units (of both sexes) attributable to an ancestral female is, on average, simply the number of females comprising an unbroken lineage of females descending from the ancestor," their focus on female lineages will allow them to "obtain an estimate of the total number of person years, male and female, that are traceable to the ancestral female" (16).

136. A key exception is Bill McKibben, who discusses the ecological consequences of reproduction in *Maybe One: A Case for Smaller Families* (New York: Penguin, 1998). As the book's title suggests, McKibben gently suggests that parents should consider having one child; he does not seriously discuss the possibility of having none.

137. Genesis 1:28. *The Holy Bible: Revised Standard Edition* (New York: Thomas Nelson & Sons, Old Testament portions copyright 1952).

138. *Flightplan*, directed by Robert Schwentke, 2005; *John Q*, directed by John Cassavetes, 2002. *John Q* goes out of its way to play fair: the father removes all bullets from his weapon in advance, ends up winning the support of all his "hostages," shows he is willing to kill himself if need be to supply the heart for his child, becomes a heroic figure for the crowd—and television audience—witnessing the ordeal, and is ultimately sentenced to serve time

for what he did. The harm he has done seems to disappear under all these considerations. Yet the fact remains he does resort to the apparent threat of violence to save his son—and the movie assumes that almost everyone will sympathize with him.

139. Cormac McCarthy, *The Road* (New York: Vintage, 2006).

Chapter 12

The God of the Whirlwind

Taking our current situation seriously requires us to reexamine our political and ethical understanding of our ordinary practices, our life decisions, our relationship to others and to all earthly life. It asks us to reimagine what we do and who we are across the entire range of our experience. As I have suggested, it even requires us to own disaster—to put the enormous environmental crisis to our own account, take responsibility for what is unfolding, and to begin the endless task of making reparation.

But as I have suggested, in taking this last, most difficult step, we must also affirm our place within the planetary and biological history that produced us. To assume responsibility for the disaster we are causing, we must also affirm much else: the debt we owe to the forces that created us, to the web of life of which we are a part.

As a result, the ethical stance I outlined above speaks also of an unreserved affirmation of those forces that ultimately reach far beyond ourselves—those aspects of the natural world that are so vast, wild, and violent that we can only submit to them in genuine humility. That affirmation, however, stretches well beyond a discussion of ethics per se; it raises questions that deserve their own treatment, challenging us with dilemmas we can understand only if we pause to consider them in their own right. If we are to absorb the full impact of climate change on our humanity, then, we need to move beyond the framework of political and ethical action and contemplate another set of questions, traditionally addressed through mythology, theology, and philosophy: What forces ultimately constitute our world, and how should we respond to them? Now that we live in a world without guarantees, possibly without a future that is livable to us, what stories should we tell about our condition? What is our place in the cosmos?

In this domain, as in all others, the near inevitability of severe climate change alters everything. The religious reassurances that once shaped many of the world's cultures no longer hold true—or at least not in the same way as before. In fact, the discoveries of climatology over the past two or three decades only sharpen what had already become a strong sense of the vulnerability of the world.

Over the course of the eighteenth century, geologists learned that Earth's history was immensely vaster than they previously suspected, that ordinary physical processes, extended over many millions of years, had given the planet's surface its present shape. Confronted with this "dark abyss of time," they could hardly encourage their audience to sustain a familiar sense of humanity's place within the history of life.[140] Cataclysms and mass extinctions, it turned out, were ordinary events; as I will discuss below, the guarantees of the rainbow covenant, in which God promises Noah never again to unleash a flood to destroy his creation, were put into question. Furthermore, since so much of the geological record bore no trace of humanity, it was no longer clear that the creation centered around human beings. This sense of human vulnerability strengthened further over the course of the nineteenth century, especially as Charles Darwin and Alfred Russel Wallace found a core mechanism—natural selection— that could drive the evolution of species and extended that mechanism to human beings. The twentieth century added many new elements to this emerging picture, notably when scientists proposed a theory of plate tectonics according to which the continents had broken away from a single primordial landmass and drifted to their present positions. The ground beneath our feet, it turned out, also moved, floating on the molten heat within the Earth.

But that is not all: in more recent decades, scientists have learned how regularly the Earth's climate has flipped back and forth between relative cold and heat, creating the conditions for ice ages and for temperate eras. At times, the Earth has been almost entirely covered in ice and snow and at others has sustained warm temperatures from pole to pole. The changes in the Earth's distance from the sun or in the tilt of its axis have routinely generated alterations in the planet's dynamic systems, producing positive feedback loops that over time cause a general warming or cooling of the atmosphere.[141] As a result of all these waves of scientific inquiry, we now have a broad sense of how Earth's dynamic systems are in constant transformation. The planet itself wobbles; the continents move; cataclysms come and go; the species appear and disappear; and the ice visits and departs. Everything ceaselessly changes.

The fact that some version of our species has lived on this planet through so many changes may give us hope. After all, if we've survived several previous big swings in the climate, it seems likely we will endure the challenges to come in the next several centuries. An enormous resilience is our ancient inheritance; it may have arisen precisely so that we could cope with very rapid, climate-driven shifts to our ecosystems.[142] We may have evolved to handle challenges something like those we'll face in the coming era. Because of our intelligence and extreme adaptability, we're a tough species to eradicate. That thought, of course, can hardly comfort us as individuals; the species will endure even if virtually all of us are wiped out, even if most people—and most societies—disappear.

But even these reflections scarcely do justice to the full import of what we face. Our evolutionary history is hardly the proper context for interpreting the present moment, for this time, rather than merely adapting to the climate change we face, we will have *caused* it. As I suggested earlier, that fact shows how little we respect the web of life from which we arose. Neither God nor Darwin, neither creation nor evolution, put us where we are today; we got here because we violated the limits imposed on us by the divine command or by our place within living systems. Thus it is entirely fitting that those who wish to honor the divine command, including Jewish, Catholic, and evangelical Christian leaders, call on us to do all we can not to contribute to climate change and to act with compassion for those who will be most harmed by it.[143]

Our actions to this point, however, have placed us in an unprecedented position. Over two decades ago, Bill McKibben rightly commented that because of climate change, we were no longer living in what we could call nature, in a world in which some ecosystems could thrive without a human imprint. Climate change shapes the conditions of life for all creatures, which cease as a result to be fully wild. In effect, he suggested, we are witnessing the end of nature.[144] Geologists designate this fact in their own way: in their view, we are moving from the Holocene into the Anthropocene, the era in which human activities determine the context of existence for all living things.

But if nature ends in one sense, it endures in another. Although we may erase a nature free of human influence, nature nevertheless persists in altered form. Our activities may ultimately force massive changes to the planet's dynamic systems, but those systems, accepting the new conditions of the biosphere, will go on doing their work. In its new mode, nature may no longer be "wild" in the sense that it is free of human interference. But because it is far outside our control, threatens the built environment in which we live, and indeed promises to shatter the cultural continuity we take for granted, it may be even *more* "wild" in the rather different sense that it is now excessively powerful and seemingly hostile to human concerns. We may ultimately have given nature a new guise as something even less hospitable to us than before, something far more capable of reminding us of our weakness and vulnerability.

Most of the time our discussions of climate change ask how we might endure in this new world by focusing on practical, technological, and ethical questions. But as I suggested a moment ago, we do not live only on those levels. We cannot grasp our situation through a bare rendition of the facts; we need stories, figures, parables—in short, myths—to make our reality come fully alive to us, to make it possible for us to do justice to our moment. The point, of course, would not be to replicate the stories by which we once lived; the myths we need today might well contest, undercut, or even destroy those familiar tales, revealing why they are no longer credible, no longer in some sense true. What stories might we tell to interpret our place in this wild domain?

One story could be the history of a mind-boggling error whereby we ruined the Earth's living systems for all creatures. This would be a fairly implausible new story of a fall, in which we once again commit a great crime and are cast out of Eden—this time, the garden of the planet's living systems over the last ten millennia.

Or we might prefer to tell the story as a tragedy. In one version, we could narrate how the technologies that enabled us to liberate ourselves from an ancient scarcity also proved to be our undoing. In a more sweeping rendition, we would see our actions as another episode in a much longer history of human ineptitude, achieving a tragic knowledge of the self-defeating, obtuse, and pathological dimensions of humanity. In either form, that story would allow us to affirm our history in the midst of defeat, for rather than merely denouncing our actions, it would find moral complexity in them, discerning a certain dignity even in our capacity to recognize that hubris.[145]

We could also move to a more visceral mode of affirmation; by telling this story as dark comedy, we could put to test the power to laugh at our radical folly. In doing so, we might learn how to endure the world we created through our great crime, to accept the unacceptable, to explode its pain through a burst of laughter. Through these and other tales we could carry out the gesture I mentioned near the end of chapter nine, daring to affirm the nullity that we are.

Writing at an earlier but comparable moment in the wake of Hiroshima and Auschwitz, Samuel Beckett explored a version of this emotional terrain. In *Waiting for Godot* and *Endgame*, he gave us masterworks of bleak farce, of hopeless slapstick, where nearly every sign of life has departed, divine promises are never to be fulfilled, and the routines of everyday life expand to fill an utterly pointless passage of time.[146] In these plays, comedy verges on making the human condition tolerable not by enabling us to affirm it outright, but far more subtly to make our peace with it by affirming it *as laughable*. Our situation may be hopelessly ridiculous, but it is one we can recognize, reenact, and through comedy, accept as our own. In these plays, we can glimpse laughter's ability to reconcile us with nearly every sort of folly and degradation.

But these plays also go a step further, showing us characters who can no longer laugh, who are no longer moved by their stories, who have lost their pleasure in rehearsing their condition; they give us moments when even comedy fails. If laughter in some sense affirms life and helps us go on, the radical absence of a future (especially visible in *Endgame*) threatens laughter itself, inspiring characters—and members of the audience—to ponder, in the midst of laughing, whether they should laugh at all. These plays put us on the edge of a condition *after* comedy, one that even its subtle stratagems cannot redeem.

What would a similar take on our present dilemma look like? Perhaps the best attempt so far is T.C. Boyle's *A Friend of the Earth*, which features a group of ecological activists whose attempts to save the world have gone astray and whose excessive love or anger wreaks havoc on their own lives.[147] Placed partly in the past, in the era of 1980's eco-terrorism, and partly in the future, when severe climate change has set in for good, the book acknowledges the attempt to bring about political transformation more openly than Beckett does but renders it comically, as if even activism is ludicrous. We could object that treating activism in this way comes close to authorizing passivity and indifference, but instead, as the novel looks back on those efforts from a defeated future, it makes comedy the antidote to a potentially overriding sense of political despair, treating even failure as part of a ridiculous and ultimately comic condition. The novel does not shrink from depicting that utter defeat, imagining a world when most large nonhuman animals are extinct or greatly endangered, fiercely intense storms are commonplace, and the forests of the American West have fallen to the earth. Yet because the book is set in a world without ecological hope, it sharpens the perspective of comedy, daring us to laugh precisely at what is irredeemable, to affirm our truly grotesque folly.

The novel focuses on the misadventures of a familiar comic type—an aging, easily enraged, sexually manipulable, often drunk white man who is well-meaning and truly loving but whose decisions almost always go wrong. By centering on this character, Boyle invites us to view the world of the novel through a position of radical error and ineptitude, using the ancient comic strategy of regarding the world from below, from that irrepressibly impulsive, desiring, persistent dimension of us that, no matter how much it might whine and complain, still endures. Here, as so often, comedy might evade a full confrontation with disaster, indulging in a literary stylization of loss, but in doing so it makes loss livable. It demonstrates how human beings might adapt to an impossible world through an entertaining performance that conquers defeat itself through the minor powers of self-mockery and absurdist play. If activism cannot ward off the ruins, laughter can convert them into the material of an art.

But even comedy has its limits. Boyle is less honest than Beckett, for he does not directly stage the possibility that the shtick will get old, that the laughter may ring a bit hollow, that the absurd life it celebrates may not go on. If we are to live in the ruins, we need something more, something beyond all the genres I have mentioned so far—a kind of wild mythology, and perhaps even a mad theology, for the ruins. Tragedy and comedy, in particular, are preoccupied with the task of affirming in retrospect the nullity of human being. But the challenge today is also to acknowledge and in some sense affirm the more intimidating, threatening, even disastrous face of nature. Comprehending the latter theme will no doubt require understanding its significance for us, to keep its impact on human beings in focus as well. Nevertheless, doing so forces us to venture beyond ourselves, to take up once again the ancient myths regarding the stability of the creation itself.

The best strategy to pursue in this regard might be to return to the theme I explored above, the transformation of nature into a force even more wild and implacable than before. What are the mythological overtones to such a shift? At first, the very attempt to interpret nature in these terms might seem impossible; the realities of Earth's systems no longer address us in an unequivocal voice. Thanks to climate change, nature no longer seems mythic to us, anchored in primordial, archaic truths; it is now historical, and like our built environment is a product of human activity. Virtually nothing in our experience now falls outside the realm of human history, thriving in a domain we cannot harm. Accordingly, we might imagine that nature's voice has fallen silent, that the old gods are dead. But as I suggested earlier, nature is not merely submissive to our will; our intervention, in fact, has caused its dynamic forces to become more powerful, less predictable, and thus more openly capable of defying human expectation.

As a result, we find ourselves in unprecedented spiritual terrain. The sacred is no longer what it used to be, but it has not simply disappeared. We might say that, like the climate itself, it has transformed. But how should we interpret that transformation? Should we imagine that divine forces have taken on a new shape and will henceforth reveal themselves to us with particularly terrifying features? No doubt those features will indeed terrify us. But if they do so, these gods are not all that unfamiliar after all. Encountering them, we may discern the return of the dark gods once defeated by the relatively humane divinities that have ruled over us for millennia. In forcing our way into a strange future, we may have revived a forgotten stage of our past.

Let me here take up the language of the central tradition of the west, the tradition that has informed all the Abrahamic religions—Judaism,

Christianity, and Islam. While the mythologies of Greece and Rome told how a given generation of the gods (the Titans, for example) were displaced by another (the Olympians), we seldom imagine that the God of the Abrahamic religions arose within any such sequence. But the early chapters of Genesis describe a sequence of another kind, a transformation in God's attitudes toward his creation. We may be used to the story that God created the world in seven days and blessed his creation outright. But we might forget that before long, in later chapters of that story, he became horrified at human sin and repented of creating humankind at all—and accordingly chose to drown the Earth and nearly all living beings beneath the waters of the flood (see Genesis, chapter 6). The God of creation, it turns out, is also the God of the deluge—one who at times utterly *hates* what he has created. Perhaps this deep ambivalence is intrinsic to omnipotent power: any power that can create can also destroy. But in that case, we are not secure in our status as creatures, for at any time God can blot us out as well. No theology can come to rest on the presence of the creation itself, for the God that brought it into being can annihilate it in a moment.

Thus the key moment in the Genesis story takes place neither at the creation nor the flood but immediately after the floodwaters recede.[148] After leaving the ark, Noah offers a burnt sacrifice to God; in response, God promises never again to destroy the world, vowing that "[w]hile the earth remains, seedtime and harvest, cold and heat, summer and winter, day and night, shall not cease" (8:22) and places a rainbow in the cloud as a "sign of the covenant" between himself and "all flesh that is upon the earth" (9:17).[149] Here, the God who has the continual option to destroy the world renounces doing so forever. Only because of *this* act can his creatures finally have confidence that the creation they know will endure. The most reassuring act is not the creation itself but the divine vow never again to undo it. The core founding moment, in effect, is the rainbow covenant.

What, then, are we to make of the fact that disasters and cataclysms of many kinds have taken place again and again over the history of the Earth? As I mentioned above, modern geological knowledge casts doubt on the rainbow covenant. It suggests that we have always been abandoned to history, living in a world without guarantees. In mythological terms, the world is under the sway of the God of creation *and* the God of the deluge—that ambivalent, dark figure who makes no promises. Nevertheless, we could argue that our sense of this dark God has retreated into a distant past, for it was once superseded by our trust in the kinder, gentler God of the covenant, whose promises seem to have been realized in the relatively stable biosphere of the Holocene. We could, in effect, match up the history of the covenant and of the Earth, construing God's promise as an appropriate sign of the very livable world we have enjoyed over the past ten millennia.

But in that case, our exit from the Holocene into the Anthropocene raises new questions. Now that our own actions will almost inevitably cause far more difficult living conditions, leading to drought, famine, and natural disasters of many kinds, we threaten to carry out the material equivalent of cancelling the covenant all by ourselves and of unleashing again the God of the deluge. Such a possibility is quite relevant in our moment because a countervailing belief in this covenant can inspire us to deny that human beings have any such power and thus to negate the reality of climate change itself. If we believe that God created the world and made the rainbow covenant with all living beings, we have a strong basis for repudiating climate change. Take as an example the statement of John Shimkus, Republican member of Congress from the state of Illinois. Speaking before the House Energy Subcommittee on Energy and Environment in March 2009, Shimkus quoted Genesis 8:22, the verse I cited a moment ago, and continued, "I believe that is the infallible word of God, and that's the way it is going to be for his creation. The earth will end only when God declares its time to be over. Man will not destroy this earth. This earth will not be destroyed by a flood."[150]

Although referring to the rainbow covenant in the midst of discussions of climate change may be unusual, we should take this gesture seriously. The passage on the covenant is a central statement on the viability of creation within the religious and cultural traditions of the West. If we are to understand the mythic resonances of climate change, we simply must grapple with that covenant's implications. Doing so may make us uncomfortable; after all, the rainbow covenant was not conditional on human behavior, for it constituted an outright promise to all creation. The possibility we could undermine the security of the creation, then, challenges divine power, as if we are in the midst of wrenching the ability to destroy the Earth out of God's hands. In his own way, Mr. Shimkus has accurately identified the aspect of climate change that threatens to undercut one version of traditional belief.

We could object that climate change does not undo that covenant; we are merely changing the climate, not destroying it. But if we take the further details of the covenant seriously, we cannot sustain this position. In fact, climate change will destroy "seedtime and harvest" in many places; what we now recognize as winter is likely to retreat ever further toward the poles, leaving more and more of us in a seasonal cycle quite unlike what we knew before—in an oscillation not between "cold and heat," but between warmth and blistering heat. Furthermore, climate change will increase the intensity of atmospheric systems, unleashing much more powerful storms and making destructive floods far more likely. This is not the world guaranteed by the covenant. However impossible it may be to conceive, then, we have dispensed with the relatively kinder God of the covenant and revived that earlier, dark God, opting for a less friendly, more demented divinity—as if, in pagan terms, we have moved from the Olympians back to the Titans. We have embraced a far more difficult fate.

Some might protest that climate change is merely a consequence of human action, another example of how sin corrupts the creation, and that it cannot alter God's power over us. But in the covenant, God takes charge over the future health of the creation; he does not concede to us any power to alter it through the sheer abundance of our sins. Others may object that God is allowing global warming to happen as a judgment on our actions; he promised to sustain the seasons "[w]hile the earth remains," so the warping of the seasons might mean that the earth will not remain, that we are witnessing a slow-motion end of the world, a strange but legitimate version of God's judgment on humankind. But the Bible always attributes the timing and substance of the final judgment to God himself, never suggesting that human beings through their own actions might force that judgment to take place. If God is allowing the end of the world to unfold, he is a mere figurehead, for that judgment is coming down upon us without his needing to do a thing.

These interpretations of the covenant, however, ultimately distract us from how it is being used in the current debate. Mr. Shimkus quotes the key verse and insists on its infallible truth in order to argue against any effort to ward off climate change. It won't happen, so we need do nothing about it. Case closed. The irony is thus quite stark: the more we believe that God guarantees the continuity of Earth's living systems, the less responsibility we take for them and the more we destroy them. Here, a reliance on biblical mythology is actually pernicious, justifying a great transgression against the divine command that we exercise stewardship over the creation.

But Representative Shimkus is not the only person caught in a contradiction. What about a position that *does* insist on stewardship—but also admits that the covenant no longer holds? In that case, what divine injunction are we carrying out if we hold firmly to the notion we must be responsible to all life? We may end up in a dilemma opposite to that of Mr. Shimkus, carrying out our role as stewards of the Earth in the absence of a covenant. We would find ourselves complying with an ethics that has no divine foundation and on an Earth that may not be subject to our control.

How might we resolve this contradiction? We could argue that the absence of that divine foundation actually makes our stewardship necessary; if God is totally in charge of the creation, what could we possibly do to assist him? Our activity *matters* precisely because there is no transcendental guarantee that all will be well. Our ethical orientation would thus arise not from a divine command but from our responsibility to the web of life from which we arose. We could do without God—and without a story of the creation—and still have a strong basis for doing justice to our fellow creatures.

This is the kind of ethical position that arises from a secular and scientific interpretation of our moment. But it does not fully take the measure of the mythic, theological challenge; because it tells no story, it leaves us without a language in which to depict our most fundamental situation. Would it be possible to resolve the contradiction in another way—one that takes seriously the presence of more-than-human forces, whatever they may be?

As it turns out, in looking at this split between the creation and a workable ethics, we are thinking about questions already asked elsewhere in the Bible, particularly in the book of Job. The book of Genesis need not be our only mythic reference in the Jewish and Christian scriptures, for the latter includes many texts and places them all within a complex, creative tension—within a spacious spiritual legacy no single statement, however sophisticated, could ever capture. That diversity of statement, which arises from within a long and varied history, makes available a range of spiritual resources for people who live within varying historical moments of their own, so that the book of Job, for example, might become more relevant to us today than Genesis as we face our own unique challenges. We who are the heirs of this tradition, whether religious or secular, may thus draw on this often neglected rendition of God to understand the face the world may take in the coming decades and in this way to sustain something more than a pragmatic relation to the infinite.

The story of Job is very simple: he is a just man, yet disaster strikes his family and property and he is stricken with boils. Why did God do these things to him? If there is some link between God's rule over the creation and his respect for just action, then Job should not suffer. Yet clearly he does. His friends sit with him and talk to him endlessly, coming up with one explanation or another for his condition, exposing the vanity of all human chatter. In the end, God himself appears to Job in a whirlwind and addresses him, asking who he is to challenge what God does. Was Job present when God laid the foundations of the earth or set bounds for the sea? Can he tame Behemoth or lead Leviathan with a fishhook? Job responds, "I had heard of thee by the hearing of the ear, but now my eye sees thee; therefore I despise myself, and repent in dust and ashes" (42:5-6). Struck with awe at divine might, he gives up any claim to being rewarded for his right action, humbles himself, and repents.

Job is the great biblical text that splits apart the wildness and terror of the creation from any notion of divine justice. God is so powerful, so stunning in what he achieves, that he need not pay any attention to human concerns. We could regard this God as a kind of divine bully, a character very fond of throwing his weight around. Or we could adopt a humbler version of this interpretation, deciding out of an excess of piety not to contradict God in any respect whatsoever, even if we have no idea how to understand him. This latter stance seems to be orthodox, of course, but its hasty submission hides an unstated resentment against the bully and thus surreptitiously agrees with the first, defiant response. But there is a third option: perhaps the creation is so stunning, the beast Leviathan so spectacularly terrifying, that we are genuinely moved, truly transported with awe, and no longer care about our petty concerns. *The creation is so splendid that we renounce our longing to live in an ethical universe in the first place.* At that point, our previous complaints look foolish, and we repent of even raising them in dust and ashes.[151]

This, I think, is the reading of Job that makes most spiritual sense. If we take it seriously, though, it leads us far beyond the story of the creation, flood, and rainbow covenant. For one thing, *this* God doesn't affirm the beauty of a creation that might submit meekly to human control; on the contrary, he celebrates the fire-breathing, iron-hearted, invulnerable monster Leviathan. In the old myths and rituals from which the creation story comes, the heroic divine being produces our world by defeating chaos—or in the Genesis version, that state in which "[t]he earth was without form and void, and darkness was upon the face of the deep" (1:2). The creator God is a tamer of chaos, a dragon slayer, a victor over monsters; what's more, the God of the covenant promises never to release the waters of the deep again, as if to reaffirm the original achievement of his creation. But in Job, God *celebrates* the monstrous. Not only does this God show utter contempt for any covenant with human beings, he points to his creation's terrifying power as the utmost sign of his sovereignty, indicating that the very thing that would violate the covenant is the most divine thing about him. It's not as if this God would unleash the flood because he despises human sin; on the contrary, he is indifferent to human assertion, for in the presence of his transcendental power, any human act has virtually no significance. It would not do, then, to regard him as the God of the deluge; he is even more threatening than that dark being.[152]

It's worth remembering that this God declaims from amidst the whirlwind, as if to make absolutely clear that he is embodied in whatever is most formless, threatening, and terrifying. But this God is *even more terrifying than chaos,* for his ability to defeat chaos and give it organic form in the monster Leviathan shows he is stronger than monstrosity itself. Rather than being a slayer of the formless, this God takes the formless as his form, takes delight in its destructive qualities, and thrusts them in the face of complaining human beings.

Anyone who has encountered *this* God might have a few choice words for Representative Shimkus. This God makes no kind promises; if anything, he authorizes his creation to humble humanity at any time. Under his sway, disasters might indeed be ordinary events, and mass extinctions—and the emergence of all kinds of Leviathan-like creatures—might become a regular part of Earth's history. I would thus suggest that we should take this God as the exact mythological counterpart of the forces that in the view of science have operated over the history of the biosphere; there is in fact little difference between the attitude the God of the whirlwind displays and the implicit tone of those dynamic systems. In our time, the gap between a mythic and a materialist sense of those superhuman forces has virtually disappeared. Both do their work on time scales and with a power far beyond human imagining; both manifest a chaotic inventiveness and casual destructiveness that dwarf our own; and both, having produced humankind, are indifferent to our well-being. This God would worry no more than biodynamic systems about the devastating consequences of climate change; if anything, to speak in mythological terms, he would point them out as further demonstrations of his wild power.

It might be tempting to repudiate this God as a being who takes delight in humiliating us. But if we responded in that way, we would not be true to an important and revelatory dimension of ourselves, a dimension realized in Job's response. We *love* wild creatures; the great predators—lions, cheetahs, tigers, sharks—move us beyond words. We take an astonished delight in the furious power unleashed in tornadoes and hurricanes—in the very forms that the God of Job chooses to clothe himself. When we see such things, we know we are in the presence of something infinitely greater than us, something that does not mind our concerns whatsoever. In such moments, we might even feel an immense relief, knowing that we will never experience the severe boredom and alienation of living within an entirely controlled environment. Our awe tells us that we *seek* transcendence, that we *rebel* against the prospect of absolute human control. We are *grateful* in knowing that Earth's living systems and nonhuman creatures do not follow any moral norms, certainly not our own.[153]

To some degree, then, we share the awe that moved Job to give up his moral claim. Furthermore, as we look forward to the coming decades, we must also recognize that the extraordinary forces that climate change will release around the biosphere will inspire awe in us as well. However devastating such forces will be, however greatly they will harm our societies and our individual lives, we can still recognize in them the signs of a supreme power.

Thus our foray in the domain of myth, which can seem to take us far afield from our core concerns, can in fact sharply transform and perhaps even reverse an initial assessment of our condition. Our awe in the presence of this demented God—or of the implacable, anonymous forces that this figure of God personifies—can enable us to make peace with our cosmic inconsequence, affirm the absence of any moral concern in the universe, and thus embrace the very features of our condition that might otherwise fill us with despair. In a few years, we may, like the characters in Beckett's *Endgame*, be numbed by the apparent futility of our actions and the blank hostility of the natural world. The book of Job teaches us to respond with awe instead—to see Earth's living systems and creatures as inhuman, even monstrous, *and for that reason all the more splendid*. If we move deeper into despair, as it were, and come out the other side, as Job does, we will at last be released into a space much vaster than our petty concerns and be stunned by a great splendor.

This release inevitably alters our sense of nearly all the themes I have discussed so far in this book. The reversal from anguish to awe, bafflement into astonished humility, can take place only if we give up our fierce arrogance, cosmic or otherwise. That renunciation, of course, would inevitably motivate us to give up our habit of subordinating the biosphere to ourselves—to carry out, on a collective and individual level, a truly ecological revolution. A transformative politics is the immediate consequence of that spiritual breakthrough, for it would put into practice the equivalent of Job's repentance.

That awe would also change our response to the consequences of severe climate change. If that change should come, we would know our actions helped trigger it—but we would also recognize that we did not create the forces that it would unleash, forces that would perpetually humble us with their power. Its onset would remind us that the very attempt to slay the dragon, to use the immense resources of the Earth for our convenience, eventually unleashes it, making the Earth less habitable. Our story would thus be much like Job's: by demanding that an indifferent universe comply with our expectations, we would have provoked it to respond with a stunning violence that revealed our true place.

Such a transformation would not put our ethical orientation into doubt but would actually give it new strength and sophistication. We who inevitably lead intentional lives, filled with a sense of responsibility, would learn not to expect that our intentions will also be those of the universe. Giving up our cosmic arrogance, we would also renounce the idea that our moral purposes for the cosmos will come true. If we choose to assume responsibility for the environmental crisis now taking place around the Earth, to own disaster, we would realize that this ethical act does not make us masters of the situation, but the reverse, for it asks us to do justice even when we are powerless to bend natural forces to our will. We would thus act with justice not because the universe will reward us or because everything will work out well for us if we do, but simply because such action is the right thing to do. This renunciation would have a double benefit: it would allow us to give the wildness of the world its due, to pursue a truly ecological ethics of humility in the face of nature, as I argued above, and would also relieve us of the notion that this wildness will necessarily operate in a manner we might expect.[154] We would thus finally live with genuine humility, affirming through our actions our due place in the creation.

Once we learned to live in this way, we might also finally place the great emphasis on the future in its proper sphere—in the world of ordinary prudence, beyond which lies an entirely different level of concern. We can and should still remain attentive to the practical matters of life, including how we emit greenhouse gases and the consequences of doing so for all forms of life. But beyond prudence lie the ultimate questions of who we are and why we are here. Our pragmatic concern for the future cannot eclipse the presence of forces that have always superseded us, that have perpetually revealed our cosmic vulnerability.

Accepting this gap between ethics and the universe, between pragmatic concerns and a sense of the sacred, between prudence and awe, we would also relinquish any myth, any religious teaching, that would attempt to unite the two. The rainbow covenant, however beautiful, can hardly serve as a resource of consolation in our time. But stepping beyond it is no small matter. If we do so, our entire sense of what religion might offer us also changes; in fact, as I have suggested above, the awe that arises out of the book of Job accords almost exactly with a humility in the presence of what a materialist science teaches us to see. It does so not because it finally reconciles faith and reason but because it pushes beyond them, cracking open both religious and secular interpretations of our condition. The God of the whirlwind demands that we give up any confidence that the universe will comply with our expectations. Awe in his presence obliterates those religious institutions that would translate his power into human terms, that would capture his voice in specific doctrines, and that would assure us of our place in an eventual cosmic triumph. By the same token, an encounter with such dark forces reveals there can be no ultimate basis for secular hope, no guarantee that utopia will come to pass, no prospect of historical closure, and no certainty that any political promise will come true. The same awe that destroys our religious arrogance would also demolish our confidence that through reason we will conquer those forces that challenge us. Through the experience of that awe, we would thus give up our confidence that God is a larger version of ourselves or that by speaking in his name we can subdue our fellow creatures—or that with greater effort we might gain a rational and systematic control over every aspect of our fate. We would be in the presence of what defeats us and for that reason takes us beyond ourselves.

By accepting our defeat, we would at last become capable of witnessing the unutterable wildness at the heart of things, the biological exuberance (as Bruce Bagemihl calls it) that proliferates in sheer crazy inventiveness and raucous excess without rhyme or reason, without hope of explanation.[155] That wildness is the sense of the sacred of our time—a version of the sacred that supersedes and devastates nearly every prior experience that went by its name. In this version of the sacred there is no solace for human beings except for our astonishment at its limitless beauty and fragility, the splendor of what arises without origin or end, what flourishes in the dark abyss of time.

Dazzled by that splendor, we can endure nearly anything that may transpire. If we act in time, as we must, we will have withdrawn what would otherwise have been a great crime—and will be blessed with the opportunity to dwell with a beautiful chaos henceforth. If we do not, as we almost inevitably will not, we can greet the coming horrors not only with regret and grief, indignation and sorrow, but also with the sense that what sweeps over us is an even more stunning revelation of the ultimate strangeness of things. In that world, which is almost upon us now, we would do well to endure the floods, embrace the ruins, and let the dragons roam—accepting our due place at last.

Notes

140. On the study of the history of the earth and the notion of the dark abyss of time see Paolo Rossi, *The Dark Abyss of Time: The History of the Earth & the History of Nations from Hooke to Vico* (Chicago: University of Chicago Press, 1984).

141. For readable overviews of Earth's highly dynamic climate systems, see Richard B. Alley, *The Two-Mile Time Machine: Ice Cores, Abrupt Climate Change, and Our Future* (Princeton: Princeton University Press, 2000), and Wallace S. Broecker and Richard Kunzig, *Fixing Climate: What Past Climate Changes Reveal About the Current Threat—and How to Counter It* (New York: Hill and Wang, 2008).

142. See William H. Calvin, *A Brain for All Seasons: Human Evolution & Abrupt Climate Change* (Chicago: University of Chicago Press, 2002).

143. For three examples among many, see "Climate Change," a resolution adopted by the Central Conference of American Rabbis in 2005, http://www.jewcology.com/resource/Central-Conference-of-American-Rabbis-Resolution-Climate-Change-2005; *Global Climate Change: A Plea for Dialogue, Prudence and the Common Good* (Washington, D.C.: United States Conference of Catholic Bishops, 2001), http://www.usccb.org/issues-and-action/human-life-and-dignity/environment/global-climate-change-a-plea-for-dialogue-prudence-and-the-common-good.cfm; and The Evangelical Climate Initiative, "Climate Change: An Evangelical Call to Action," available as a pdf document online.

144. Bill McKibben, *The End of Nature* (New York: Random House, 1989).

145. This tragic knowledge would be akin to that which speaks in Sophocles' tragedy *Antigone*, whose Chorus celebrates our capacity to move forward into no future that will actually happen and to rely on resources that leave us bereft. Here I draw upon a discussion and loose translation of key lines of the play in Jacques Lacan, *The Seminar of Jacques Lacan*, edited by Jacques-Alain

Miller, *Book VII: The Ethics of Psychoanalysis*, translated by Dennis Porter (New York: Norton, 1992), 274–75.

146. Samuel Beckett, *Waiting for Godot: Tragicomedy in Two Acts* (New York: Grove Press, 1954); *Endgame, A Play in One Act, Followed by Act Without Words, A Mime for One Player* (New York: Grove Press, 1958).

147. T. C. Boyle, *A Friend of the Earth* (New York: Viking Penguin, 2000).

148. For my analyses of this subject in another context, see "After the Covenant: Romanticism, Secularization, and Disastrous Transcendence," *European Romantic Review* 21 (2010): 345–61.

149. All biblical quotations in this chapter are taken from *The Holy Bible: Revised Standard Edition* (New York: Thomas Nelson & Sons, Old Testament portions copyright 1952).

150. "'The planet won't be destroyed by global warming because God promised Noah,' says politician bidding to chair U.S. energy committee," *[Daily] Mail Online*, November 10, 2010, http://www.dailymail.co.uk/news/article-1328366/John-Shimkus-Global-warming-wont-destroy-planet-God-promised-Noah.html.

151. For an exemplary reading of Job along these lines, see Stephen Mitchell, Introduction, *The Book of Job*, translated by Mitchell (New York: HarperCollins, 1987), vii–xxxii.

152. As a result, even though Job eventually recovers his property and family, we should not assume that this happy ending arises as a *consequence* of his moment of humility. In fact, the divine repudiation of justice renders that happy ending trivial by comparison.

153. Some readers might ponder whether awe is a version of the aesthetics of the sublime. In his influential account, Immanuel Kant argues that in the sublime we respond to the infinite capacity of the mind, not of nature. The book of Job instead depicts a response to what truly exceeds us. For Kant's discussion, see *Critique of the Power of Judgment*, edited by Paul Guyer, translated by Guyer and Eric Matthews (Cambridge: Cambridge University Press, 2000), 128–159.

154. For a reading of Job that brings out the environmentalist overtones of its attack on anthropocentrism, see Bill McKibben, *The Comforting Whirlwind: God, Job, and the Scale of Creation* (Grand Rapids: Eerdmans, 1994).

155. Bruce Bagemihl, *Biological Exuberance: Animal Homosexuality and Natural Diversity* (New York: St. Martin's Press, 1999); see especially 252–262.

Climate Change Is Real

What is the fundamental situation with climate change? Is it actually happening? Are human beings causing it? How much of climate science is truly reliable enough for us to accept?

This appendix is designed to help readers work through initial questions about climate science. It will rely in part on the background research and in part on common sense. I will organize it in reply to various objections in the hope that it will respond to the kinds of misgivings readers may have, or questions they have heard, about the basics of our situation.

The first objection is this: *It isn't real.* A fully "skeptical" response would suggest, right from the start, that global warming is not happening and that in consequence there is no need for us to worry about the effects of climate change; we can put the entire subject aside and get on with the rest of our lives.

Right on the face of it, this position is wildly implausible. "Skeptics" like to suggest that the science on climate change is unsettled, that there are many grounds for doubt, that the current consensus among researchers is full of holes. But in fact, there is virtually no serious dissent from this consensus among qualified specialists in the relevant fields, specialists who are doing good research recognized as such by their peers.

Because of the controversy about climate change, several scholars have surveyed publications in the field to see how many scientists are raising doubts about the basic consensus, and they repeatedly find that the number of qualified dissidents is extremely small. One recent study examined research by scholars who have published at least twenty articles on the topic and ranked them by the number of articles they have published. They concluded that only one of the top fifty relevant scientists, only three of the top one hundred, and only five of the top two hundred are "unconvinced by the evidence." These findings closely match surveys of expert scientists, 97 percent of whom state that they share the consensus view. Although there are dissidents from that view, they are primarily scientists in other fields, scholars no longer doing active research, journalists, or laymen—in short, people who do not have as clear a knowledge of contemporary research as those centrally in the relevant fields.[156]

A series of similar reviews of the literature have taken place over many years and inevitably point to the same result.[157] Yet a significant portion of the public continues to think that scientists are still in doubt about global warming. Researchers on climate change are of course acutely aware of public attitudes and are highly motivated to correct this false impression. Accordingly, organizations of scientists in several dozen nations and in specialties all across climate change science have issued clear, strong declarations on climate change.[158]

What's more, given the urgency of this research for public policy analysis, the international community has organized the Intergovernmental Panel on Climate Change (IPCC) to summarize contemporary science every few years for public consumption. The scientific portions of each IPCC report are written by scientists and the summary portions by others for the benefit of government officials around the world. Scientists of various persuasions complain that the IPCC reports omit important aspects of their research, whether by ignoring important questions about the consensus view or by refusing to endorse the most alarming recent research.[159] Such complaints are inevitable about any document that strives to capture the most representative views within a vast field of knowledge. It's also inevitable that a document this immense and complex will contain at least minor errors. No human enterprise is infallible. But it does not follow that the entire consensus is therefore incorrect.

"Skeptics" nevertheless insist that the consensus view is unconvincing or false. Some of those who repudiate this view argue that most researchers act from venal motives, from the attempt to comply with the wishes of power-hungry bureaucrats, well-funded public agencies, and other parties offering money, power, and fame to scientists who endorse the mainstream view. Perhaps the most vocal advocate for this argument is the MIT atmospheric scientist Richard Lindzen, who scorns what he calls the fraudulence and hysteria of the consensus.[160] But the notion that researchers benefit from a conspiracy, that they collude with those in power and with each other for mutual benefit, flies in the face of reality. It can hardly explain why scientists in so many different nations around the world, in such a wide variety of disciplines, and with so many contrasting relationships to funding agencies agree on the basic claims. The world of climate change science is far too large and complex for such a conspiracy to work.

This refusal to accept the validity of the overwhelming majority of scientific findings is not really motivated by skepticism but by a distorting, self-flattering tale about the lone wolf who defies The Man, who goes up against The Establishment and beats it at its own game. It calls out to the contrarian streak in all of us, our love of the tiny, heroic minority that exposes the foolishness of the mindless drones in power. This sensational scenario is splashed across the title pages of countless books promising to enlighten readers about the climate change conspiracy, the hysteria and fraud of those supporting the consensus view, or the science "they" don't want you to know. Although ninety-seven of the top one hundred scientists accept the idea of human-caused climate change and only three scientists raise doubts, "skeptics" clearly want us to believe that these three lonely researchers—*and only these three*—are correct. Doing so may be especially foolish, for it's not clear whether those three even agree with each other or are assured that an alternative paradigm is necessarily correct. Their doubts about the dominant view may be motivated by hesitation rather than defiance. Nevertheless, "skeptics" capitalize on that hesitation, hoping that it can justify repudiating the reality of climate change outright, as if the refusal to accept the consensus view is a sufficient reason to commit to an alternative. It's clear that the position of heroic opposition hardly qualifies as a cautious, deliberative, and truly *skeptical* viewpoint: it is actually much more like a risky, defiant, and absolute *faith*—a faith that simply *knows* that climate change cannot be real.

This idealization of the contrarian scientist collapses as soon as one examines the science carefully. For one thing, researchers have been examining climate change with special intensity for the last couple of decades, and the ideas of the dissenters have of course received serious attention during that time. The more carefully researchers look at dissenters' objections and replicate earlier studies to correct for possible errors and flaws, the more accurate and persuasive their findings become and the firmer the basis for the overall consensus. The drift in climate science over time has been toward *greater*, not lesser, conviction. Each succeeding IPCC report indicates as much, for the statements on the likelihood that climate change is caused by human activity have become increasingly confident. The Third Assessment (2001) was still somewhat hesitant: "There is new and stronger evidence that most of the warming observed over the last 50 years is attributable to human activities." The Fourth Assessment (2007), however, was much stronger, stating, "Most of the observed increase in global average temperatures since the mid-20th century is very likely due to the observed increase in anthropogenic greenhouse gas concentrations," with "very likely" elsewhere defined as a likelihood of 90 through 99 percent.[161]

Nevertheless, some "skeptical" observers are unimpressed—or have evolved new ways to contest the consensus. Recently, contrarians have begun to concede that climate change is real and is caused by human beings, but insist that it will do far less damage than is claimed—and that with our current technology we can't address the problem to any serious extent anyway. In effect, they have changed their tactics, pretending to accept the basic science but finding yet another way to dispute its significance. This new style of resistance may be found in a wide range of "skeptical" writings, the best example of which—and one that I will discuss here—may well be a book by Patrick J. Michaels and Robert C. Balling, Jr.

Michaels and Balling hold that the virtual unanimity of the consensus results from the institutional structure of science. The nature of publication in the sciences, they argue, tends to exclude negative findings (those that find no correlation between variables or no statistically significant results), creating an intrinsic bias in favor of any prevalent theory, including the consensus view. Moreover, in their interpretation of the operations of normal scientific research, scientists who adhere to a reigning paradigm tend to exclude alternative views. Finally, following the tenets of "public choice theory," which holds that people tend to choose political and economic options that promise "more" rather than "less," preferring big claims over small ones, they argue that a systematic bias pervades decisions about publication, public funding, and career advancement in the field.[162]

These authors draw on credible ideas about how science operates, but they do not apply those ideas to the climate change controversy with sufficient care. In the context of that controversy, research that undermines the prevailing view would be a *positive* finding, for it *would* establish a statistically significant result. The IPCC incorporates many findings of this kind, taking care to list many instances where research suggests that certain factors may not be causing climate change, or at least not through any clearly demonstrated mechanism (for example, atmospheric aerosols), and that certain consequences one might expect, such as the thinning of ice over the East Antarctic landmass, are not taking place.

Furthermore, researchers do not operate as if they are so many sheep; they take delight when they encounter convincing arguments to the contrary, when they see data that upsets the established view in the field. Scientists are interested in examining the dominant research paradigm, to be sure, but they also know that it can be more important and groundbreaking to create a new one. Most of the major reputations in science are made when a researcher finds something genuinely different from what has gone before, shifting the general orientation of the field in a new direction.

Finally, the claim that the consensus view is not credible is itself an example of "more" rather than "less," for it inevitably gets an outsize share of public attention. To suggest that people would prefer *not* to hear a "skeptical" viewpoint simply ignores the public—and scientific—response, since the public is just as interested in a contrary view as in the consensus. The popularity of "skeptical" books—including the one Michaels and Balling themselves wrote—exemplifies that pattern.

The relatively cogent ideas put forward by Michaels and Balling are more apparently responsible—and thus ultimately more devious—than Lindzen's charge of a climate change conspiracy. But at least Lindzen attempts to explain what might motivate a conspiracy at all: a wish to corner the market on public funding for research. The problem with his theory is that it's difficult to see why scientists would conspire to give the world such consistently bad news. If they might be tempted (according to this theory) by the promise of more grant money, nearly everything else in their lives would tell them to *disprove* the consensus. Do any of us—outside of hardcore disaster freaks—really have incentives to *accept* climate change? We enjoy our lives as they are, and typically we would like to be more wealthy, consume more energy, travel greater distances more often, and contribute to and benefit from steadily increasing economic growth. Nearly everyone from the poorest to the most wealthy likes the idea of an ever increasing abundance—an abundance, of course, that with current technology also implies an increasing emission of greenhouse gases. Who, exactly, wants to bother with rebooting the industrial capacity at the basis of all this abundance? For most of us, climate change is the *last* thing we want to see happen. Our lives would be much easier and more casual, far more relaxed and enjoyable, if we didn't have to worry about it at all. *Nearly all the incentives are on the side of the contrarians.*

Follow the money. If the entire global economic system is on one side, and a handful of granting agencies is (hypothetically) on the other, which one wins? In the face of such an immense tide of longing for more wealth, the conspiracy of a handful of scientists for their own self-interest would soon be swept away. But that's assuming scientists would ever wish to participate in this scheme in the first place. Scientists are people too: their assumptions, training, laboratories, and institutions are fully bound up with the technologies of an advanced industrial society and thus with the very economic systems that are also causing climate change. What they are discovering, in short, is inconvenient to *them* as people, too. In fact, it is *especially* inconvenient to them, for a change in our industrial economies would affect their technical labor quite directly. It's ludicrous to imagine that they are concocting the tale of climate change for personal benefit. On the contrary, they are laying out findings that the entire international community would rather *not* accept. Instead of denouncing them as conspirators, we should see them as reluctantly discovering and investigating something that even *they* might prefer were not true.

Given the enormous incentives for all of us *not* to accept the science of climate change, it would be much more plausible to ponder whether the small group of dissenters is concocting *their* science for personal benefit. Dissenters, after all, have the entire world potentially with them, especially business-oriented groups such as the U.S. Chamber of Commerce, which continually pressures the U.S. Congress to take as mild a course of action as possible, and corporate advocates for the fossil-fuel industry, who of course dread the thought that the world might eventually wean itself of oil. One might expect such groups—which ultimately represent some aspect of consumer preference in which we are all implicated—to put their weight behind denying or dismissing climate change science, and indeed some of them have already done so. As James Hoggan demonstrates in his book, *Climate Cover-Up*, starting around 1991, businesses such as the Western Fuels Association and the National Coal Association funded a massive public relations campaign to distort the science, mislead the public, and delay the adoption of public policies meant to address the problem. In a parallel effort, the Exxon corporation created groups to funnel support to various conservative "think tanks" for similar purposes.[163] This effort had significant results: one study showed that over 92 percent of English-language books expressing skepticism about climate change between 1972 and 2005 were "published by conservative think tanks, written by authors affiliated with those think tanks, or both."[164] A good example is the aforementioned book by Michaels and Balling, which was published by the Cato Institute, the well-known conservative think tank in Washington, D.C. Through these and associated efforts, national business associations and major fossil-fuel corporations successfully persuaded mainstream media outlets that there was a credible debate about climate change, with genuinely accomplished scientists on "both sides" of the question.[165]

In doing so, these groups relied on a sophisticated strategy that they and others had long used in postwar America. In this instance, as in others, they relied on the gap between how scientists and the public see uncertainty. Scientists seek out areas where knowledge is not settled in order to refine and deepen their understanding, whereas the public often confuses that level of uncertainty with doubt on the basic facts themselves. As the historians of science Naomi Oreskes and Erik M. Conway show in their devastating book, *Merchants of Doubt*, since World War II conservative obstructionists have relied on a small number of scientists to exploit this gap and create the perception of doubt again and again. Climate change is only one of the most recent instances in a long sequence of public policy questions in which doctrinaire opponents of action have set aside a solid scientific consensus in the name of a supposed uncertainty. Over the decades, these "merchants of doubt" have suggested there really was no strict link between smoking and a host of health problems, industrial air pollution and the problem of acid rain, or CFCs and the growing ozone hole over the Antarctic. They sought to undermine research showing how an exchange of nuclear warheads could lead to nuclear winter, and in recent years have even suggested that the ban on DDT was a mistake. All these campaigns took roughly the same shape, and all were effective in shaping public opinion: they show that once you suggest that a consensus position is "bad science," prompting responsible scientists to reply and defend research in the field, you create a public debate where there is none to speak of within the scientific community itself, produce the impression of uncertainty, and thus create the basis for inaction. The situation today around climate change is no different.[166]

At one point a few years ago, however, many of the "skeptics" behind these efforts abandoned their intransigence. Frank Luntz, the Republican pollster, spinmeister, and leading participant in a public relations campaign against action on climate change, recanted his "skeptical" views in 2006, and in 2008 or so Exxon stopped funding the group behind most of that campaign's activities.[167] Around the same time, President George W. Bush, who doubted whether human activities are contributing to global warming and whose White House had often doctored statements about climate change by scientists working for the federal government, spoke of the urgent need to take steps to "confront the serious challenge of global climate change" in his 2007 State of the Union message.[168] By this point, the increasing confidence of climate change science was beginning to change even resistant minds.

Despite the tendency of even well-known public figures to recant or soften their resistance to action, a portion of the public remains unconvinced and is likely to stick with that position, no matter what scientists or policy professionals might say. This group, generally associated with the Republican party, is now *permanently* committed to a "skeptical" position, despite the partial change of heart by leaders as prominent as former President Bush. Candidates for office as Republicans are now virtually required to deny the human contributions to climate change if they are to receive the support of voters in that party, whatever the evidence may show. Apparently, "conservatives" are not terribly interested in conserving the planet, even though the preservation of cherished traditions—the core of the conservative position—will be impossible if we don't also conserve the environments we live in.

By now, "skeptical" opinion has very little going for it: the scientific research doesn't support it, its leading spokespeople have been largely discredited, many of its former leaders have recanted or altered their positions, and a vast majority subscribes to the consensus view. Nevertheless, as a result many contrarians hold to their views with greater intransigence. No doubt a certain lazy style of media coverage—which continues to speak of "both sides" of a so-called "debate"—helps sustain this degree of public misperception. But media coverage alone cannot account for that deep resistance. The ferocity of the rhetoric attacking climate change scientists, the hostility to all the suggestions for how to address the problem, and the general intolerance for the concerns of environmental justice suggest that something else is at stake.

For some lay "skeptics," the idea of climate change undermines the belief that God protects and sustains his creation. Acknowledging the consensus view would require giving up a particular version of the theology of creation. In another version of this resistance, Lindzen is reluctant to give up his belief that nature is intrinsically capable of balancing out its own systems.[169] For other "skeptics," the consensus poses a threat to the notion of individual liberty guaranteed by the U.S. Constitution, and the prospect that the government might take action to decrease our emissions smacks to them of an unwarranted intrusion into our private lives. This position amounts to a civil religion in which liberty trumps all other concerns, including the "general welfare" of the Preamble to that very Constitution. People committed to these fundamental positions have ample motive to seize upon the least doubt regarding the consensus to justify their "skepticism." Clearly, what is at stake for them goes much further than a reading of the science. (I discuss these aspects of the debate in depth in chapters four and twelve.)

Linked to these deep sources of resistance is another: a suspicion of the political and cultural power of experts. For good reasons, common people around the world instinctively mistrust the power of highly educated people, whatever their profession, to understand and govern them. The inevitable failure of those in the governing class to reflect on the sources of their authority, as well as the willingness of those in that class to intrude into long established ways, to scoff at folk wisdom and received cultural values, and to demand compliance with the latest form of social improvement, have always been more than a little offensive, even if expert knowledge has often brought real benefits to common people. Popular ambivalence over expertise is deep, for it is intrinsic to the vexed relation between people of different social classes and different ways of seeing the world. Yet this ambivalence is not a feature only of certain social classes; it is present in nearly anyone who secretly defies doctor's orders, follows an unhealthy diet, or finds a purely scientific definition of the world and the human mind limiting.

For all these reasons, the attempt to persuade "skeptics" through the endless rehearsal of scientific findings does not get at their real concerns. The conversation must take up questions about our bedrock values. In the end, a person fully committed to the "skeptical" position may simply resist the authority of science as such or acknowledge it only insofar as it complies with more important loyalties. But those who dismiss such "skepticism" too readily may also miss something essential, for none of us is truly free of the impulse to resort to similarly intransigent, and often unacknowledged, loyalties. We all have abundant reasons to evade the implications of climate change; we all on some level feel a deep surprise and resistance. In reflecting on the intransigence of the "skeptics," then, we would do well to consider our own convenient evasions, our own hesitation to take the transformation in the world seriously.

The outright denial that climate change is taking place is only the most overt form of evading its claims. There is an entire series of increasingly subtle denials of what researchers have found, each of which is instructive. Perhaps the next version of resistance arises in someone who doesn't wish to be so harsh in repudiating the science but doesn't want to accept it, either. Even if the "skeptics" are wrong to be so stubborn, a person might think, they are right to point out how much we still don't know about the Earth's climate. Accordingly, in this view *there is simply too much uncertainty in the science for us to act now.*

Hesitation of this kind is ordinarily a good thing. In fact, the position of so-called "skeptics" betrays the promise of a *genuine* skepticism. A truly cautious dissent from the claim that human beings are causing climate change is beneficial to the public, for it forces researchers to account for their way of gathering and analyzing data much more carefully and to sharpen their research methods as well. Even the research—not the rhetoric—of contrarian scientists such as Lindzen who cultivate the lone wolf persona continues to benefit climate research today, for his challenge to the consensus view helps it sharpen its own account of climate change and prevent it from becoming too uncritical of its findings. Such contrarian viewpoints serve an important public function. Because the news is so bad, and has such a huge potential impact on our lives, it's only natural that we'd resist it with everything we've got—and force the experts to listen to a wide range of objections and doubts. Making researchers defend their findings is a good thing: there is no reason to let their work influence our lives until they make a case that is truly convincing. Skepticism here, as in so many walks of life, can be a real boon.

But skepticism of *this* sort is non-dogmatic, open-minded, and curious; when it is true to itself, it hesitates to endorse *any* of the findings outright, including the work of contrarian scientists. (Nor would it, like Lindzen, describe those who accept the consensus as venal or hysterical.) This kind of skepticism, in fact, permeates the scientific community; it is the lifeblood of research, its motivating force. No self-respecting researcher could get up in the morning without the perpetual suspicion that earlier work in the field was incomplete, that there are huge gaps in existing knowledge, and that another angle might reveal more. Because of this attitude, the statements about climate change that scientists give to the public even today are not declarations of absolute faith but carefully phrased descriptions of a plausible scenario, descriptions that have probability and hesitation built into them as a matter of course.

Such doubts are not present merely out of habit, merely because scientists just can't commit. On the contrary, it's quite clear that there are, in fact, vast gaps in our knowledge. Nobody really understands what causes clouds to form, what effect climate change might have in creating more or fewer of them, and whether the ability of clouds to reflect potentially warming sunlight back into space may increase or decrease in the future (and thus affect the planet's warming in some manner).[170] Furthermore, the computer models that predict future warming are not yet capable of describing the incredibly complex, dynamic systems of the planet with utter accuracy, and as a result there is no firm consensus on exactly how much warming a certain level of atmospheric carbon dioxide would cause. Specialists in each field related to climate change studies can easily add to this list.

Yet those specialists have also declared their conviction that global warming is happening and is being caused by human beings. We can only conclude that for them *this* much is certain; the uncertainties arise in how to *describe* some of the mechanisms by which warming takes place, in *how much* warming might take place under certain circumstances, and what *exact* consequences might emerge in the course of time.[171] The limitations in our knowledge do not undercut the fundamental reality that we are changing Earth's climate in an unprecedented way. The consensus position, in short, is now seen as so elementary, so difficult to dispute, that it is taken for granted by scientists in the field, who have moved on to examine other questions.

But the hesitation with regard to certainty nevertheless does reveal something crucial about our current dilemma. After all, very few of us have ever been asked to assess the state of scientific expertise before making up our minds about something central to our lives. We're not used to being in this position. What's more, while scientists live with uncertainty as part of their profession, we laymen typically think in a different way: we want clear, concise answers and ask our politicians, journalists, and leading figures to supply them as often as possible. We don't like the mismatch between scientific caution and our everyday demand for clarity. Our dissatisfaction with the scientific response to our demand for certainty comes out of this mismatch.

But it's worth asking whether our defensiveness on climate makes sense. Do we truly seek certainty in every area of our own lives? For example, do we buy fire insurance only if we know for *sure* we'll need it down the line? When we go on a trip, do we take only those items we can *prove* we'll need? As a nation, do we demand military preparedness only if we know *precisely* what other forces will threaten us—and when they will do so?

When we think about our situation in this light, it's pretty clear that insisting on total certainty about climate change before we act gets everything backwards. What would you do if you were told that if you drove down a particular street at a certain hour, you'd face a 1 to 10 percent chance you'd have a terrible accident? Very few of us would take that chance. Those who insist on certainty, however, suggest that if there is somewhere between a 90 and 99 percent chance of a crash, we should *still* go down that road. After all, there is still a small chance we'd make it through without injury.

Such a response is ludicrous. When faced with the possibility of major harm, most sane adults would want to play it safe, to have an out, a Plan B, or at least good insurance and excellent medical care. We aren't simply indifferent if there is a high likelihood something horrible will happen to us. Yet in the climate change debate, we've managed to get the whole thing upside down. A supposed uncertainty in the science has covered up a far more frightening uncertainty about our futures: are we going to make it through the next few decades in good shape? Do we actually *have* a future? *That's* the real uncertainty we should face, and if we think about it in *those* terms, our answer gets obvious very fast.

The question is not whether scientists have absolute proof that human beings are causing climate change. The core question is instead whether we are sure we are *not* putting our own lives and futures into doubt by how we live, especially by how we emit greenhouse gases. Even if you think the science on this subject could be sharper, you have to admit it's already telling a pretty dire tale. Just hanging out until the consensus is even stronger isn't very smart.

But wait a minute, another person might object, *global warming is real, but we aren't the cause.* Earth's climate has changed dramatically over its history, thanks to any number of natural causes; our present moment is no exception. For us to attribute climate change to ourselves is merely a sign of our own arrogance. We live on an unstable planet, this person might say; there's nothing we can do about that fact. The cyclic changes in distance between the Earth and sun, the changes in the tilt of the polar axes, and variations in the brightness of the sun all change the amount of sunlight entering the atmosphere, alter the planet's warmth, and over time lead to immense changes in climate.

This objection has a great deal behind it. Research has in fact demonstrated, for example, that the slight changes in solar intensity (due to sunspots and changes in the sun's brightness) have enormous effects on temperature and climate systems and that these variations are routine events over the vast stretches of the planet's history. But because those factors are relevant, scientists have worked hard to take them into account. Looking into this very question, scientists found that an increase in solar radiation caused the rise in temperatures up to the 1940s and that a decrease in that intensity—possibly along with the release of aerosols into the atmosphere, which may counteract warming—led to the global cooling from the 1940s to the 1970s. But average sunspot activity has not increased since then, while global temperatures have risen at a good pace, suggesting that solar intensity is not in fact a primary factor in the global warming of recent decades.[172] The current change in temperature is anomalous, is taking place far more quickly than in the past, and is primarily caused by human activities.

But this direct response to the objection may not do it justice. Evidently, many people feel that if climate change has happened before, we shouldn't get too upset if it is happening again. This attitude may motivate responses to charts showing how much temperatures have risen since the late 1970s: for some observers, if current temperatures remain within the zone of temperature variation familiar in the planet's history, what we see today is by definition *not* anomalous and thus not a source of concern.[173] As a result, if they can show that current temperatures really aren't higher today than they were at some point in the past, they feel they have refuted the consensus view.

But this logic just doesn't hold true. If we say for the sake of argument that the planet may have been this warm or even warmer in the very distant past, that fact does not mean that the current warming is "natural," part of the ordinary course of things. Nonhuman causes may have led to great warming in another era; it doesn't follow that the current warming is "natural," too.

This answer is already a sufficient response. But it is interesting to try a thought experiment as well—to take the contrarian objection at its word and see what happens. Suppose that the current warming *is* "natural," that it is entirely the result of forces entirely outside our control. Does it really follow that we have nothing to worry about? Rather than helping us dismiss climate change, this argument only *reinforces* the problem—and makes it even *harder* for us to do anything about it.

This position is ultimately quite puzzling. It's just not plausible to assume that if sometime in Earth's history it was as warm as it is today, we can relax. For hundreds of thousands of years, Earth's average temperatures have varied widely, far more than most of us learned in science classes. Until recently, in fact, the history of Earth's climate had barely registered in the popular mind. A good look at charts of temperatures over the past 70,000 years or so—not to mention the last 600,000 years—will certainly get one's attention: the lines on those charts bounce around far more than one might initially have thought, slowing down into relative stability only in the very recent past, in the 10,000 years or so since the most recent Ice Age—the period geologists call the Holocene.[174] Civilization as we know it arose on a planet pretty much with its current characteristics. In this rather brief, exceptional period, the Earth's climate has created conditions that are ideal for certain kinds of human activities to flourish. "Nature" for us is highly specific, very recent, and quite vulnerable. Even for the first several thousand years after the Ice Age, we lived in mobile hunter-gatherer communities and could adapt to new conditions by changing our habitat. But with the rise and spread of the great sedentary, built civilizations, we are now rooted in specific places, much less flexible, and deeply reliant on the endurance of our familiar landscapes. The return of an Ice Age or the coming of a fully tropical planet, both with ample precedent in Earth's history, would be an immense danger to our way of life. Nothing we are used to, and no aspect of contemporary civilization, would be the same if Earth entered one of these scenarios. Rather than allowing us to dismiss the danger of climate change, then, this version of "skepticism" only makes clearer how fragile civilization is, how recent and potentially temporary.

If we are merely caught in yet another climatic shift, we must still imagine how to cope. For the most part, those who claim that climate change is not caused by human activities fight against efforts to do anything substantial about our situation. Such a position is indeed consistent with their sense that human action is not the cause of recent warming. But if that warming is taking place and we can do nothing about it, then how should we face the coming decades?

Anybody who actually believes that the current warming is entirely natural should pause and think about the consequences of that claim. If it is true, then our attempts to reduce our contributions to climate change will have no effect and our future is truly bleak. Such a person should also be very interested in reflecting—at least in some fashion—on what it is like to live in a world with a disappearing future. The thought experiment in imagining this alternative rendition of our present dilemma ultimately takes us right back to the central questions of this book.

Very well, one might say, *climate change is real and is caused by human beings, but the rise in temperatures isn't that great—not enough for us to worry about.* Some observers argue that if we gather data about Earth's temperatures more carefully, for example by filtering out the "urban heat effect" (the drift toward higher temperatures caused by urban encroachment into areas where weather data is collected), we'd find that the Earth simply isn't warming as much as we thought.[175]

At first, this sounds like an intriguing objection. What if the data about warming is exaggerated? On this score, skeptical inquiry is justified: shouldn't we be fairly certain that we measure global temperature shifts accurately if we are to have a clue in understanding the present biosphere?

Richard A. Muller of the University of California at Berkeley found enough flaws in previous studies of global temperatures that he led a research team in examining the entire question. As a result of this effort, he published an opinion piece in July, 2012, that began, "Call me a converted skeptic." Taking up a series of objections raised by climate change skeptics (regarding the urban heat effect, faulty data selection, and human bias) and subjecting them all to a comprehensive statistical analysis, that team ultimately found that none of these objections held true—and that the emission of greenhouse gases has indeed forced an increase in global temperatures of two and one half degrees Fahrenheit over the past 250 years and of one and one half degrees over the past fifty.[176] That group further found that no explanation other than human activity better accounted for this rise in temperatures—not even a change in solar intensity. Such a serious, apparently neutral, and thorough examination of the question should remove most doubts on this score.

But it's also important to recognize that objecting to the reality of climate change on this basis misses the point. It looks for certainty in how we *measure* climate change rather than thinking about its *results*. The best response to this objection is to try out another thought experiment. Let's say this objection is correct: what follows?

The answer is immediate and quite damning. Evidently, the rise in temperature, however high or low, is already having surprising effects. As I mentioned in the first pages of this book, the sea ice in the Arctic—and the methane clathrates on an Arctic continental shelf—are both melting far more quickly than scientists predicted just a few years ago, suggesting that the effect of the warming we've already experienced is more severe than we recently suspected. If such massive Earth systems can transform so greatly and so soon, the rise in the planet's average temperature, whatever the precise numbers might be, are enough to get our attention. Is it really wise to keep disputing how to gather temperature data for another decade or so and let the world's ecosystems just take care of themselves?

There is very little doubt that we have a serious problem on our hands. Scientists have arrived at an overwhelming, nearly unanimous consensus that we're causing climate change and that it is already causing devastating changes to Earth's living systems. The fact that our knowledge about how it works is not yet absolute should not encourage us to ignore it for the time being, since the very great uncertainty about whether we'll have a future dramatically outweighs the relatively technical uncertainties in our knowledge. The fundamentals of climate change science, in short, tell us that this problem is real.

Notes

156. William R. L. Anderegg and others, "Expert credibility in climate change," *Proceedings of the National Academy of Sciences of the United States of America*, volume 107, number 27 (June 21, 2010), 12107–12109, doi:10.1073/pnas.1003187107.

157. For a widely cited early example, see Naomi Oreskes, "The Scientific Consensus on Climate Change," *Science*, volume 306, number 5702 (December 3, 2004), 1686, doi:10.1126/science.1103618.

158. For a representative attempt by scientists to demonstrate their sense of the urgency of the crisis and the need for public action, see the National Academies' joint statement, "Climate change and the transformation of energy technologies for a low carbon future," May 2009, available online as a pdf document.

159. For a representative complaint about the IPCC from a "skeptical" perspective, see the discussion of Christopher Landsea's experience as a contributor to the second IPCC report (1995) in Lawrence Solomon, *The Deniers: The World-Renowned Scientists Who Stood Up Against Global Warming Hysteria, Political Persecution, and Fraud* (Richard Vigilante Books, 2010), 29–36. For a complaint from those who argue the IPCC is too cautious, see the account of new assessments of the Greenland ice sheet by Richard Schlesinger and others in Fred Pearce, *With Speed and Violence: Why Scientists Fear Tipping Points in Climate Change* (Boston: Beacon Press, 2007), 39–45, 145–46; see also Glenn Scherer, "Eight examples of where the IPCC has missed the mark on its predictions and projections," The Daily Climate, December 6, 2012, http://www.dailyclimate.org/tdc-newsroom/2012/12/ ipcc-prediction-fact-check.

160. For a representative statement, see Richard S. Lindzen, "Resisting Climate Hysteria: A Case Against Precipitous Climate Action," http://www.quadrant. org.au/blogs/doomed-planet/2009/07/resisting-climate-hysteria.

161. See the IPCC Third Assessment Report, Working Group I: The Scientific Basis, Summary for Policymakers, page three, initial portal available at http://www.grida.no/publications/other/ipcc_tar/, and the IPCC Fourth Assessment Report, Working Group I: The Scientific Basis, Summary for Policymakers, Understanding and Attributing Climate Change, http://www.ipcc.ch/publications_and_data/ar4/wg1/en/spmsspm-understanding-and.html.

162. Patrick J. Michaels and Robert C. Balling, Jr., *Climate of Extremes: Global Warming Science They Don't Want You to Know* (Washington, D.C.: Cato Institute, 2009), 195–209.

163. For a discussion of both efforts, see James Hoggan, *Climate Cover-up: The Crusade to Deny Global Warming* (Berkeley: Greystone Books, 2009), 31–87.

164. Hoggan, *Climate Cover-up*, 81.

165. For another, particularly devastating treatment of these corporately funded efforts to discredit climate change science, see George Monbiot, *Heat: How to Stop the Planet from Burning* (Cambridge, Massachusetts: South End Press, 2009), 20–42.

166. Naomi Oreskes and Erik M. Conway, *Merchants of Doubt: How a Handful of Scientists Obscured the Truth on Issues from Tobacco Smoke to Global Warming* (New York: Bloomsbury Press, 2010).

167. On Luntz, see Hoggan, *Climate Cover-up*, 72; on Exxon, see Hoggan, 84.

168. President George W. Bush, State of the Union Address, January 23, 2007, http://georgewbush-whitehouse.archives.gov/news/ releases/2007/01/20070123-2.html.

169. Hansen, *Storms of My Grandchildren*, 55. On the uncertainties surrounding clouds and climate change, see Fred Pearce, *With Speed and Violence: Why Scientists Fear Tipping Points in Climate Change* (Boston: Beacon Press, 2007), 105–114.

170. For a balanced statement that combines an endorsement of the mainstream view with a strong sense of its limitations, see Claire L. Parkinson, *Coming Climate Crisis? Consider the Past, Beware of the Big Fix* (New York: Rowman & Littlefield, 2010). On these dimensions of uncertainty see Michael Oppenheimer and others, "The Limits of Consensus," *Science*, volume 317, number 5844 (September 14, 2007), 1505–1506, doi:10.1126/science.1144831, and the letter in response by Susan Solomon and others, "A Closer Look at the IPCC Report," *Science*, volume 319, number 5862 (January 25, 2008), 409–410, doi:10.1126/science.319.5862.409c.

171. Spencer R. Weart, *The Discovery of Global Warming*, revised and expanded edition (Cambridge: Harvard University Press, 2008), 167–68. For a representative research article on the influence of solar irradiation, volcanic activity, aerosols, and greenhouse gases on global temperatures, see Thomas J. Crowley, "Causes of Climate Change Over the Past 1000 Years," *Science*, volume 289, number 5477, (July 14, 2000), 270–77, doi:10.1126/science.289.5477.270.

172. For a skeptical view of the famous "hockey stick" chart and related topics, see Solomon, *The Deniers*, 9–21; 57–74. For a representative mainstream account of the Michael Mann controversy, see Fred Pearce, *With Speed and Violence*, 204–209.

173. For good examples of such charts, see Richard B. Alley, *The Two-Mile Time Machine: Ice Cores, Abrupt Climate Change, and Our Future* (Princeton: Princeton University Press, 2000), 123, and Wallace S. Broecker and Robert Kunzig, *Fixing Climate: What Past Climate Changes Reveal About the Current Threat—And How to Counter It* (New York: Hill and Wang, 2008), 118.

174. Michaels and Balling, *Climate of Extremes*, 58–64.

175. Richard A. Muller, "The Conversion of a Climate Change Skeptic," *The New York Times*, July 28, 2012, http://www.nytimes.com/2012/07/30/opinion/the-conversion-of-a-climate-change-skeptic.html?pagewanted=all&_r=0. For the full research behind Muller's statement, see the papers at Berkeley Earth Inc., http://berkeleyearth.org/.

Acknowledgments

Early in this book I wrote that climate change interrupts us, throws us off at every turn. It has certainly done so with me: it interrupted my scholarly career, demanding that I suspend my usual engagements to address matters of overwhelming common concern. I thus wish to acknowledge from the start the signal support of Bowdoin College, which not only provided financial support through the Faculty Leave Supplement to enable me to research and write the book but also explicitly encourages faculty to take on the broader mission of enlarging what it calls "the common good." I truly appreciate the College's rare support for the public dimension of learning.

I owe a great debt to those scientists who continue to describe the contours of climate change to a resistant and at times hostile public. Their persistence in carrying out this task despite the odds sets a high standard for ethical courage today. I am equally grateful to my forebears in the humanities, especially those in the deconstructive, Lacanian, and leftist traditions who have modelled the ethically courageous capacity to tarry with the negative despite deep-seated resistance of another kind. I hope that this book in some measure makes visible the deep affinities of these two intellectual traditions.

I am grateful to my colleagues in the study of Romanticism and adjacent fields who, through the rigor of their work and their capacity for searching conversation, continue to model the best possibilities of our shared vocation. I especially wish to thank Tilottama Rajan, Thomas Pfau, William Galperin, Frances Ferguson, David Clark, James Engell, Theresa Kelley, Orrin Wang, Rob Mitchell, Jacques Khalip, Nancy Yousef, Vivasvan Soni, Anne-Lise Francois, Tilar Mazzeo, Elizabeth Fay, Scott Juengel, Jennifer Fay, Joan Steigerwald, Rei Terada, Arkady Plotnitsky, Richard Sha, Nick Halmi, Colin Jager, Mark Canuel, Joel Faflak, Tres Pyle, Josh Wilner, Eugene Stelzig, David Baulch, Ron Broglio, Tobias

Menely, Andrew Warren, Alexander Schlutz, George Erving, Andy Burkett, Allison Dushane, Jennifer Horan, Christopher Bundock, and Jacob Risinger. Their responses to my work in recent years have greatly influenced this book, distant as it may be from the language in which we usually speak.

Bowdoin College has provided a lively intellectual community within which this project could take shape. Gen Creedon, who encouraged me to pursue this project, and Thom Cote, who gave me helpful suggestions for revision at a crucial juncture, have been especially important interlocutors. I am grateful to the late Tom Cornell, Susan Wegner, and David Hecht for their concrete suggestions as I researched the book; John Lichter, Phil Camill, Mary Hunter, Collin Roesler, Elizabeth Pritchard, Matt Klingle, Emily Peterman, Casey Meehan, Anne Witty, and Kate Stern for their support for and response to the project; my colleagues in English, Environmental Studies, Gay and Lesbian Studies, and Gender and Women's Studies, whose sense of ethically engaged scholarship continues to inspire me; and the students in several of my courses in recent years, especially advanced seminars, for the freshness, intensity, and clarity of their thought on the book's central themes. I give a warm thanks to Celeste Goodridge, Liz Muther, Guy Mark Foster, Louisa Slowiaczek, and Rich Kreiner for the depth and sustaining power of their friendship. I am grateful to those in the broader community of coastal Maine and beyond whose friendship and conversation have often helped lay the foundations for this project or illuminated its contours anew; foremost among them are Lucinda Cole, Robert Markley, Frank Wicks, Sukanya Rahman, and Gerard Dorian.

I am delighted to acknowledge my debt to Claire Colebrook and Tom Cohen, editors of the Critical Climate Change series, for seeing the value of this book and bringing it into a growing body of work from the humanities on climate change, and my gratitude for the exemplary work of the volunteer collective at Open Humanities Press, from Sigi Jöttkandt and David Ottina, co-founders and co-directors of the press, to Marcia LaBrenz, Kelly Witchen, and others at Michigan Publishing, who steered this project through many phases and helped get the contents and the cover of the book into publishable form.

My deepest thanks go to Terri Nickel for the rigor of her response to this project at every stage, her endless patience in reading with fresh attention each new draft, and most of all, her unique talent for tenderness and joy—one that has made the task of articulating even these dark thoughts into an affirmative venture. Without her bedrock support and brilliant responsiveness, my writing this book would never have been possible. Truly in this as in all other endeavors she is my mind's and my heart's companion.

Works Cited

Alley, Richard B. *The Two-Mile Time Machine: Ice Cores, Abrupt Climate Change, and Our Future.* Princeton: Princeton University Press, 2000.

Anderegg, William R. L. and others. "Expert credibility in climate change," *Proceedings of the National Academy of Sciences of the United States of America,* volume 107, number 27 (June 21, 2010): 12107–12109. doi:10.1073/pnas.1003187107.

Bagemihl, Bruce. *Biological Exuberance: Animal Homosexuality and Natural Diversity.* New York: St. Martin's Press, 1999.

Baker, Peter and David M. Herszenhorn. "Senate Democrats to Pursue a Smaller Energy Bill." *New York Times,* July 15, 2010. http://www.nytimes.com/2010/07/15/us/politics/15energy.html.

Barringer, Felicity. "A Grand Experiment to Rein In Climate Change." *New York Times,* October 13, 2012. http://www.nytimes.com/2012/10/14/science/earth/in-california-a-grand-experiment-to-rein-in-climate-change.html?pagewanted=all.

Beckett, Samuel. *Endgame, A Play in One Act, Followed by Act Without Words, A Mime for One Player.* New York: Grove Press, 1958.

Beckett, Samuel. *Waiting for Godot: Tragicomedy in Two Acts.* New York: Grove Press, 1954.

Berkeley Earth Inc. http://berkeleyearth.org/.

Black, Richard. "World's oceans in 'shocking' decline." *BBC News,* June 20, 2011. http://www.bbc.co.uk/news/science-environment-13796479.

Blunier, Thomas. "'Frozen' Methane Escapes from the Sea Floor." *Science,* volume 288, number 5463 (April 7, 2000): 68–69. doi:10.1126/science.288.5463.68.

Bond, T. C. and others. "Bounding the role of black carbon in the climate system: A scientific assessment." *Journal of Geophysical Research: Atmospheres,* 118 (June 6, 2013): 1–173. doi: 10.1002/jgrd.50171.

Boyce, Daniel G., Marlon R. Lewis, and Boris Worm. "Global phytoplankton decline over the past century." *Nature* 466 (July 29, 2010): 591–596. doi:10.1038/nature09268.

Boyle, T. C. *A Friend of the Earth.* New York: Viking Penguin, 2000.

Broder, John M. "White House Energy Session Changes No Minds." *New York Times*, June 29, 2010. http://www.nytimes.com/2010/06/30/science/earth/30energy. html.

Broecker, Wallace S. and Robert Kunzig. *Fixing Climate: What Past Climate Changes Reveal About the Current Threat—And How to Counter It*. New York: Hill and Wang, 2008.

Brysse, Keynyn and others. "Climate change prediction: Erring on the side of least drama?" *Global Environmental Change*, volume 23, issue 1 (February 2013): 327–337.

Bush, President George W. State of the Union Address, January 23, 2007. http:// georgewbush-whitehouse.archives.gov/news/releases/2007/01/20070123-2. html.

Calvin, William H. *A Brain for All Seasons: Human Evolution & Abrupt Climate Change*. Chicago: University of Chicago Press, 2002.

Carana, Sam. "The potential for methane releases in the Arctic to cause runaway global warming." *Arctic News*, December 20, 2011, updated January 29, 2012. http://arctic-news.blogspot.com/p/potential-for-methane-release.html.

Catton, William R., Jr. *Overshoot: The Ecological Basis of Revolutionary Change*. Urbana: University of Illinois Press, 1982.

Central Conference of American Rabbis. "Climate Change." Resolution adopted in 2005. http://www.jewcology.com/resource/ Central-Conference-of-American-Rabbis-Resolution-Climate-Change-2005.

Chen, I-Ching and others. "Rapid Range Shifts of Species Associated with High Levels of Climate Warming." *Science* 333 (August 19, 2011): 1024–26. doi:10.1126/science.1206432.

CO2now. http://co2now.org/.

Cohen, Tom. "Anecographics: Climate Change and 'Late' Deconstruction." In *Impasses of the Post-Global: Theory in the Era of Climate Change*, volume 2, edited by Henry Sussman. MPublishing, University of Michigan Library; Open Humanities Press, 2012. http://quod.lib.umich.edu/o/ohp/10803281.0001.001/1:3/-- impasses-of-the-post-global-theory-in-the-era-of-climate?rgn=div1;view=fullt ext.

Collings, David. "After the Covenant: Romanticism, Secularization, and Disastrous Transcendence." *European Romantic Review* 21 (2010): 345–61.

Connor, Steve. "Vast methane 'plumes' seen in Arctic ocean as sea ice retreats." *The Independent*, December 13, 2011. http://www.independent.co.uk/news/science/ vast-methane-plumes-seen-in-arctic-ocean-as-sea-ice-retreats-6276278.html.

Crane, David and Robert F. Kennedy, Jr. "Solar Panels for Every Home." *New York Times*, December 12, 2012. http://www.nytimes.com/2012/12/13/opinion/solar-panels-for-every-home.html.

Critchley, Simon. *Infinitely Demanding: Ethics of Commitment, Politics of Resistance*. New York: Verso, 2007.

Crowley, Thomas J. "Causes of Climate Change Over the Past 1000 Years." *Science*, volume 289, number 5477 (July 14, 2000): 270–77. doi:10.1126/science.289.5477.270.

Dallaire, Roméo and Brent Beardsley. *Shake Hands with the Devil: The Failure of Humanity in Rwanda*. New York: Carroll & Graf, 2004.

Davis, Mike. *Late Victorian Holocausts: El Niño Famines and the Making of the Third World*. New York: Verso, 2001.

Derrida, Jacques. *The Gift of Death*, second edition, and *Literature in Secret*. Translated by David Wills. Chicago: University of Chicago Press, 2008.

Devall, Bill and George Sessions. *Deep Ecology: Living as if Nature Mattered*. Salt Lake City: G. M. Smith, 1985.

Diamond, Jared. *Collapse: How Societies Choose to Fail or Succeed*. New York: Penguin, 2006.

Eaton, Marie. "Environmental Trauma and Grief." Curriculum for the Bioregion Initiative, Science Education Resource Center at Carleton College, August 2012. http://serc.carleton.edu/bioregion/sustain_contemp_lc/essays/67207.html.

Eisenberg, Anne. "Pulling Carbon Dioxide Out of Thin Air." *New York Times*, January 5, 2013. http://www.nytimes.com/2013/01/06/business/pilot-plant-in-the-works-for-carbon-dioxide-cleansing.html.

Environment America Research and Policy Center. "When it Rains, it Pours: Global Warming and the Increase in Extreme Precipitation from 1948 to 2011." July 31, 2012. http://www.environmentamerica.org/reports/ame/when-it-rains-it-pours.

Evangelical Climate Initiative. "Climate Change: An Evangelical Call to Action." Available as a pdf document online.

Faris, Stephan. *Forecast: The Consequences of Climate Change, from the Amazon to the Arctic, from Darfur to Napa Valley*. New York: Holt, 2009.

Feldman, Shoshana and Dori Laub. *Testimony: Crises of Witnessing in Literature, Psychoanalysis and History*. New York: Routledge, 1992.

Fitzgibbons, Athol. *Adam Smith's System of Liberty, Wealth and Virtue: The Moral and Political Foundations of* The Wealth of Nations. Oxford: Clarendon Press, 1995.

Flightplan. Directed by Robert Schwentke. Buena Vista Pictures, 2005.

Flint, Julie and Alex De Waal. *Darfur: A New History of a Long War*. Revised edition. New York: Zed Books, 2008.

Francis, Jennifer A. and Stephen J. Vavrus. "Evidence linking Arctic amplification to extreme weather in mid-latitudes." *Geophysical Research Letters*, volume 39, issue 6 (March 2012): L06801. doi:10.1029/2012GL051000.

Freedman, Andrew. "Arctic Warming is Altering Weather Patterns, Study Shows." Climate Central, April 3, 2012. http://www.climatecentral.org/news/ arctic-warming-is-altering-weather-patterns-study-shows.

Friedman, Thomas L. *Hot, Flat, and Crowded: Why We Need a Green Revolution—and How It Can Renew America*. Release 2.0. New York: Farrar, Straus and Giroux, 2009.

Garvey, James. *The Ethics of Climate Change: Right and Wrong in a Warming World*. New York: Continuum, 2008.

Gillis, Justin. "Carbon Emissions Show Biggest Jump Ever Recorded." *New York Times*, December 4, 2011. http://www.nytimes.com/2011/12/05/science/ earth/record-jump-in-emissions-in-2010-study-finds.html.

Gillis, Justin. "With Deaths of Forests, a Loss of Key Climate Protectors." *New York Times*, October 1, 2011. http://www.nytimes.com/2011/10/01/science/ earth/01forest.html?pagewanted=all.

Gore, Al. *An Inconvenient Truth: The Planetary Emergency of Global Warming and What We Can Do About It*. Emmaus, Pennsylvania: Rodale, 2006.

Gore, Al. *Our Choice: A Plan to Solve the Climate Crisis*. Emmaus, Pennsylvania: Rodale, 2009.

Gould, Stephen Jay. *Ever Since Darwin: Reflections in Natural History*. New York: Norton, 1977.

Greider, William. *The Soul of Capitalism: Opening Paths to a Moral Economy*. New York: Simon & Schuster, 2003.

Hamilton, Clive. *Requiem for a Species: Why We Resist the Truth about Climate Change*. Washington, DC: Earthscan, 2010.

Hansen, James. *Storms of My Grandchildren: The Truth About the Coming Climate Catastrophe and Our Last Chance to Save Humanity*. New York: Bloomsbury, 2009.

Heidegger, Martin. *Being and Time*. Translated by John Macquarrie and Edward Robinson. London: SCM Press, 1962.

Henson, Robert. *The Rough Guide to Climate Change*. London: Rough Guides, 2006.

Hoffert, Martin I. "Farewell to Fossil Fuels?" *Science,* volume 329, number 5997 (September 10, 2010): 1292–1294. doi:10.1126/science.1195449.

Hoggan, James. *Climate Cover-up: The Crusade to Deny Global Warming.* Berkeley: Greystone Books, 2009.

Holy Bible: Revised Standard Edition. New York: Thomas Nelson & Sons, Old Testament portions copyright 1952.

Hughes, Patrick J. "Geothermal (Ground-Source) Heat Pumps: Market Status, Barriers to Adoption, and Actions to Overcome Barriers." Oak Ridge National Laboratory, U.S. Department of Energy Publications. December, 2008.

Hughes, Robert. *The Fatal Shore: The Epic of Australia's Founding.* New York: Knopf, 1987.

Hulme, Mike. *Why We Disagree About Climate Change: Understanding Controversy, Inaction and Opportunity.* Cambridge, England: Cambridge University Press, 2009.

Hulse, Carl and David M. Herszenhorn. "Democrats Call Off Climate Bill Effort." *New York Times,* July 22, 2010. http://www.nytimes.com/2010/07/23/us/politics/23cong.html.

IdiotTracker. "Semiletov and Shakhova report." December 27, 2011. http://theidiottracker.blogspot.com/2011/12/semiletov-and-shakhova-report.html.

International Programme on the State of the Ocean. http://www.stateoftheocean.org/.

Intergovernmental Panel on Climate Change (IPCC). *Fourth Assessment Report.* 2007. *Synthesis Report.* http://www.ipcc.ch/publications_and_data/ar4/syr/en/main.html

IPCC. *Fourth Assessment Report.* 2007. Working Group I: *The Physical Science Basis.* Chapter Ten: Global Climate Projections. http://www.ipcc.ch/publications_and_data/ar4/wg1/en/ch10.html.

IPCC. *Fourth Assessment Report.* 2007. Working Group I: *The Physical Science Basis. Summary for Policymakers.* http://www.ipcc.ch/publications_and_data/ar4/wg1/en/spm.html.

IPCC. Special Report. *Aviation and the Global Atmosphere.* 1999. http://www.ipcc.ch/ipccreports/sres/aviation/index.php?idp=0.

IPCC. *Third Assessment Report.* Working Group I: *The Scientific Basis. Summary for Policymakers.* 2001. http://www.grida.no/publications/other/ipcc_tar/.

Jackson, Tim. *Prosperity Without Growth: Economics for a Finite Planet.* Sterling, Virginia: Earthscan, 2009.

Jameson, Fredric. "Future City." *New Left Review*, volume 21 (2003): 65–79.

Jensen, Derrick. *Endgame: Volume I, The Problem of Civilization*, and *Volume II, Resistance*. New York: Seven Stories Press, 2006.

Jensen, Robert. "Hope is for the Lazy: The Challenge of Our Dead World." *Counterpunch*, July 9, 2012. http://www.counterpunch.org/2012/07/09/hope-is-for-the-lazy/.

John Q. Directed by John Cassavetes. New Line Cinema, 2002.

Kant, Immanuel. *Critique of the Power of Judgment*. Edited by Paul Guyer. Translated by Guyer and Eric Matthews. Cambridge: Cambridge University Press, 2000.

Kerr, Richard. "Arctic Summer Sea Ice Could Vanish Soon But Not Suddenly." *Science*, volume 323, number 5922 (March 27, 2009): 1655. doi:10.1126/science.323.5922.1655.

Kerr, Richard. "Ocean Acidification Unprecedented, Unsettling." *Science*, volume 328, number 5985 (June 18, 2010): 1500–1501. doi:10.1126/science.328.5985.1500.

Kevorkian, Kristine. "Environmental Grief." *Ecology Global Network*, February 15, 2012. http://www.ecology.com/2012/02/15/environmental-grief/.

Kolbert, Elizabeth. *Field Notes from a Catastrophe: Man, Nature, and Climate Change*. New York: Bloomsbury, 2006.

Kovel, Joel. *The Enemy of Nature: The End of Capitalism or the End of the World?* New York: Zed Books, 2002.

Kozloff, Nikolas. *No Rain in the Amazon: How South America's Climate Change Affects the Entire Planet*. New York: Palgrave Macmillan, 2010.

Krosnick, Jon. "The Climate Majority." *New York Times*, June 8, 2010. http://www.nytimes.com/2010/06/09/opinion/09krosnick.html?pagewanted=all&_r=0.

Krupp, Fred and Miriam Horn. *Earth: The Sequel: The Race to Reinvent Energy and Stop Global Warming*. New York: Norton, 2009.

Kurz, W. A. and others. "Mountain pine beetle and forest carbon feedback to climate change." *Nature* 452 (April 24, 2008): 987–990. doi:10.1038/nature06777.

Lacan, Jacques. *The Seminar of Jacques Lacan*. Edited by Jacques-Alain Miller. *Book VII: The Ethics of Psychoanalysis*. Translated by Dennis Porter. New York: Norton, 1992.

Laden, Greg. "Top Climate Stories of 2012." ScienceBlogs, December 28, 2012. http://scienceblogs.com/gregladen/2012/12/28/top-climate-stories-of-2012/.

Lal, Rattan. "Soil Carbon Sequestration Impacts on Global Climate Change and Food Security." *Science*, volume 304, number 5677 (June 11, 2004): 1623–1627. doi:10.1126/science.1097396.

Levinas, Emmanuel. *Otherwise Than Being: Beyond Essence*. Translated by Alphonso Lingis. Pittsburgh: Duquesne University Press, 1998.

Levinas, Emmanuel. *Totality and Infinity: An Essay on Exteriority*. Translated by Alphonso Lingis. Pittsburgh: Duquesne University Press, 1969.

Lewis, Simon L. and others. "The 2010 Amazon Drought." *Science*, volume 331, number 6017 (February 4, 2011): 554. doi:10.1126/science.1200807.

Leys, Ruth. *Trauma: A Genealogy*. Chicago: University of Chicago Press, 2000.

Library of Congress, Bill Summary and Status, 105th Congress (1997–1998), S. Res 98. http://thomas.loc.gov/cgi-bin/bdquery/z?d105:S.RES.98:.

Lilley, Sasha and others. *Catastrophism: The Apocalyptic Politics of Collapse and Rebirth*. Oakland: PM Press, 2012.

Lindzen, Richard S. "Resisting Climate Hysteria: A Case Against Precipitous Climate Action." http://www.quadrant.org.au/blogs/doomed-planet/2009/07/resisting-climate-hysteria.

Lovelock, James. *The Revenge of Gaia: Earth's Climate Crisis & the Fate of Humanity*. New York: Basic Books, 2006.

Lovins, Amory and L. Hunter Lovins. *Climate: Making Sense and Making Money*. Old Snowmass, Colorado: Rocky Mountain Institute, 1997. http://www.rmi.org/Knowledge-Center/Library/C97-13_ClimateSenseMoney.

Lubasz, Heinz. "Adam Smith and the 'Free Market.'" In *Adam Smith's* Wealth of Nations: *New Interdisciplinary Essays*, edited by Stephen Copley and Kathryn Sutherland, 45–69. New York: Manchester University Press, 1995.

Lynas, Mark. *Six Degrees: Our Future on a Hotter Planet*. Washington, D.C.: National Geographic, 2008.

MacIntyre, Alasdair. *After Virtue: A Study in Moral Theory*. Third edition. Notre Dame: University of Notre Dame Press, 2007.

MacKay, David J. C. *Sustainable Energy—Without the Hot Air*. Cambridge, England: UIT Cambridge, 2009.

Malhi, Yadvinder and others. "Persistent effects of a severe drought on Amazonian forest canopy." *Proceedings of the National Academy of Sciences of the United States of America*, volume 110, number 2 (December 24, 2012), 565–570. doi:10.1073/pnas.1204651110.

Mantgem, Phillip J. van and others. "Widespread Increase of Tree Mortality Rates in the Western United States." *Science*, volume 323, number 5913 (January 23, 2009): 521–24. doi:10.1126/science.1165000.

Mark Hertsgaard. *Hot: Living Through the Next Fifty Years on Earth*. Boston: Houghton Mifflin Harcourt, 2011.

Mason, John. "Arctic methane outgassing on the East Siberian Arctic Shelf. Part 2. An interview with Dr Natalia Shakhova." Skeptical Science, January 19, 2012. http://www.skepticalscience.com/arctic-methane-outgassing-e-siberian-shelf-part2.html.

McCarthy, Cormac. *The Road*. New York: Vintage, 2006.

McKibben, Bill. *Deep Economy: The Wealth of Communities and the Durable Future*. New York: Henry Holt, 2007.

McKibben, Bill. *Eaarth: Making a Life on a Tough New Planet*. New York: Times Books, 2010.

McKibben, Bill. "Global Warming's Terrifying New Math." *Rolling Stone*, July 19, 2012. http://www.rollingstone.com/politics/news/global-warmings-terrifying-new-math-20120719.

McKibben, Bill. *Maybe One: A Case for Smaller Families*. New York: Penguin, 1998.

McKibben, Bill. *The Comforting Whirlwind: God, Job, and the Scale of Creation*. Grand Rapids: Eerdmans, 1994.

McKibben, Bill. *The End of Nature*. New York: Random House, 1989.

Michaels, Patrick J. and Robert C. Balling, Jr. *Climate of Extremes: Global Warming Science They Don't Want You to Know*. Washington, DC: Cato Institute, 2009.

Mitchell, Stephen. Introduction. *The Book of Job*. Translated by Mitchell. New York: HarperCollins, 1987, vii–xxxii.

Monbiot, George. *Heat: How to Stop the Planet from Burning*. Cambridge, Massachusetts: South End Press, 2009.

Montaigne, Fen. "Arctic Tipping Point: A North Pole Without Ice." Yale360, August 30, 2012. http://e360.yale.edu/feature/tipping_point_arctic_heads_to_ice_free_summers/2567/.

Muller, Richard A. "The Conversion of a Climate Change Skeptic." *The New York Times*, July 28, 2012. http://www.nytimes.com/2012/07/30/opinion/the-conversion-of-a-climate-change-skeptic.html?pagewanted=all&_r=0.

Murtaugh, Paul A. and Michael G. Schlax. "Reproduction and the Carbon Legacies of Individuals." *Global Environmental Change* volume 19, issue 1 (February 2009): 14–20, available as a pdf document online.

National Academies. "Climate change and the transformation of energy technologies for a low carbon future." May 2009, available as a pdf document online.

National Science Foundation. "Methane Releases From Arctic Shelf May Be Much Larger and Faster Than Anticipated." March 4, 2010. http://www.nsf.gov/news/news_summ.jsp?cntn_id=116532.

Olusoga, David and Casper W. Erichsen. *The Kaiser's Holocaust: Germany's Forgotten Genocide.* London: Faber and Faber, 2010.

Oppenheimer, Michael, and others. "The Limits of Consensus." *Science,* volume 317, number 5844 (September 14, 2007): 1505–1506. doi:10.1126/science.1144831.

Oreskes, Naomi and Erik M. Conway. *Merchants of Doubt: How a Handful of Scientists Obscured the Truth on Issues from Tobacco Smoke to Global Warming.* New York: Bloomsbury Press, 2010.

Oreskes, Naomi. "The Scientific Consensus on Climate Change." *Science,* volume 306, number 5702 (December 3, 2004):1686. doi:10.1126/science.1103618.

Pacala, S. and R. Socolow. "Stabilization Wedges: Solving the Climate Problem for the Next 50 Years with Current Technologies." *Science,* volume 305, number 5686 (August 13, 2004): 968–972. doi:10.1126/science.1100103.

Parkinson, Claire L. *Coming Climate Crisis? Consider the Past, Beware of the Big Fix.* New York: Rowman & Littlefield, 2010.

Pearce, Fred. *With Speed and Violence: Why Scientists Fear Tipping Points in Climate Change.* Boston: Beacon Press, 2007.

"'The planet won't be destroyed by global warming because God promised Noah,' says politician bidding to chair U.S. energy committee." *[Daily] Mail Online,* November 10, 2010. http://www.dailymail.co.uk/news/article-1328366/John-Shimkus-Global-warming-wont-destroy-planet-God-promised-Noah.html.

Ponting, Clive. *A Green History of the World: The Environment and the Collapse of Great Civilizations.* New York: Penguin, 1991.

Rashid, Salim. *The Myth of Adam Smith.* Northampton, Massachusetts: Edward Elgar, 1998.

Ridgwell, Andy and Daniela N. Schmidt. "Past constraints on the vulnerability of marine calcifiers to massive carbon dioxide release." *Nature Geoscience,* volume 3, number 3 (March 2010): 196–200. doi:10.1038/ngeo745.

Roberts, D. and others, "Interannual variability of pteropod shell weights in the high-CO2 Southern Ocean." *Biogeosciences Discussions* 5 (2008): 4453–4480. doi:10.5194/bgd-5-4453-2008.

Rockström, Johan and others. "A Safe Operating Space for Humanity." *Nature* 461 (September 23, 2009): 472–475. doi:10.1038/461472a.

Romm, Joe. "Bridge to Nowhere? NOAA Confirms High Methane Leakage Rate Up To 9% From Gas Fields, Gutting Climate Benefit." Climate Progress, January 2, 2013. http://thinkprogress.org/climate/2013/01/02/1388021/bridge-to-nowhere-noaa-confirms-high-methane-leakage-rate-up-to-9-from-gas-fields-gutting-climate-benefit/.

Rosenthal, Elizabeth. "As Biofuel Demand Grows, So Do Guatemala's Hunger Pangs." *New York Times*, January 5, 2013. http://www.nytimes.com/2013/01/06/science/earth/in-fields-and-markets-guatemalans-feel-squeeze-of-biofuel-demand.html?pagewanted=all.

Rosenthal, Elizabeth. "Burning Fuel Particles Do More Damage to Climate Than Thought, Study Says." *New York Times*, January 15, 2013. http://www.nytimes.com/2013/01/16/science/earth/burning-fuel-particles-do-more-damage-to-climate-than-thought-study-says.html?_r=0.

Rosenthal, Elizabeth. "Carbon Taxes Make Ireland Even Greener." *New York Times*, December 27, 2012. http://www.nytimes.com/2012/12/28/science/earth/in-ireland-carbon-taxes-pay-off.html?pagewanted=all.

Rosenthal, Elizabeth. "U. N. Chief Seeks More Climate Change Leadership." *New York Times*, November 18, 2007. http://www.nytimes.com/2007/11/18/science/earth/18climatenew.html?pagewanted=all&_r=0.

Rosenthal, Elizabeth. "Using Waste, Swedish City Cuts Its Fossil Fuel Use." *New York Times*, December 10, 2010. http://www.nytimes.com/2010/12/11/science/earth/11fossil.html?pagewanted=all.

Rossi, Paolo. *The Dark Abyss of Time: The History of the Earth & the History of Nations from Hooke to Vico*. Chicago: University of Chicago Press, 1984.

Royal Commission on Environmental Pollution. Special Report. *The Environmental Effects of Civil Aircraft in Flight*, 2002, available as a pdf document online.

Ruttiman, Jacqueline. "Sick Seas." *Nature* 442 (August 31, 2006): 978–980. doi:10.1038/442978a.

Schaefer, Kevin and others. "Amount and timing of permafrost carbon release in response to climate warming." *Tellus B*, volume 63, Issue 2 (April 2011): 165–180. doi:10.1111/j.1600–0889.2011.00527.x.

Scheffler, Samuel. *Death and the Afterlife*. New York: Oxford University Press, 2013.

Scherer, Glenn. "Eight examples of where the IPCC has missed the mark on its predictions and projections." The Daily Climate, December 6, 2012. http://www.dailyclimate.org/tdc-newsroom/2012/12/ipcc-prediction-fact-check.

Semple, Robert P., Jr. "Remember Kyoto? Most Nations Don't." *New York Times*, December 3, 2011. http://www.nytimes.com/2011/12/04/opinion/sunday/remember-kyoto-most-nations-dont.html?_r=0.

Sessions, George, editor. *Deep Ecology for the 21st Century: Readings on the Philosophy and Practice of the New Environmentalism*. Boston: Shambhala, 1995.

Shakhova, Natalia and others. "Extensive Methane Venting to the Atmosphere from Sediments of the East Siberian Arctic Shelf." *Science*, volume 327, number 5970 (March 5, 2010): 1246–1250. doi:10.1126/science.1182221.

Shelley, Percy Bysshe. *Shelley's Poetry and Prose*. Edited by Donald H. Reiman and Neil Fraistat. Second edition. New York: Norton, 2002.

Shi, Dalin and others. "Effect of Ocean Acidification on Iron Availability to Marine Phytoplankton." *Science*, volume 327, number 5966 (February 5, 2010): 676–679. doi:10.1126/science.1183517.

Shiva, Vandana. *Earth Democracy: Justice, Sustainability, and Peace*. Cambridge, Massachusetts: South End Press, 2005.

Slavoj Žižek, Eric L. Santner, and Kenneth Reinhard. *The Neighbor: Three Inquiries in Political Theology*. Chicago: University of Chicago Press, 2006.

Solnit, Rebecca. *A Paradise Built in Hell: The Extraordinary Communities that Arise in Disaster*. New York: Penguin, 2009.

Solnit, Rebecca. *Hope in the Dark: Untold Histories, Wild Possibilities*. New York: Nation Books, 2004.

Solomon, Lawrence. *The Deniers: The World-Renowned Scientists Who Stood Up Against Global Warming Hysteria, Political Persecution, and Fraud*. Minneapolis: Richard Vigilante Books, 2010.

Solomon, Susan and others. "A Closer Look at the IPCC Report." *Science*, volume 319, number 5862 (January 25, 2008): 409–410. doi:10.1126/science.319.5862.409c.

Solomon, Susan and others. "Irreversible Climate Change Due to Carbon Dioxide Emissions." *Proceedings of the National Academy of Sciences of the United States of America*, volume 106, number 6 (February 10, 2009): 1704–1709. doi:10.1073/pnas.0812721106.

Spratt, David. "Big call: Cambridge prof. predicts Arctic summer sea ice 'all gone by 2015.'" Climate Code Red, August 30, 2012. http://www.climatecodered. org/2012/08/big-call-cambridge-prof-predicts-arctic.html.

Stevenson, Richard W. and John M. Broder. "Speech Gives Climate Goals Center Stage." New York Times, January 21, 2013. http://www.nytimes. com/2013/01/22/us/politics/climate-change-prominent-in-obamas-inaugural-address.html.

Stoft, Steven. Carbonomics: How to Fix the Climate and Charge It to OPEC. Nantucket, Massachusetts: Diamond Press, 2008.

Stuber, Nicola and others. "The Importance of the Diurnal and Annual Cycle of Air Traffic for Contrail Radiative Forcing." Nature 441 (June 15, 2006): 864–67. doi:10.1038/nature04877.

The Others. Directed by Alejandro Amenábar. Dimension Films, 2001.

Thomas, Chris D. and others. "Extinction Risk from Climate Change." Nature 427 (January 8, 2004): 145–148. doi:10.1038/nature02121.

United States Conference of Catholic Bishops. Global Climate Change: A Plea for Dialogue, Prudence and the Common Good. Washington, D.C.: 2001. http://www. usccb.org/issues-and-action/human-life-and-dignity/environment/global-climate-change-a-plea-for-dialogue-prudence-and-the-common-good.cfm.

United States Department of Energy. "Geothermal Heat Pumps." Available at Whole Building Design Guide. http://www.wbdg.org/resources/geothermalheatpumps. php.

United States Global Change Research Program. Global Climate Change Impacts in the U.S., 2009 Report. http://nca2009.globalchange.gov/.

Wadhams, Peter. "Geoengineering May Be Our Best Chance to Save Sea Ice." Scientific American, November 13, 2012. http://www.scientificamerican.com/ article.cfm?id=geoengineering-last-chance-save-sea-ice

Wadhams, Peter. "Imminent collapse of Arctic sea ice drives danger of accelerated methane thaw." Arctic News, March 7, 2012. http://arctic-news.blogspot. com/2012/03/rebuttal-imminent-collapse-of-arctic.html.

Wald, Matthew L. "With Natural Gas Plentiful and Cheap, Carbon Capture Projects Stumble." New York Times, May 18, 2012. http://www.nytimes. com/2012/05/19/business/energy-environment/low-natural-gas-prices-threaten-carbon-capture-projects.html.

Weart, Spencer R. The Discovery of Global Warming. Revised and expanded edition. Cambridge: Harvard University Press, 2008.

Whindle, Phyllis. "The Ecology of Grief." In *Ecopsychology: Restoring the Earth, Healing the Mind*. Edited by Thomas Roszak, Mary Gomes, and Allen Kanner. New York: Sierra Club Books, 1995, 136–149.

Willcox, Nathan. "Extreme downpours up 30%. Scientists link trend to global warming." Environment America, July 31, 2012. http://www. environmentamerica.org/news/ame/new-report-extreme-downpours-30-percent.

Wines, Michael. "An Ailing Russia Lives a Tough Life That's Getting Shorter." *New York Times*, December 3, 2000. http://www.nytimes.com/2000/12/03/ world/an-ailing-russia-lives-a-tough-life-that-s-getting-shorter. html?pagewanted=all&src=pm.

Žižek, Slavoj. *In Defense of Lost Causes*. New York: Verso, 2008.

Žižek, Slavoj. *The Sublime Object of Ideology*. New York: Verso, 1989.

Žižek, Slavoj. *The Ticklish Subject: The Absent Centre of Political Ontology*. New York: Verso, 1999.

Made in the USA
Lexington, KY
24 July 2014